The Love Story
in Shakespearean
Comedy

The Love Story in Shakespearean Comedy

ANTHONY J. LEWIS

THE UNIVERSITY PRESS OF KENTUCKY

Copyright © 1992 by The University Press of Kentucky
Scholarly publisher for the Commonwealth,
serving Bellarmine College, Berea College, Centre
College of Kentucky, Eastern Kentucky University,
The Filson Club, Georgetown College, Kentucky
Historical Society, Kentucky State University,
Morehead State University, Murray State University,
Northern Kentucky University, Transylvania University,
University of Kentucky, University of Louisville,
and Western Kentucky University.

Editorial and Sales Offices: Lexington, Kentucky 40508-4008

Library of Congress Cataloging-in-Publication Data

Lewis, Anthony J.,
   The love story in Shakespearean comedy / Anthony J. Lewis.
      p.   cm.
   Includes bibliographical references and index.
   ISBN 0-8131-1786-0 :
   1. Shakespeare, William, 1564-1616—Comedies.   2. Love in
literature.   3. Comedy.   I. Title.
PR2981.L49   1992
822.3'3—dc20   91-45643
                                                       CIP

This book is printed on acid-free paper meeting
the requirements of the American National Standard
for Permanence of Paper for Printed Library Materials.

∞

To my mother,
LILLIAN LEWIS,
and to the memory of my father,
CARLTON H. LEWIS

"Everything in this world, said my father, is big with jest,—and has wit in it, and instruction too,—if we can but find it out."
—Laurence Sterne
Tristram Shandy

Contents

Acknowledgments

I wish to thank the Research Foundation of the State University of New York for two Faculty Research Grants, which allowed me to read and write in leisure. The library of the Facoltà di Lettere e Filosofia at the Università degli Studi di Siena offered a perfect Tuscan setting for the arduous work of revising, and Signora Poggialini at the university's Ufficio di Rapporti Internazionali provided welcome secretarial assistance.

Portions of this book were previously published in *Texas Studies in Literature and Language* and in *Essays in Literature*, and I am grateful to these journals for permission to reprint them here.

I am delighted, at long last, to thank my mentors at the University of Wisconsin, Madeleine Doran, Mark Eccles, and Standish Henning; their example of scholarship and teaching taught me the joy of meticulous reading and the sheer fun of studying Shakespeare. Professors Diane Dreher of Santa Clara University, and J.A. Bryant, Jr., of the University of Kentucky, read the manuscript with care, and I am most grateful for their perceptive and detailed suggestions for its improvement. The personal and professional support of my colleagues, Ann Colley, John Dwyer, and David Lampe, has meant a great deal to me.

My friends Cathy Carter and Bob Groves taught me a lesson for life, as for literature, that comedy's truest function is to warm the heart. Percy Katz's understated and gentle way of simplifying all problems I will not soon forget. I am indebted to my sister, Barbara Trecker, and her husband, Jim Trecker, for countless favors, not least of which include allowing me to turn their house into a second office.

It is fitting that an author who reads comedy's happy ending as a product of familial forces should owe his deepest debt of gratitude to his own family. My wife, Rachel, a social worker and therapist, helped me to understand and appreciate the nature of family dynamics; she read the manuscript, smoothed awkward passages, and was an enthusiastic and encouraging partner throughout. My children, Miriam and Raphael, helped as only they could, by providing daily and sustaining examples of the decency, good humor, and spirit of adventure comedy always celebrates.

Introduction

When he entered the Maine woods in 1846, Henry David Thoreau, not a man ordinarily given to the rhapsodic, exclaimed, "Talk of mysteries!—Think of our life in nature . . . the *solid* earth! the *actual* world! the *common sense! Contact! Contact! Who* are we? *where* are we?" [1] Traipsing along Tinker Creek Annie Dillard asks, "what's going on here?" [2]; Edward Abbey simply wonders, "What does it mean?" as he looks across the deserts of the American Southwest; [3] while Peter Matthiessen, searching for the snow leopard in the Himalayas, is asked by Nepalese children, "Where are you-a going?" [4] The wonder of our world, of "our life in nature"—the sheer "pizzazz" of it all, as Dillard puts it—reduces most of us to sentences out of grade school primers. [5] Confronted by the ebullience of the world of Shakespeare's comedies, its pizzazz and diversity, we too might ask, "What's going on here?" and gasp "Where are we?" Noblemen become peasants, noblewomen become men; there are bears, lions, and snakes, fairies, love potions, sleeping potions, cakes and ale, deadly enmity—death itself—and the beauty of wisdom, trust, and love. Before venturing to explicate this text and to describe the geography of this world, the critic would do well to ask himself, "Where are you-a going?"

Shakespeare's comedies are mysterious and startling love stories, utterly unlike anything written before or since. They have their analogues, of course, and from a distance seem comfortably familiar, for scholarship has revealed sources and Shakespeare has been placed in a genealogical tree. *The Comedy of Errors* seems a romanticized version of Plautus's *Menaechmi, The Taming of the Shrew* more sophisticated than Gascoigne's *Supposes, The Winter's Tale* a deepening of Greene's *Pandosto.* But Shakespeare's comedies are not simply "better" than those of his predecessors, or some sort of easily understood natural development from their work. There is no smooth progression from Plautus or Renaissance novellas to Shakespeare, and studying his sources can take us just so far and no further. At some point we must leap from one level of comedy to another so removed as to be a different kind of comedy. Shakespeare is so far from being a natural evolutionary step, he is so fully an anomaly, an exception to a line that recapitulated itself from Menander to Neil Simon, that he seems one of those "sudden appearances" by which Stephen Jay Gould describes Darwinism.[6]

Though we have recently come to appreciate the seriousness and complexity of Shakespeare's comedies (paralleling the rise in critical attention given comedy in general), it is clear that they effect their happy ending in a profoundly different way from that of other comedies. Shakespeare deepened familiar love stories, which derive ultimately from New Comedy and from Greek romance, in a series of extraordinary ways, and this book is an attempt to describe those ways. Such stories are, of course, primarily love stories (though their focus may shift) and their central goal is the marriage or the sexual bonding of a man and a woman. The characteristic feature of stories in this tradition, simply put, is that "The course of true love never did run smooth" (*MND*, I.i.134). They detail, often in exciting and imaginative ways, the shifts to which lovers are put, or stratagems parents use, or the heartrending vagaries of fate on the bumpy road to love. Greek and Roman New Comedy, in a rather unsentimental way, tend to focus on father/son rivalry and on the importance and power of the purse strings, while the romance tradition accents the marvelous and fortuitous, shipwrecks, birthmarks and tokens, ogres and beasts. In both, the waters of love are riffled by the external impediments of which Northrop Frye, in particular, has written so persuasively, and our interest in these stories has to do with lovers overcoming great odds and attaining safe harbor in marriage.

What distinguishes Shakespeare's approach to the time-honored stories he inherited, however, is that in his comedies the lovers' problems are primarily internal, and it is the hero himself who is love's own worst enemy.[7] Locating the central conflict in the hero rather than in an angry father or a tempest at sea is a radical shift that alters the love story by deepening characterization and by making the happy ending a product of the relationship between lovers rather than of an accidental discovery or the trickery of a servant. In one bold stroke Shakespeare transformed external threats into subtle and complex motivations, and in so doing the heroine ceased to be an inert prize and the hero a one-dimensional pawn, such as Mucedorus in the most popular of all romantic comedies, or a superficial schemer, such as Mirabel in Fletcher's *The Wild-Goose Chase.* It is not that Shakespeare jettisoned the familiar catalog of impediments, the fathers and bears and wicked dukes, any more than he eliminated ghosts from tragedy, for from first to last, from the shipwreck in *The Comedy of Errors* to the interfering father in *The Tempest,* his plays retain all the conventional elements we associate with romantic comedy. Indeed, the conventional threats to true love in these plays only serve to emphasize the power of the real problems: a man's perceived need to "read" a woman (*CYM*, V. v. 48), his wandering eye, and his consequent mistreatment of the woman he loves.

One of the choices I made when I began this book was to treat the various love stories in Shakespearean comedy synoptically, as though they were one story presented differently in each play, and to devote a chapter to each phase of that story, much as Joseph Campbell treats the lives of mythological heroes in *The Hero with a Thousand Faces*. I thought that the alternative approach, devoting a chapter to each of the comedies, would soon prove as tiresome to write as to read, for I am one of those who studies Shakespearean comedy, not Shakespeare's comedies. For me, as for many scholars nowadays, especially those whose approaches are sociological or psychoanalytical, Shakespeare's plays evince attitudes toward self and others that appear not to have changed throughout his career. The way in which Shakespeare tells his love story certainly changes: he matures as a poet, his imagery develops and his prose becomes a more sensitive instrument, he grows more adept at working various plots into a cohesive play, and, most importantly, characterization becomes deeper, more three-dimensional. Yet, for all their differences in tone, setting, and theme, the comedies present a cast of characters who relate to one another in complex though consistently similar ways.

I am aware of the price one pays for seeing "the pattern in Shakespeare's carpet," as T.S. Eliot put it.[8] For C.L. Barber, "There is in the pointing out of patterns something that is opposed to life and art. . . . And yet the fact remains that it is as we see the design that we see design outdone and brought alive."[9] No two plays could be less alike than *The Two Gentlemen of Verona* and *Measure for Measure*, and yet, in each, a man forsakes the woman he will eventually marry for a sexual attraction to an unavailable woman, and a woman who is restrained by disguises or convent walls eventually wins that man by virtue of her own willingness to take extraordinary actions, to humiliate herself and sacrifice a sure sense of her own identity. What is lost in any such analysis of similarities is, of course, the individual tone of each play, the earlier play's lightheartedness and the latter's somber and brooding quality, as well as its penetrating look at themes that were, after all, quite important to Shakespeare: the relation between justice and mercy, and appearance and reality. What is gained by abstracting the love stories from their settings is, I trust, a deeper understanding of the ways in which men and women relate to one another in plays that are, in fact, love stories, and an appreciation for the variety of ways in which Shakespeare repeatedly attempted to work through what he saw as the impediments to the sort of marriage that signaled great affection, mutual respect, and trust.

My approach to the comedies is obviously sociological in emphasis, for my interest lies in gender relations. Thus, although I treat Shakespeare's love story in five phases, I pause twice to consider the same phase from both gender points of view. Chapters 1 and 2 describe the social situations of hero and heroine and their different reactions to romance; Chapter 3 describes the ways in which lovers part; and in Chapters 4 and 5, I discuss the psychosocial effects of that separation, again treating each sex independently. Chapter 6 examines the varieties of communication between separated lovers; and in Chapter 7, I analyze the face-to-face reunions with which these plays conclude. Although I discuss all the comedies and romances, I use key texts and focus in particular on *Cymbeline*, which I think the clearest example of Shakespeare's idiosyncratic presentation of the New Comedy love story. In the following summary, which I hope will prove useful both as an overview and as a guide to the reading of individual chapters, I use that play occasionally to illustrate the salient features of my argument.

Although New Comedy, in general, may be said to be built on the boy-meets-girl, boy-loses-girl, boy-gets-girl formula, Shakespearean comedy begins with the separation of a man from his father. CHAPTER 1 compares the kinds of separations effected in classical comedy with those in Shakespeare—primarily the death of the father—and discusses the consequences of that separation on the newly independent son. I draw a distinction between those young men who are invigorated by their freedom to travel and to contract themselves in marriage, and those who seem burdened by a sense of themselves as the vector through whom family name and honor are to be transferred to posterity from a long line of mythicized ancestors. Often ambivalent about himself as an independent adult and about the woman with whom he shortly falls in love, the hero experiences and verbalizes his disorientation as an external threat, perceiving his task as a need to define women and to distinguish between what he sees as female moral types. Posthumus, whose father and brothers had died before he was born, and whose mother died in childbirth, cannot be delved "to the root" (*CYM*, I.i.28). His separation from a father thought by all to have been exemplary brings on precisely that ambivalent state of mind in which, loving Imogen, he nonetheless doubts her fidelity.

The familial and social situation of the heroine when the play begins is quite clearly the opposite of the hero's. CHAPTER 2 contrasts her static position before she meets him with her vigorous actions once she does fall in love. Restrained by patriarchal convention and occasionally imprisoned as well, she is immured literally and figuratively, forced to pursue those indoor and domestic arts that typify and often plague female characters. The ties restricting Shakespeare's heroine, however, belie her condition, for hers is latent power rather than impotence. Her social status is often higher than the hero's; when she is not the favored child of the ruling family she is thought to possess quasi-magical powers or is associated with the leading religious figure in the play. In her connection with the other-worldly, as in so much else, the heroine finds herself in the condition of a nun, and her story echoes medieval *chansons de nonnes,* which lament the sterile sequestration of the convent and celebrate the ruses that free women to elope and marry their lovers.

In love with a man, the heroine is a wonder of courage and action. And it is here, as the lovers meet, that Shakespearean comedy reveals the very different way it treats man and woman from that of its sources and analogues. As the heroine generously gives tokens and promises herself and her fortune to a man, he hesitates, revealing a tendency to pull back as she expands. His rejection of her is occasionally implicit, as when Bassanio wins Portia but sees in the picture of her hair a deadly threat, "A golden mesh t' entrap the hearts of men / Faster than gnats in cobwebs" (*MV,* III.ii.122-23). More often the rejection is explicit, as when Navarre closes his "gates" (*LLL,* II.i.171) and denies the ladies of France "fair harbor" (174) in his house. Occasionally, it is violent and vengeful, and the hero—Posthumus most clearly—thinking his lover slippery or indeed a whore, seeks her death.

CHAPTER 3 focuses on the particularly Shakespearean nature of that rejection and on the inevitable separation of lovers. I argue that, from the first, in *The Comedy of Errors,* Shakespeare's heroes reveal those contradictory impulses—entirely absent from classical New Comedy—which propel them toward a woman and lead them to debase and abandon her at the same time. Antipholus's love for, and fear of, Luciana, for example, indicate early on his psychological complexity; his habits of mind and action prefigure those of Posthumus, in whom we see all too clearly the earlier character's insecurity, suspicion, and readiness to accuse a woman. Indeed, in terms of their attitudes toward women very little separates the heroes of the earliest plays from those of the latest. The lover's illogical response to attraction, and the relative unimportance of external threats to romance, define Shakespeare's more profound approach to human relationships.

In CHAPTER 4 I focus on the confused man, who, separated from father and family, shrinking from woman and marriage, begins a descent that affects him socially and psychologically. Some heroes adopt disguises and pseudonyms, others work as servants or drudges or wander like vagabonds without a name or those tokens, jewelry and such, that would connect them to father and family history. All tend, to a greater or lesser degree, to an approximation of the attitudes and lifestyle of the stereotypical bastard in Elizabethan drama and occasionally adopt, quite self-consciously, views Jenny Teichman describes as typical of the "ideologically illegitimate" in literature,[10] reducing themselves by thinking male friends faithless and women whores. In their separation from father, their self-righteous misogyny, and their disenfranchisement, the men seem Elizabethan versions of Euripides' or Seneca's Hippolytus, the bastard hero who flees from sexuality and opts for misogyny as the only way of life possible for a good man on a planet corrupted by the fact of female sexuality. Posthumus, who slanders his mother by declaring, "We are all bastards," and bemoans the fact that human generation requires the detested woman, is an Hippolytan male par excellence, pushing to its furthest point that separation from father that characterized his birth and led the King and Cloten to call him "base." In Shakespearean comedy, I suggest, even the more fortunate, privileged heroes, Bertram no less than Florizel, drive toward that bastardy of which Posthumus despairs.

As the hero tends toward the ideology or position of the illegitimate, the heroine, separated from her lover or husband, undergoes her own remarkable journey, and that progress I examine in CHAPTER 5. Instead of biding her time, waiting for a man to come to his senses and accept her, the heroine acts in precipitous ways, ultimately saving a man bent on his own destruction. Starting with Julia in *The Two Gentlemen of Verona*, Shakespeare sees the trials of the woman as a response to the flight of the man and as the crucial first step in an evolving solution to the problems between lovers. Julia prefigures the actions of later heroines not only in her disguising herself as a man, but also in her revealing the psychosocial price such disguise and fictions about self necessarily demand. Shakespeare's heroines don male disguise and "conceal" themselves, to use Viola's word (*TN*, I.ii.53), in a variety of ways, incorporating in one personality attitudes and characteristics associated with both men and women. At one and the same time, such heroines are outwardly active and yet harbor within a stultifying vision of themselves as passive, or dead, buried beneath male clothes and frozen in time, like a statue of Patience on a marble monument. The iconography of Patience, in fact, with its emphasis on hope and its use of stone as primary symbol, I compare to the active heroine's descriptions of herself as inanimate. This active passivity, so to speak, characterizes Imogen, who combines male and female stereotypes in so perfect a way that actresses these days are hard pressed to capture its special quality. Her journey and suffering parallel Posthumus's, though he sinks psychologically and she only physically. The stories of Shakespeare's heroines thus seem latter-day versions of Euripides' *Alcestis*, accounts of women who journey like men and sacrifice like women.

CHAPTER 6 suggests that it is gender role reversal on the part of males, too, that changes ambivalence to trust and leads to the reunions of act 5. Active heroines save marriages and relationships from the regressive pull of men whose second thoughts, outright misogyny, or unconscious fears have, ironically, rendered them as passive and prayerful as votarists of Diana or dutiful wives sojourning at monasteries. But if the course of true love has been impeded by changeable men who then sequester themselves, locking up, as Claudio does, "All the gates of love" (*MAdo*, IV.i.105), it is their very living and suffering like women, immured and penitential or simply hopeful and patient, that helps them gain faith in women and reflects a wholesale change in attitude. Posthumus, for example, languishes in prison—much as Imogen had in act 1—though it is there, in fetters, that he forgives her and establishes once and for all a relationship with parents he had never seen.

The hero's renewed faith is prompted and encouraged by Shakespeare's woman, who leaps between a man and his worst intentions, receiving rings meant for others, even making love (through the bedtrick) with the very man who detests her, debasing herself in ways Carol Thomas Neely calls "painfully humiliating."[11] Thus, Shakespeare's separated lovers communicate with one another, sometimes physically, at other times in more spiritual ways. The rueful Posthumus, for example, falls asleep in prison declaring, "O Imogen, / I'll speak to thee in silence" (V.iv.28-29). The contact is always instructional, as W. Thomas MacCary reminds us,[12] the men being tutored, quite self-consciously in *Love's Labour's Lost*, *The Two Gentlemen of Verona*, and *As You Like It*, more subtly in *The Merchant of Venice*, when Portia and Nerissa give their errant husbands a second chance as the play ends. Understanding flows from women to men and is largely about women, sexuality, and the nature of marriage. Its effect is to clear the hero's eyes, so to speak, to help him see women more accurately, and to teach him that love and trust go hand in hand.

In CHAPTER 7 we see that as the hero revives from his stupor and tends toward mental health, he ascends in society, assuming the title and responsibilities—connection to father, family, and governance—he had lost earlier. Posthumus dreams that his father, mother, and brothers intercede on his behalf with Jupiter and gains for the first time a lost, half-mythical family. When he awakens, it is to a "golden chance" (V.iv.132) that leads to his reunion with Imogen. We see the hero legitimatized, both in terms of his accepting himself as his father's son and, more importantly, in terms of his ideology. Women cease to be the enemy, and celibacy is forsaken for heterosexuality. Thus, Shakespearean comedy ends with a second reversal of sexual stereotypes, for men grow active once again in the external worlds of finance and governance, dress in clothing befitting their rank and class, and women relinquish control, ceding authority to men, becoming more stereotypically feminine if only by changing into gender-appropriate clothing. But the play's return to the Elizabethan status quo is a return only in general terms. The nature of the trials the woman has undergone, the loyalty and strength she has demonstrated, make it virtually impossible for these plays to end without ceding to her a large measure of power on the interpersonal level, power that is less public and practical than political power but that is, nevertheless, remarkably telling both to the male characters and to the audience.

On this most crucial of issues for understanding Shakespeare's attitude toward female characters and gender relations in general, a good deal has been written in the last fifteen years. Although in this last chapter I describe the final arrangement—familial, social, political—as a positive response to the values held by the female characters, and therefore as a concession to their abilities, even to what is perceived in these plays as their "wonder," I am by no means unaware of the patriarchy's power, for example, in *Measure for Measure* or *Pericles*, and of its jealous aggrandizement especially of "real" estate and political sway. Like Juliet Dusinberre, I am perhaps not significantly more sanguine about the final situation of the heroines than are other commentators, in particular Marianne Novy, who argues that women gain and lose as the comedies end.[13] Yet, surely, these plays do conclude with more than just a token pat on the back to the female characters. How can *Cymbeline*, for example, leave us with any other impression than that Imogen is, or appears to be, mysterious, wonderful, and, most importantly, morally superior? And in its ending *Cymbeline* is typical of Shakespearean comedy where the stories of women make it seem as though they are both dead and alive, male and female, and capable of being in two places at the same time. Though the audience almost always knows that what appears to be is not what is, the male characters infrequently do, and these plays typically end before the men learn how the women have performed their wonders.

It is precisely that fifth act feeling of wonder shared by characters and audience that affects our perceptions of the lovers' traditional roles in marriage as husband and wife. By what stretch of the imagination can we apprehend the profligate and ambivalent Bassanio as Portia's "lord, her governor, her king" (III. ii.165) or Navarre and his lords as the equals of the intelligent and clear-sighted Princess of France and her ladies? How can the "Elizabethan world picture" and its biased views of men and women be taken as a guide to the marriages finally made between Proteus and Julia,

Duke Orsino and Viola, Claudio and Hero, Bertram and Helena, Angelo and Mariana, Posthumus and Imogen, Leontes and Hermione? As the final act winds down, the marriages toward which the whole action of the play has led are felt to be, at the very least, unions between equals rather than mere affirmations of stereotypical assumptions about how men and women relate. What we tend to believe as a Shakespearean comedy ends is that a marriage between such partners will be skewed so that new outbursts by insecure men are much less likely to happen. Viewed in this way, Shakespearean comedy can be said to work through those problems that, in other contexts, cause the disasters of tragedy. In act 3 Othello says of Desdemona, "Perdition catch my soul / But I do love thee! and when I love thee not, / Chaos is come again" (iii.90-92). When comedy ends, the chaos of disaffection, suspicion, hatred, and death has been averted by loving women and men adaptable enough to learn and change.

To summarize the action of these plays as I have is to recognize that Shakespeare makes romance contingent upon social setting—family relationships, in the first place, but also assumptions about gender- and class-appropriate behavior—and thus radically transforms the love story he inherited from his Roman and continental models. In his insistence that it be the young man himself who impedes his developing relationship with the woman he loves, Shakespeare creates a story far more reflective of the complexity of human interaction than those that sunder love through the external agency of angry fathers, raging rivers, hungry lions. And yet, having located the impediment to true love in the social circumstances of the hero, Shakespeare was, happily, constrained to solve the problems of romance internally as well. That is, if the causes of the rupture have to do with a man's relationship with his father and with his assumptions about female sexuality, the meaning of marriage, and the appropriateness of gender politics, its repair necessarily involves a reeducation so thorough as to render him metamorphosed as the play ends and he embraces the heroine. The primary agent of that deep change is the evolving relationship itself, while the nature of the change is an ability to see the world as a woman does, more accurately and less fantastically, and to develop relationships, as Coppélia Kahn puts it, "based on the union of his and her separate identities, in which trust and reciprocity mediate that separateness."[14]

Time and again Shakespeare's heroes mistrust and simply misapprehend, missing what is there, as Proteus misses Julia's beauty and charm, and seeing what is not, as Claudio sees Hero as Venus rather than as Diana. For a man to see as a woman does is to avoid being pulled down into a world reminiscent of the tragedies, where dream overwhelms reality and madness enslaves reason. In their madness, men struggle with contradictory views of women, and in play after play we are asked to choose between two ways of seeing the heroine, as proper wife or shrew, patient Griselda or impatient scold, virgin or whore, Diana or Venus. Were there such variety among moral types in the comedies, Shakespeare's heroes might be justified in their frantic search, their suspicions, their flightiness, and these plays would be about a young man's steering his way around the external threats of mermaids and sirens, or past golden caskets hiding the death's-head of female lust. Were the women genuinely threatening, who would blame Navarre for denying the Princess of France "fair harbor," or Benedick for vowing to live a bachelor, or Antipholus for hastening to the abbey, or Claudio for believing his eyes, or Posthumus his ears? It was Shakespeare's great genius, however, not to see two sorts of women, but only one sort viewed by men in two contradictory ways. The love story in Shakespearean comedy thus shows us in affecting, compelling fashion, how a man comes to see the world and women aright.

1

"The Spirit of My Father"

Shakespeare's version of the typical New Comedy love story begins not with boy meeting girl, as we might expect, but rather with the separation of a young man from his father.[1] Though this division between parent and child is ordinarily cordial and no sign of a change in either the son's or the father's loyalties, it has a profound effect on the young man's social position, attitudes, and feelings, and therefore on his relationship with the woman he will soon meet and eventually wish to marry.

It is not surprising that Shakespeare's comedies begin with such father/son divisions, inasmuch as a salient feature of Shakespeare's sources is father/son interactions of all sorts. For Madeleine Doran the central theme of Roman New Comedy, plundered and adapted by sixteenth century Europe, is the "contest between high-living young men, deeply involved in an apparently discreditable love affair . . . and their conservative fathers, who are, of course, anxious to have their sons settle down as sober householders."[2] Terence, whose plays had a lasting effect on Shakespeare and on Elizabethan drama (and on medieval and Renaissance critical theory), had a particular fondness for describing and analyzing father/son relationships.[3] *Phormio* begins with Geta's lament to his fellow slave Davus, that the young man of his household, Antipho, has met and married a young girl while his father has been visiting a friend in Cilicia; and *Heautontimorumenos* begins with Menedemus's complaint that after an argument with his son the boy traveled to Asia and joined the army. Terence, in turn, may have been influenced indirectly by Aristophanes who occasionally particularized the opposition between youth and age as a conflict between father and son, especially in the *Wasps* and the *Clouds*.[4] Such separations are common in Plautus, too, as we might expect. *Mercator* begins with Charinus's return to Athens after a two years' sojourn at Rhodes—at his father's insistence—during which time he has fallen in love with and purchased a maidservant; and *Casina* begins with a young man already far from home, vying with his father for their maid and the *droit du seigneur.* Plautus's *Menaechmi,* probably the most popular Roman comedy in the Renaissance, begins with the story of a separation between father and son, as does one of its Shakespearean descendants, *The Comedy of Errors*.[5]

The devices used by Shakespeare to separate fathers and sons are traditional and of various origins, most from Greek New Comedy through Roman comedy, some from medieval romance.[6] In *The Two Gentlemen of Verona*, when Antonio insists that his son Proteus follow Valentine to the ducal court in Milan, his servant Panthino supports him and spells out some of the ways in which comedy divorces father and son in his observation that other men

> Put forth their sons to seek preferment out:
> Some to the wars, to try their fortune there;
> Some to discover islands far away;
> Some to the studious universities. [I.iii.7-10]

Such methods of separating sons and fathers are found throughout Elizabethan drama and in continental Renaissance comedy, as well as in the nondramatic literature of the period, though it is the death of the father that most often separates his son from him in Shakespearean comedy. "Antonio, my father, is deceas'd" (I.ii.54), Petruchio tells us early in *The Taming of the Shrew;* he now seeks his fortune "farther than at home, / Where small experience grows" (51-2). Sebastian, in *Twelfth Night*, comes ashore in Illyria and is soon approached by Olivia, but not before we learn, in his second speech—"my father was that Sebastian of Messaline" (II.i.17-18)—that his father is deceased. *All's Well That Ends Well* begins with Bertram's leaving his mother to serve the King in Paris shortly after his father has died and while the Countess is still in mourning, all of which is made abundantly clear when the Countess declares in the play's opening line, "In delivering my son from me, I bury a second husband." By virtue of his name alone Posthumus Leonatus in *Cymbeline* is defined by his father's death; Orlando tells us in the first speech in *As You Like It*, indeed, in the first sentence of the play, that his father is dead; and "young lord Pericles" rules Tyre because he has inherited the crown following his illustrious father's death. Indeed, only eight of the major male characters in Shakespearean comedy have fathers who are alive when the play begins.[7] We know that the other twenty or so young men are fatherless either because they tell us so explicitly, because they are titled (most titles "normally passed downward in tail male from the first holder,"[8] and are hereditary—King of Navarre, Count Claudio, Duke Orsino) or because they exercise prerogatives in marrying or in concluding marriage contracts. In this regard, Shakespeare's comedies differ markedly from those of Plautus and Terence where the old father, though separated from his son, is generally alive and very much a vital force in a direct and physical way. In *Casina*, for example, it is the son, in fact, who is absent; Euthynicus is spoken of occasionally yet never appears on stage because, as the Prologue tells us, "Plautus would not have it so—he broke down a bridge that lay on the youth's route" to Athens.[9]

Thus, more often than not, Shakespeare's heroes are in a significantly different position from that of their counterparts in Roman comedy. Separated from their fathers by the stark fact of death, they are less susceptible to the external pressures fathers so often exercise in Roman comedy. Shakespeare's plays tend, therefore, to focus on consequential matters, those that are internal and psychological—the force of memory, conflicts arising from the contradiction between a son's financial independence and his immaturity, inhibitions and loss of confidence that result from invidious comparisons between father and son—rather than on simple external motives—winning a father's blessing, scheming for a large allowance, undermining parental authority. Even in those six plays in which a young man's father is alive, his power to affect the son in tangible ways is considerably diminished, primarily because Shakespeare physically distances the two. Although they all wind up in Ephesus on the same day, Antipholus of Syracuse and Egeon have not seen each other for five years, and Antipholus's brother has been separated from his father since infancy. Proteus travels to Milan in act 1, Lucentio to Padua, and Florizel to Sicilia. Ferdinand and Alonso each thinks the other dead and are on different parts of the island for most of *The Tempest,* and in *Troilus and Cressida* Shakespeare, constrained by a familiar literary tradition, nonetheless keeps father and son apart. As far as the love story between Troilus and Cressida goes, Priam is simply irrelevant.

The many fatherless young men of Shakespearean comedy seem to agree with Claudius in *Hamlet* that "obstinate condolement is a course / Of impious stubbornness" (I.ii.93-4) and are quick to accept harsh reality and occasionally to turn their fathers' deaths into something useful in what has become a new world of independence and adventure. This, in fact, is the critical aspect of the death of the father in Shakespearean comedy: the young man is now responsible for, and to, himself, especially with regard to marriage and money matters, which were, of course, intimately related for the nobility and the rising middle class in the sixteenth and seventeenth centuries. The death of the father, therefore, very often "makes" the son, turning him into a financially independent adult, unless he is a younger son (Orlando in *As You Like It*) or the son of a man without great means (Posthumus Leonatus). Lawrence Stone points out that the "high adult mortality rate provided many children with some freedom of choice by removing their parents from the scene at an early age. If a boy was the heir to the estate, he was then more or less free to suit himself."[10] In *The Tempest*, Ferdinand encounters Miranda and falls in love with her even as he laments "the King my father's wrack" (I.ii.391). His distress at what he believes to be the King's death, however, is soon eclipsed by his infatuation, and personal and national tragedy are transformed into a lover's plea:

> My prime request,
> Which I do last pronounce, is (O you wonder!)
> If you be maid or no?
> *Mir.*   No wonder, sir,
> But certainly a maid.
> *Fer.*   My language? heavens!
> I am the best of them that speak this speech,
> Were I but where 'tis spoken.
> *Pros.*   How? the best?
> What wert thou, if the King of Naples heard thee? [426-32]

Similarly, in *The Winter's Tale* Florizel uses the promise of a kingdom for romantic purposes, going as far as to enrage his disguised father, Polixenes, in a scene reminiscent of Prince Harry's removing King Henry's crown in 2 *Henry IV.* In asking Perdita's stepfather for her hand, Florizel declares,

> One being dead,
> I shall have more than you can dream of yet,
> Enough then for your wonder. But come on,
> Contract us 'fore these witnesses.
> *Shep.*   Come, your hand;
> And, daughter, yours.
> *Pol.*   Soft, swain, awhile, beseech you.
> Have you a father?
> *Flo.*   I have; but what of him? [IV.iv.387-92]

There is something in these sentiments that reminds us of Petruchio's brag to Gremio, "My father dead, my fortune lives for me" (I.ii.191). Stone points out that "for the elder sons, their entrepreneurial drive was sapped by the certainty of the inheritance to come, until which time they were condemned to live a kind of shadow existence waiting for their father to die, when they would at last come into their own."[11] What we sense in Shakespeare's young men, however, is less callousness or even presumption than the simple desire to be independent, to make significant decisions on their own.

Occasionally, their decisions are merely childish and amount to little more than running through their patrimony. Bassanio has been "something too prodigal" (I.i.129) and is in debt when *The Merchant of Venice* opens; Sir Andrew Aguecheek, a suitor, though hardly a hero, is "a very fool and a prodigal" in *Twelfth Night* (I.iii.24), and Fenton in *The Merry Wives of Windsor* is a gentleman "of no having" (III.ii.72) whose state has been "gall'd" (III.iv.5) with expense from his "riots" and "wild societies" (8) and who is considered, consequently, an undesirable suitor for Anne Page by her father. Though the prodigal son was enormously popular as a stereotype on the Elizabethan and Jacobean stages, Shakespeare focused more often not on the profligacy of sons per se but rather on the profligacy of their emotions after their fathers' deaths.[12] Shakespearean heroes more typically express their independence by falling in love and choosing to marry than by foolish spending. Petruchio, for one, with "crowns" in his purse and "goods at home" (I.ii.57) is free to "wive" (56), as is Pericles, or Ferdinand in *The Tempest* when he thinks his father dead, an action Florizel in *The Winter's Tale* or Lucentio can undertake only in disguise.

If these young men are like Claudius in their easy acceptance of nature's inevitable ways, they are nonetheless like Hamlet in venerating their fathers. The two attitudes are not contradictory, for the young man's estimate of himself, in Shakespearean comedy as in tragedy, is based upon his estimate of his father, living or dead. In his first speech in *The Taming of the Shrew*, Lucentio carefully defines himself by describing both family history and his father, "A merchant of great traffic through the world, / Vincentio, come of the Bentivolii" (I.i.12-13). In *The Two Gentlemen of Verona* the Duke of Milan is pleased to welcome Proteus to his court, in part because Valentine spoke so well of his friend's father as a gentleman "of worth and worthy estimation, / And not without desert so well reputed" (II.iv.56-57). Petruchio refers to his father twice in act 1; in act 2 he introduces himself to Baptista as "Antonio's son, / A man well known throughout all Italy" (II.i.68-69). Baptista's response, "I know him well; you are welcome for his sake" (70), indicates the power of Antonio's reputation, and yet Petruchio reiterates the connection between his father and himself forty-seven lines later: "You knew my father well, and in him me" (116). The family connection is precisely the point, and Marianne Novy quite rightly sees that "the younger characters' words about tradition, loyalty, and hierarchy in general, as well as patriarchy, are frequently in pursuit of their own ends."[13] Petruchio expects others, particularly Baptista, to respect him as they respected his father, and he freely spends the coin of his father's reputation to achieve that end and, in fact, to win Kate. He assumes, after all, that his father has left him "soly heir to all his lands and goods" (II.i.117) so that he may "thrive" (I.ii.56) and thus repeat in himself the success that was his father's. Knowing Petruchio's pedigree, of course, makes Baptista's decision to entrust him with his daughter relatively uncomplicated.

However, when it seems to the fatherless son, as it often does at the start of these plays, that his own accomplishments are insignificant or that his station in life is demeaning, his venerated father haunts him, a silent reminder of his inadequacy. This scenario suggests *Hamlet*, though it ought to suggest just as clearly some of the comedies. In *As You Like It*, Orlando's revolt against Oliver and his acceptance of Charles' challenge to wrestle in act 1 have to do primarily with his awareness of not having fulfilled himself as the son of the renowned Sir Rowland de Boys. His education had been planned by Sir Rowland and is his birthright. To Oliver he complains,

> The spirit of my father grows strong in me, and I will no longer endure it; therefore allow me such exercises as may become a gentleman, or give me the poor allottery my father left me by testament, with that I will go buy my fortunes. [I.i.70-74]

Typical of those comedies in which the hero is orphaned and disenfranchised at the start, *As You Like It* presents a world ringing with praise for the young man's father. Even Orlando, in acts 1 and 2, describes himself as a son struggling to become the kind of man he believes his father to have been. He constantly invokes his father's "spirit" as the cause of his rebellion against Oliver, and his remarks are underscored by Adam who calls him "you memory / Of old Sir Rowland!" (II.iii.3-4).[14] The Duke exiles him because his father was an enemy, but Rosalind claims her father "lov'd Sir Rowland as his soul, / And all the world was of my father's mind" (I.ii.235-36). On the other hand, though Sir Rowland's reputation serves to emphasize Orlando's destitution, at the same time it helps him to see himself as a special and important man. Apparently—so the romance tradition will have it—sons of great fathers chafe against the restraints of poverty even when they are unaware of their high birth. In *Cymbeline*, although Guiderius and Arviragus, the King's two kidnapped sons, think themselves the exiled Belarius's sons, "their thoughts do hit / The roofs of palaces" (III.iii.83-84), and they are restless with their lowly life and with being denied "the courtesy" their "cradle promis'd" (IV.iv.28).

The situation is similar though more complicated in *All's Well That Ends Well*, where the reputation of the dead Count of Rossillion appears only to stifle any sense of pride in himself Bertram has when the play begins as he leaves his mother and home for the court in Paris. The sickly King of France greets Bertram as though the young Count were his father reborn, and not a man in his own right:

> Youth, thou bear'st thy father's face,
> Frank Nature, rather curious than in haste,
> Hath well compos'd thee. Thy father's moral parts
> Mayst thou inherit too! Welcome to Paris. [I.ii.19-22]

As the scene develops, the King wistfully recounts Bertram's father's glories, physical and spiritual, as though he no longer expects to see such a man. After declaring his dead friend an exceptional warrior who "lasted long" (28), the King forbids Bertram to travel to the wars in Italy with the other young men of the court, a decision that, in Bertram's eyes, leaves him with "no sword worn / But one to dance with!" (II.i.32-33). Bertram, who seems to most critics callous and immature, appears at the very least ambivalent about his father as "copy to these younger times" (I.ii.46) and about his being son and heir to so great a man.15

The same tension between who the father was and who the son is develops in *Measure for Measure* when Isabella visits Claudio, in jail, to inform him that Angelo will spare his life only if she consents to go to bed with him. When he appears ready to "encounter darkness as a bride" (III.i.83), Isabella remarks, "there my father's grave / Did utter forth a voice" (85-86). Yet fifty lines later, after Claudio begs, "Sweet sister, let me live" (132), Isabella's condemnation of her brother rests partly on a comparison between him and their father, from whom, she says, "such a warped slip of wilderness / Ne'er issu'd" (141-42). In *Measure for Measure*, as elsewhere, "A son is a father's grave."16 Posthumus Leonatus, in *Cymbeline*, is separated from his father, impoverished, and thought to have obscure origins, and although he never denigrates himself in comparison with his father, the audience cannot help but compare him, an exile thought to be a "basest thing" (I.i.124), with his father, whose valor gained him "the sur-addition Leonatus" (33).

Pericles too thinks himself far less a man than he imagines his father to have been at his age. Even after winning Thaisa and the tournament at Pentapolis, no mean accomplishments for a man cut off from home, friends, and family, he cannot refrain from seeing himself as a "glow-worm in the night" when he looks at Thaisa's father:

> [Yon] king's to me like to my father's picture,
> Which tells [me] in that glory once he was;
> Had princes sit like stars about his throne,
> And he the sun for them to reverence;
> None that beheld him but, like lesser lights,
> Did vail their crowns to his supremacy;

> Where now his [son's] like a glow-worm in the night,
> The which hath fire in darkness, none in light. [II.iii.37-44]

Perhaps Hamlet has some reason to chastise himself in this way; Pericles has not.

For Bertram, Orlando, Pericles, and Posthumus, comparisons between father and son are double-edged swords, for the greatness of the father not only defines the son and spurs his ambition but also magnifies his present insignificance, in his own eyes and, as he imagines, in his dead father's as well. This seems especially to be the case for those sons whose problems, like Hamlet's, appear to be less the result of outside forces than of what they see as their own inbred disposition to failure or torpor. For example, Orlando, whose problems are all external, knows that there is little he can do to rise in the world without his inheritance; perhaps for that reason he retains some sense of himself as noble and valiant. Philaster, in Beaumont and Fletcher's play, is similarly blocked from the outside rather than by a sense of himself as inept. His disenfranchisement only spurs his ambition:

> This earth you tread upon
> (A dowry, as you hope, with this fair princess),
> By my dead father (oh, I had a father,
> Whose memory I bow to!) was not left
> To your inheritance, and I up and living—
> Having myself about me and my sword,
> The souls of all my name and memories,
> These arms and some few friends besides the gods—
> To part so calmly with it, and sit still
> And say, "I might have been."[17]

Orlando and Philaster remind us of Faulconbridge, in *King John*, who would rather be the bastard son of a great man (Richard Cordelion) than "good old Sir Robert's wive's eldest son" (I.i.158).

The predicament shared by all sons who see themselves as less than their fathers were at their time of life, is that they also believe their present humiliation prefigures ruin for their posterity. In the world of Shakespeare's plays, as in the world of the Renaissance nobility in general, the male line is felt to reach back in time to that "first father," an almost mythical figure, and forward to all one's descendants. Thus, at one and the same time, the young man feels caught between the honored past, an endless line of "mythicized" fathers, and the prospect of a future shamed by generations of failing sons.[18] The husband in *A Yorkshire Tragedy* is told that his immorality dishonors his family's past, "Thy father's and forefathers' worthy honors, / Which were our country monuments, our grace, / Follies in thee begin now to deface," but is also warned that he threatens his family's future: "heap not wrongful shame / On . . . your posterity."[19] In *A Woman Killed with Kindness*, Sir Charles Mountford's fall "to this base estate," the fact that he let his "name lie fettered in disgrace," is all the more awful considering his pride, earlier, in himself as the most recent in a long line of male heirs:

> this house successively
> Hath 'longed to me and my progenitors
> Three hundred year. My great-great-grandfather,
> He in whom first our gentle style began,
> Dwelt here, and in this ground increased this mole-hill
> Unto that mountain which my father left me.
> Where he the first of all our house began,
> I now the last will end and keep this house,
> This virgin title never yet deflowered
> By any unthrift of the Mountford's line.[20]

In *The Shoemaker's Holiday*, the Earl of Lincoln can only lament of his nephew, Rowland Lacy, "thy name / Lived once in honour, now dead in shame!"[21]

Georges Duby writes of the relationship between father and son in medieval France, "The purpose of marriage was to unite a valiant progenitor to a wife in such a manner that his legitimate son, bearer of the blood and name of a valorous ancestor, should be able to bring that ancestor back to life again in his own purpose."[22] It is difficult for us to conceive of how important patrilinear descent was to aristocratic families during the Renaissance, and of the effects of primogeniture. Whether the fundamental issue is one of preserving family power, as Mark Girouard suggests,[23] or of preserving the family seat, land, heirlooms, name, and hereditary title, as Lawrence Stone thinks, or of a Darwinian and biological impulse predisposing individuals to protect their own genes, "the prime preoccupation of a wealthy English landed squire was somehow to contrive to preserve his family inheritance intact and to pass it on to the next generation according to the principle of primogeniture in tail male."[24] To cause a rupture in one's family line, to be the male who destroys family name, loses its holdings, and causes "social derogation," was an unthinkable ignominy.[25] It is, of course, irrelevant that Hamlet and Pericles, as well as Orlando and other unhappy heroes of Shakespearean comedy, are greatly admired by most of those around them (and by the audience), and are, in fact, thought to be flattering incarnations of their dead ancestors ("you memory / Of old Sir Rowland!"). One of the ironies of Pericles' speech of self-derision quoted above is that it comes immediately after Thaisa tells us in an aside that compared to the other knights who seek her hand, "he seems like diamond to glass" (II.iii.36), and that her father, the King, admires him only.

Separated from their fathers by death, distance, or disguise, the young men of Shakespearean comedy seem ripe for adventure. Petruchio is typically ingenuous and spirited; his complaint, "small experience grows" (I.ii.52) at home, announces with a metaphor from agriculture his arrival on "such wind as scatters young men through the world" (50). His images remind us of Valentine's valedictory to Proteus, "Home-keeping youth have ever homely wits" (I.i.2), and of Bassanio's telling Antonio that "the four winds blow in from every coast / Renowned suitors" (I.i.168-69) for Portia. Petruchio's describing himself as seed is obviously appropriate to comedy and to beginnings, as is the indirect comparison between himself and Theseus a few lines later, when he explains, "I have thrust myself into this maze, / Happily to wive and thrive as best I may" (55-56). Perhaps in Petruchio's classical allusion, Shakespeare is recalling Lucentio's earlier comparison between Jove, disguised as a white bull, and himself when he first arrives in Padua and sees Bianca: "O, yes, I saw sweet beauty in her face, / Such as the daughter of Agenor had, / That made great Jove to humble him to her hand, / When with his knees he kiss'd the Cretan strond" (I.i.167-70). These allusions to myth, familiar to Elizabethans from many sources but especially from Arthur Golding's translation of Ovid's *Metamorphoses*, help to define Petruchio and Lucentio as young lovers who conceive of themselves as heroic figures undergoing dangerous and difficult journeys, in part, at least, for a woman's love. Petruchio's winning of Kate is prefigured—in mock-epic terms—in Theseus's entering the maze, slaying the minotaur, and escaping with Ariadne; Lucentio's winning of Bianca is prefigured in his reference to Jove rising from the sea to seduce Europa. Both allusions emphasize the adventure of a journey, with its possible rewards and risks, and elevate courtship to heroic levels.

Shakespeare's young men are certainly conventional in their drawing self-conscious comparisons between themselves and the heroes of mythology. In *The Merchant of Venice* Bassanio and Gratiano "are the Jasons" (III.ii.241); when Bassanio chooses among the caskets at Belmont, he alludes to Hercules, Mars, and Midas, and Portia too compares him to the "young Alcides" (55). In *Much Ado about Nothing* when Don Pedro woos Hero for Claudio, his visor is "Philemon's roof, within the house is Jove" (II.i.96-97). Even Falstaff, in *The Merry Wives of Windsor*, can milk the tradition by asking "the hot-bloodied gods" (V.v.2) to assist him: "Remember, Jove, thou wast a bull for thy Europa, love set on thy horns. O powerful love, that in some respects makes a beast a man; in some other, a man a beast. You were also, Jupiter, a swan for the love of Leda" (3-7).

If disguise and physical changes are the very essence of the New Comedy tradition, a deeper and more telling sort of transformation is at the heart of Shakespeare's version of that tradition. When Florizel woos Perdita, he too uses the gods in Ovid's pantheon as models and encouragement:

> Apprehend
> Nothing but jollity. The gods themselves,
> Humbling their deities to love, have taken
> The shapes of beasts upon them. Jupiter
> Became a bull and bellowed; the green Neptune
> A ram, and bleated; and the fire-rob'd god,
> Golden Apollo, a poor humble swain,
> As I seem now. Their transformations
> Were never for a piece of beauty rarer. [IV.iv.25-32]

In Florizel's mouth, however, the allusions to heroes of mythology seem to signify more than merely an inflated way of apprehending himself. Jupiter and Neptune may be his models in their disguising and descending for love but not in terms of their behavior or goal, mere sexual triumph, as they are for Falstaff. In his next speech, Florizel drops the self-conscious references in favor of a straightforward admission of the stakes for which he plays in courting Perdita. The young Prince tells her that disguise is more than simply a stratagem to elude the King and elope with her:

> Thou dear'st Perdita,
> With these forc'd thoughts I prithee darken not
> The mirth o' th' feast. Or I'll be thine, my fair,
> Or not my father's; for I cannot be
> Mine own, nor any thing to any, if
> I be not thine. To this I am most constant,
> Though destiny say no. [40-46]

Here Florizel suggests that marrying Perdita has to do with discovering and freeing himself, creating and affirming an identity that goes far beyond mere changes of apparel, and that failing to win her means a kind of death, the inability to be "any thing to any." Thus, Florizel's transformation, his humbling, most obvious to the audience in his change of clothes (he dresses first as a shepherd and later changes clothes with the thief Auto-lycus), seems a necessary shedding and an attempt to begin afresh.[26]

Though in Falstaff all we can sense are rhetorical games, the profounder use to which Florizel puts the stories of the gods' escapades indicates a more serious side to the adventurousness of the young man as he leaves home and separates from his father. Even in Shakespeare's earliest comedies, spirited and ambitious men betray a concern for self that necessarily deepens these familiar love stories. In Petruchio's reference to Padua as "this maze" we hear at least a hint of ambivalence about life on his own. As *The Taming of the Shrew* begins, Petruchio seems to be the hero par excellence, a young man caught between the death of his father and the birth of his own sure conception of himself. His intention is to marry and "thrive," yet the journey from his home to Padua seems to be a significant enough change to be compared by him with Theseus's wanderings in the labyrinth. Even in his bragging Petruchio seems apprehensive, as though, unlike Lucentio, he were aware on some level of crossing a threshold. On his wedding day he disguises himself in "mad attire" (III.ii.124)—like the gods' "Humbling their deities for love"—not to win Kate, for she is already won and standing outside the church long before he arrives, but rather as a stratagem having to do with self-protection: "To me she's married, not unto my clothes. / Could I repair what she will wear in me / As I can change these poor accoutrements, / 'Twere well for Kate, and better for myself" (117-120). In his disguise and deception, Petruchio follows Jove's lead but in a far more psychologically revealing manner. Unlike Jove, who risks nothing and changes only his appearance, Petruchio is concerned with what Kate will "wear," i.e., "wear out," in him. In *The Taming of a Shrew*, which either served as one of Shakespeare's sources for *The Taming of the Shrew* or derived independently from a common source, Ferando, Petruchio's counterpart, also dresses in "base attire" on his wedding day, but only to confuse his future bride and to protect his expensive wardrobe: "For when my wife and I am married once, / Shees such a shrew, if we should once fal out, / Sheele pul my costlie sutes over mine eares, / And therefore am I thus attired awhile."[27] There is no hint of disguise as a necessary device employed on behalf of the hero's psychological well-being, no hint that there are parts of Ferando he feels need protecting. Plays that use disguise as a means to a sexual end—or for a variety of other rather practical purposes, such as Dekker's *Patient Grissil*, where the Marquess dons a peasant's weeds to test his wife's constancy—were, of course, legion in the sixteenth and early seventeenth centuries. It is Shakespeare who sensed ambivalence and insecurity beneath a man's new clothes and his allusions to the gods.

Shakespeare's deepening of what in classical comedy and in his Italian sources is mere high jinks is clear as well in his treatment of Lucentio, perhaps his most lighthearted and simple lover, for even Lucentio is a fuller and more important character than his counterpart, Erostrato, in a source for the play, Gascoigne's *Supposes*, a translation of Ariosto's *I Suppositi*. Shakespeare allows us to see Lucentio enter Padua as a student, espy Bianca, and fall in love. We are with him when he and Tranio hit on the notion of changing roles and identities, we see him "tutor" Bianca, we are privy to their plans for marriage, and in act 5 we see them as a married couple. On the other hand, when *Supposes* begins Erostrato has been in Ferrara for two years and has "passed so many pleasant nightes togither" with his love, Polynesta. [28] Erostrato has none of Lucentio's *joie de vivre*, and there is no sense that he is embarking on an adventure, great or small, or that he thinks of himself at all in heroic terms. His relationship with Polynesta is subordinated to the problems of his maintaining his disguise as Dulipa, his servant, and we see him with Polynesta only once, in the last scene, during which he speaks two words and she none. In fact, Polynesta appears in only two scenes, the first and the last, and the overall impression is not so much of a love story with boy and girl striving together to shape a future as of a play detailing in realistic fashion the machinations of a host of one-dimensional characters. Shakespeare's direction throughout *The Taming of the Shrew* is characteristic of his handling of source material for most of the comedies: he pulls our attention to the problems of lovers, and here especially to those of Petruchio and Lucentio, rather than to those of their fathers. In *Supposes*, the problems and wishes of Phylogano, Erostrato's father, together with those of Cleander, Dulipa's father, shape most of the second half of the play, whereas in *The Taming of the Shrew* Lucentio's father arrives only after his son has secretly married. The machinations of the lovers are almost always of less consequence to Shakespeare than the inner turmoil produced by the love relationship itself.

Shakespeare's young men, however strongly identified with the heroic, often begin their journey toward marriage with ambivalent feelings if not with outright reluctance, as one critic describes it. [29] Petruchio's "maze" is never very clearly defined, though other lovers are less subtle in their response to the choices made possible by their newfound and often unsought independence from father. Proteus, for example, responds halfheartedly to his father's demand that he follow Valentine and serve the duke in Milan: "Why, this it is: my heart accords thereto, / And yet a thousand times it answers 'no'" (I.iii.90-91). Journeying to Milan means leaving Julia, but staying in Verona with Julia implies that loss of honor he laments earlier, when Valentine leaves: "He after honor hunts, I after love" (I.i.63). Antipholus of Syracuse, in *The Comedy of Errors*, is an early and complex example. At eighteen, we are told, he left his father to search for mother and brother and has been wandering ever since. When he first enters in I.ii, he sounds the familiar note. As a newcomer to Ephesus, he will "view the manners of the town, / Peruse the traders, gaze upon the buildings" (12-13). Fifteen lines later, the same intentions are expressed metaphorically, "I will go lose myself, / And wander up and down to view the city" (30-31), but in soliloquy, four lines later, the same traveler's urge melts into a self-conscious simile, which comments, albeit clumsily, on his sense of who he is:

> I to the world am like a drop of water,
> That in the ocean seeks another drop,
> Who, falling there to find his fellow forth
> (Unseen, inquisitive), confounds himself.
> So I, to find a mother and a brother,
> In quest of them (unhappy), ah, lose myself. [35-40]

In II.ii, the next scene in which he appears, Antipholus is approached by Adriana and her sister Luciana who mistake him for his twin brother. Without her knowing it, however, Adriana speaks to him in terms best suited to his psychological needs, and perhaps this is why he acquiesces when she insists that he come home to dinner. Adriana claims that they are "undividable incorporate" (122) as husband and wife and pleads,

> do not tear away thyself from me;
> For know, my love, as easy mayst thou fall
> A drop of water in the breaking gulf,
> And take unmingled thence that drop again,
> Without addition or diminishing,
> As take from me thyself and not me too. [124-29]

Antipholus had assumed that he would be "lost" in his search for his family; he hears now that to be lost "in the breaking gulf" of marriage is to remain "undividable incorporate." Though he will shortly recoil from the supposed mysteries of Ephesus and the familiarity of these women, he understandably allows himself the pleasure of staying with women who seem to want and need the same security for which he yearns.[30] As an attempt to explain that he is a stranger, his response, "In Ephesus I am but two hours old" (148), is disregarded by the sisters, yet, like Petruchio, who describes himself as seed, and Lucentio, who "kiss'd the Cretan strond," Antipholus speaks more tellingly than he is aware. Separation from his father, confusion, and freedom combine to produce fear and exhilaration as he senses, perhaps subliminally, that one way of life is dying and another being born.

Just as Antipholus describes his emotional state through images of water, so too does Lucentio, newly arrived in Padua: "I have Pisa left / And am to Padua come, as he that leaves / A shallow plash to plunge him in the deep, / And with saciety seeks to quench his thirst" (I.i.21-24). Lucentio's simile expresses his exuberance at the prospect of plunging "in the deep," while Antipholus's comparison ("I to the world am like a drop of water") only indicates anxiety and fear of loss. In most of Shakespeare's young men imagery and tone suggest a sense of risk, and sometimes outright hesitation and even fear at the start of their great adventures separated from their fathers and accountable, if only temporarily, to themselves alone. Being submerged in water or "scattered" by the four winds can mean death by drowning or disintegration as easily as transformation and rebirth on a far shore, for to these men the victories of Jove often seem balanced by the death of Leander.

In *The Two Gentlemen of Verona*, when Proteus is forced by his father to leave Julia and travel to Milan (which, as H.V. Morton reminds us, once had a port),[31] he complains, "Thus have I shunn'd the fire for fear of burning, / And drench'd me in the sea, where I am drown'd" (I.iii.78-79). All he means, of course, is that by trying to prevent one evil, his father's discovery of his love for Julia, he has created a second, the command that he leave Verona. However, the predicament caused by his infatuation with Silvia later in the play creates in him that sensation of loss he had feared earlier and that in *The Comedy of Errors* and *The Taming of the Shrew* we associate with water and with being "drench'd." For Shakespeare's male characters, love seems to imply, one way or another, both gain and loss, life and death: "Julia I lose, and Valentine I lose: / If I keep them, I needs must lose myself; / If I lose them, thus find I by their loss— / For Valentine, myself; for Julia, Silvia" (II.vi.19-22). Here Proteus tells us explicitly that to "keep" Julia he must "lose" himself, that being faithful to Julia will force him to disobey his own desire to woo Silvia. What he is also implying, however, is that meeting Silvia has raised questions about his own identity, about where his truest sense of self resides. In *Love's Labour's Lost*, Berowne thinks in much the same terms when he argues that the courtiers of Navarre should turn from their segregated academy to the Princess of France and her ladies: "[Let] us once lose our oaths to find ourselves, / Or else we lose ourselves to keep our oaths" (IV.iii.358-59). Berowne echoes Proteus's formula, for he too argues that a man is "lost" without a woman. In this belief he is in agreement with Adriana and Luciana, who argue for marriage as "incorporation." Although the men in these plays almost always rationalize about motives and intentions, their sense of loss seems real enough.

Images of wind and water, and their inevitable suggestions of disintegration, are two among several important metaphors describing the geography of the male psyche at the beginning of Shakespeare's version of the New Comedy love story. Frequently, the hero feels as though life has become a dream, where both his senses and thought processes are either useless or misleading, and where only trust in a benevolent universe or faith in a woman can be his guide. Accosted by Adriana, Antipholus becomes confused, almost ready to believe that he is two people: "What, was I married to her in my dream? / Or sleep I now and think I hear all this? / What error drives our eyes and ears amiss?" (II.ii.182-84). The doubts about sanity and the sensation of dreaming in *The Comedy of Errors* derive ultimately from *Menaechmi*, where several characters, and especially Menaechmus of Epidamnus, the traveler, begin to assume that they must be asleep. The same sense of disorientation is clear in Plautus's *Amphityron* too, when Mercury tricks Sosia by presenting himself as the slave's double, and in other plays where tricks or deceptions are standard plot features. What distinguishes Shakespeare's treatment of this subject from Plautus's is that Antipholus, and Sebastian in *Twelfth Night*—a play similarly based on Plautine originals—seem to be genuinely groping for answers rather than merely posing the rhetorical question, "Am I dreaming?" In addition, their disorientation has to do primarily with the assumptions made by Adriana, Luciana, and Olivia, as possible sexual and marital partners, rather than with those of peripheral characters, such as slaves, merchants, or seamen. Their confusion makes much more meaningful their decision to enter the homes of the women, to test the water, so to speak, a gesture that seems merely opportunistic in Roman comedy, as when Menaechmus of Syracuse takes advantage of the courtesan's mistake, enters her house, is wined and dined, and sleeps with her only to mock her afterward. The sensation in *The Comedy of Errors*, then, is of a "sure uncertainty" (185), a phrase suggesting ambivalence as effectively as drowning and scattering do:

> Am I in earth, in heaven, or in hell?
> Sleeping or waking, mad or well-advis'd?
> Known unto these, and to myself disguis'd?
> I'll say as they say, and persever so,
> And in this mist at all adventures go. [212-16]

Of course, Antipholus does have good reason to be stunned by the apparent aggressiveness of Adriana, though his reactions are only exaggerations of the reactions of other males to more demure women. For him to enter the woman's house he must be less defensive and relax his grip on the world and reality as he knows it.

Though doubting, Antipholus is willing to try this adventure in a world of "mist," just as Petruchio is willing to tread a "maze." In *Twelfth Night*, based in part on Plautus's *Menaechmi* though written a decade later than *The Comedy of Errors*, we can see in Sebastian clear echoes of Antipholus of Syracuse, and though Sebastian is more fully delineated, there is little in his response to Olivia that is not obvious in the earlier character's response to Luciana. Sebastian's visit to a strange town where he had only hoped to see "the things of fame / That do renown this city" (III.iii.23-24), like Antipholus's sojourn in Ephesus, soon becomes a venture his reason cannot fathom. Olivia's command, "Go with me to my house" (IV.i.54), shakes his equilibrium and his trust in his senses: "What relish is in this? How runs the stream? / Or I am mad, or else this is a dream. / Let fancy still my sense in Lethe steep; / If it be thus to dream, still let me sleep" (60-63). The allusion to Lethe, dreaming, and "the stream" suggest further that he is being seduced to his own destruction, perhaps by drowning, and remind us of Antipholus and Lucentio. Shakespeare's more serious handling of the hero's emotions just as he meets a woman is even clearer when we compare Sebastian with Fabrizio, his counterpart in *Gl' Ingannati*, one of the probable sources for *Twelfth Night*, written by members of the Academy of the Thunderstruck (Intronati) in Siena, and acted in 1531. Like Sebastian, Fabrizio is called from the streets by a complete stranger, a woman who can only seem either insane or brazen. But unlike Sebastian or, for that matter, Antipholus, Fabrizio is at most mildly curious; there is no sense of his being disoriented, of his slipping into a distant and strange world where his very identity may be in jeopardy. Compare the passage quoted above from *Twelfth Night* with the following from *Gl' Ingannati*, spoken by Fabrizio: "I will stay and see what comes of this fairy-tale. Perhaps this woman is the servant of some courtesan, and hopes to relieve me of a few crowns. In that case she is a bad judge, for I am a pupil of the Spaniards, and am more likely to want a crown from her than to give her a shilling of my own. One of us will not be rooked anyway. If I move away from the house a little I can take note what people go in and out, and so discover what sort of woman she is."[32] Fabrizio's is the practical approach to romance that the Tuscan playwrights of the Cinquecento inherited from their Roman ancestors. It is only slightly less opportunistic and commercial than Menaechmus of Syracuse's fleecing of Erotium in *Menaechmi*.

Not satisfied with Sebastian's reaction to Olivia's apparent boldness, Shakespeare devotes another scene, IV.iii, to further examination of his confusion. Just before Olivia swoops down on him with a priest, Sebastian tries once again to understand this new and strange situation, which finds his soul at odds with his sense. He can only conclude, "there's something in't / That is deceivable" (20-21). Instead of spying on her house to "discover what sort of woman she is," Sebastian simply gives in: "I'll follow this good man, and go with you, / And having sworn truth, ever will be true" (32-33). In *Twelfth Night* a woman's invitation is treated neither as an opportunity for sexual conquest, as in *Gl' Ingannati,* nor as one for sexual conquest and robbery, as in *Menaechmi,* but simply as a "flood of fortune" (11) leading a man to question himself, his reason, and senses. This is as near as the comedies come to the syllogistic reasoning of the tragedies, and this is as it should be, for the young man's decision either to back off or to yield to sensation and go where the flood will take him—to risk drowning for the chance to stand like Jove on the "Cretan strond"—is as much at the heart of Shakespeare's comic vision as the hero's more serious decision to "rough hew" his future is to his tragic vision.

What Sebastian willingly submits to here in entering her house with Olivia and the priest, the courtiers of Navarre arm themselves against, and the operant metaphor in *Love's Labour's Lost* is indeed military. The play begins with the king and his three courtiers openly rejecting, or rather postponing, marriage and sexual contact with women. The men swear to support the principles of an academy, to war against "the huge army of the world's desires" (I.i.10), by which means they hope to achieve "fame" (1). The central "desire" their vows pledge them to conquer, however, has only to do with women. Navarre, who urges his men to wage war against their affections, seems to equate victory over physical temptation with gaining wisdom, as though education were simply abstinence and he the hermit in Milton's "Il Penseroso." Although all four courtiers agree to "study, fast, not sleep" (48), they chafe against the edict's demand that they agree "not to see a woman" (37) for three years. The academy reflects a state of mind in which women are the enemy against whom the men ought to be armed. Thus Navarre's academy is not so much a unit dedicated to positive advances as a fortress or an armed cloister, a kind of last stand against the mating ritual. Appropriately, the imagery in the play often suggests circles, with the court like an island whose perimeter the Princess and her ladies cannot penetrate. It is an imagery more traditionally associated with female characters than with male, as in *The Merry Wives of Windsor,* when Ford, as "Brook," asks Falstaff to "lay an amiable siege to the honesty of this Ford's wife" (II.ii.234) so that he himself might be able to "drive her then from the ward of her purity, her reputation, her marriage vow, and a thousand other her defenses, which now are too too strongly embattled against me" (248-51); or in *Cymbeline,* when the Second Lord prays, for Imogen, that "The heavens hold firm / The walls of thy dear honor"

(II.i.62-63), or when Cloten is advised that in wooing women music "will penetrate" (II.iii.11). To the men in *Love's Labour's Lost*, however, the ladies are the attacking force and are made to camp outside the court, beyond Navarre's "forbidden gates" (II.i.26) in tents, as though they were Tamburlaine and his horde threatening Damascus. To Boyet, the King's intentions are only too apparent:

> Marry, thus much have I learnt:
> He means rather to lodge you in the field,
> Like one that comes here to besiege his court,
> Than seek a dispensation for his oath,
> To let you enter his [unpeopled] house. [84-88]

Navarre himself tells the Princess, "You may not come, fair Princess, within my gates, / But here without you shall be so receiv'd / As you shall deem yourself lodg'd in my heart, / Though so denied fair harbour in my house" (171-74). His rationale for such incivility is that he must be true to his oath, but the effect of that fidelity is to prevent him from getting on with the business of comedy by committing himself to union with a woman.

In a long speech arguing against the courtiers' oaths, Berowne claims that "love, first learned in a lady's eyes, / Lives not alone immured in the brain" (IV.iii.324). However, when the men decide to forgo the principles of their academy, to open their "gates" and to visit the extramural world, they retain the military attitude, and approach the women as attacking troops rather than as dedicated and trusting lovers. The soldiers defending their academy have taken the offensive and are now "affection's men-at-arms" (286) advancing on the ladies. This, then, is how man meets woman in *Love's Labour's Lost*:

> *King.* Saint Cupid, then! and, soldiers, to the field!
> *Ber.* Advance your standards, and upon them, lords!
> Pell-mell, down with them! but be first advis'd,
> In conflict that you get the sun of them. [363-66]

What these men soon learn is that they simply cannot have it both ways: either a woman is the "queen of queens" (39), a "goddess" (63), a tutor, from whom "doth spring the true Promethean fire" (300), as they suggest throughout act 4 when they decide to woo, or she is the enemy to be distrusted and conquered. The play is almost schizophrenic in this parallel set of images describing the women as an alien force and yet at the same time as the source of all learning, wisdom, and fame.

Shakespeare's great interest in the ways in which psychological aspects of character derive in part from sociological circumstances, is what, in the first place, distinguishes his treatment of the New Comedy love story from that of his sources, where external impediments, and external and superficial changes in response to those impediments—a disguise to confuse a father, for example—are the sum total of what happens in a comedy. In Shakespeare, father/son separation reveals those complex associations peculiar to societies that invest the patrilinear with special obligations. To the son, women are goddesses, Ariadne, Europa, and Leda, but also the enemy for whom he must place himself in jeopardy or against whom he must be armed. Thus, a central issue that emerges from the way Shakespeare develops his love stories has to do with male notions about the nature of women. To say, as I have throughout this chapter, that the men are ambivalent about their adventures, independence, and women, or that they explicitly reject heterosexual life, as Navarre and his courtiers do (or as Benedick does in *Much Ado about Nothing* or Angelo in *Measure for Measure*), is really to say that the men seem unable to settle on a clear view of women. When Cymbeline learns in act 5 that his Queen "confess'd she never lov'd" him (v.37), he calls her a "most delicate fiend" (47) and asks, "Who is't can read a woman?" (48). Repeatedly, almost obsessively, Shakespeare's comedies present worlds in which men stagger from one view of women to its opposite, alternately offensive and defensive, enraptured and enraged, adoring women and degrading them, as though the problem for men, and the issue for the play, were simply how to "read" a woman and then how to act accordingly. Poor, pitiful, confused Cymbeline is left musing,

> Mine eyes
> Were not in fault, for she was beautiful;
> Mine ears, that [heard] her flattery, nor my heart,
> That thought her like her seeming. It had been vicious
> To have mistrusted her. [62-66]

Though it is that dichotomous vision that accounts, by and large, for the difficulties and separations comprising the plots of these plays, Shakespeare's genius permitted him, ultimately, to see the split, not in women, but in male views of those women, and to write plays that describe the various and complex ways in which the male psyche heals itself and is reintegrated. While the young men of Shakespearean comedy are busy assessing the usefulness of "eyes" and "ears" ("What error drives our eyes and ears amiss?") and the reactions of their hearts, faithful women are at work helping to mend the broken males.

2

"We Cannot Fight for Love"

In *Reinventing Womanhood*, Carolyn G. Heilbrun suggests that "the stories of women are the stories of acceptance, and passivity,"[1] and Rachel Brownstein, in *Becoming a Heroine*, tells us that "a beautiful virgin walled off from an imperfect real world is the central figure in romance."[2] Feminist criticism has argued persuasively that the heroines of literature are at least virginal and passive, waiting like so many Sleeping Beauties for the liberating and vivifying influence of a heroic man. Bound by stultifying paternalistic codes, the women are free only to fulfill preordained roles leading to marriage and motherhood or to sequestration in a convent. Beatrice in *The Changeling* calls being a man "the soul of freedom";[3] Emma Bovary wants to bear a male child, for a "man is free, at least—free to range the passions and the world, to surmount obstacles, to taste the rarest pleasures. Whereas a woman is continually thwarted. Inert, compliant, she has to struggle against her physical weakness and legal subjection. Her will, like the veil tied to her hat, quivers with every breeze: there is always a desire that entices, always a convention that restrains."[4] Isabel Archer, in *The Portrait of a Lady*, tells her cousin, Ralph Touchett, "I'm not in the least an adventurous spirit. Women are not like men."[5]

More often than not, the hero of Shakespearean comedy falls in love with a woman who seems at first just such an unadventurous, beautiful, and imprisoned virgin. Her actions appear circumscribed, first of all, in physical terms, for she is often restricted to her room or house. Miranda in *The Tempest* is trapped on an uncharted island, though Silvia's plight in *The Two Gentlemen of Verona* is more common, "Her chamber is aloft, far from the ground" (III.i.114). Bianca in *The Taming of the Shrew* is restrained and must stay indoors; though unhappy, she obeys her father, declaring, "My books and instruments shall be my company" (I.i.82). Jessica, in *The Merchant of Venice*, is told to "go in" (II.V.51) by her father; "Do as I bid you," Shylock demands, "shut doors after you; / Fast bind, fast find" (53-54).[6] The same strength of purpose can be seen in the first scene of *Cymbeline*, as we learn that Imogen has been "imprison'd" (I.i.8) by her father for having married Posthumus Leonatus; Isabella, in *Measure for*

Measure, has chosen the convent; and Olivia, in *Twelfth Night,* has voluntarily turned her house into a kind of cloister. Mourning the deaths of father and brother twelve months earlier, Olivia has let it be known that for seven years even the "element itself" "Shall not behold her face at ample view; / But like a cloistress she will veiled walk, / And water once a day her chamber round / With eye-offending brine" (I.i.25-29). Like Bianca, most women are simply presented to us as creatures of an indoor world. The first line Anne Page speaks in *The Merry Wives of Windsor* is an invitation on her father's behalf to Slender, Shallow, and Sir Hugh Evans for dinner, "Will't please your worship to come in, sir?" (I.i.266), just as the first we hear from Adriana, through the Dromio of Ephesus, is that "she is so hot, because the meat is cold: / The meat is cold, because you come not home" (I.ii.47-48).

The physical restraints on these women, whether imposed from without or self-imposed, reflect, of course, a traditional attitude toward woman's place in society. And though recent studies indicate that some women in the Middle Ages and the Renaissance were perhaps more influential and active than has been generally assumed, literature reflects a more conservative view.[7] Indeed, in some senses Elizabethan and Jacobean drama reads embarrassingly like a history of female incarceration. From *The Spanish Tragedy's* Bel-Imperia, who is "sequestered" by her brother and who moans, "Well, force perforce, I must constrain myself / To patience, and apply me to the time, / Till heaven, as I have hoped, shall set me free,"[8] to Isabella in *The Changeling,* who can only joke to her husband's man, "If you / Keep me in a cage, pray whistle to me,"[9] to Penthea in *The Broken Heart,* whose husband has her "window next the street damm'd up,"[10] women are kept in and down by real physical pressures as well as by the more daunting pressures of custom and psychology. Before he is confronted by Brabantio, Othello describes marriage in terms that define traditional male and female roles:

> for know, Iago,
> But that I love the gentle Desdemona,
> I would not my unhoused free condition
> Put into circumscription and confine
> For the sea's worth. [I.ii.24-28]

The New Variorum *Othello* describes the sentiments here as "natural to an adventurer,"[11] though they are typical of most male heroes in Shakespearean comedy who, as we have seen, expect (or are expected) to travel, study, or war far from home. Marriage, identified with women, is described as a limiting institution antithetical to the "free condition" in which a man ought to live, as Bertram takes it in refusing forced marriage to Helena, "O my Parolles, they have married me! / I'll to the Tuscan wars, and never bed her" (II.iii.272-73). A married man is a limited man, circumscribed by his "house" rather than free and wandering the seas. In marriage—even in a marriage for love, such as Othello's—the male becomes "housed," a husband, the interior world of the house being understood as the natural province of the woman, and the exterior world as that of the man.[12]

Societal norms demanded that women develop the domestic arts and stay indoors. In figurative ways as well, women were restrained. From gowns and veils to disguises, coffins, and statues, Shakespeare's women are contained, covered, and bound. It is little wonder, then, that an analogy was often drawn between literature's sequestered virgin and nun in cloister or convent. The plain fact is that Shakespeare's heroines are compared so often to nuns, and occasionally become novices, sisters, and votaresses indeed, because like nuns they are immured, wear disguises, and often undergo the sorts of trials associated with sacrifices for religion. Metaphorically, nunneries and the conventual way of life suggested sterility and death, and thus were useful indicators of the tragic possibilities at the center of a comedy. With heroines imprisoned by walls and conventions in act 1 and by disguises and "death" in act 3, we ought not be surprised to find that comedies, in fact, appear similar in plot and structure to *chansons de nonnes* and other forms of popular literature written and sung about convent life in the Middle Ages. The two great themes of such literature, according to Eileen Power's invaluable compendium, *Medieval English Nunneries*, are "the nun unwillingly professed" and "the broken-hearted wife or lover, Guinevere hiding her sorrows in the silent cloister."[13] Both themes have their parallels in plots used by Shakespeare and his contemporaries. For example, Hermia is threatened by Theseus with "the livery of a nun, / For aye to be in shady cloister mew'd, / To live a barren sister all your life, / Chaunting faint hymns to the cold fruitless moon" (I.i.70-73). In similar ways, other heroines seem to be "unwillingly professed." Imogen is imprisoned, Silvia, Bianca, and Jessica locked in their rooms, Hero forced to play dead by the Friar, Hermione trapped in a sarcophagus in a chapel and as a statue in a gallery, and Miranda marooned on an island on a sort of perpetual retreat. Indeed, most of Shakespeare's heroines are in distress in act 1 precisely because they feel confined by convention, walls, and clothing, as nuns in fact are.

That songs written about nuns and convent life in Europe in the Middle Ages read surprisingly like summaries of Shakespeare's comedies tells us how deeply Shakespeare isolates, in one way or another, the young woman in comedy. Power's translation of a thirteenth-century French poem reads like the typical plot of Renaissance comedies in its content if not in its tone:

> The curse of Jesus on him who made me a nun! All unwillingly say I vespers and compline; more fain were I to lead a happy life of gaiety and love. *I feel the delicious pangs beneath my bosom. The curse of God on him who made me be a nun!* She cried, God's curse on him who put me in this abbey. But by our Lady I will flee away from it and never will I wear this gown and habit. *I feel, etc.* I will send for him whose love I am and bid him come seek me in this abbey. We will go to Paris and lead a gay life, for he is fair and I am young. *I feel, etc.* When her lover heard her words, he leapt for joy and his heart beat fast. He came to the gate of that abbey, and stole away his darling love. *I feel, etc.*[14]

The nun's lament and its story of the trapped and angry woman captures the mood of Hermia and Silvia, and that of countless other daughters and wives in Renaissance drama. It is an important plot element in *The Merry Devil of Edmonton,* for example, where Millisent's father, Sir Arthur Clare, sends his daughter to a nunnery to keep her from Raymond Mounchensey, whom he considers beneath her. Mounchensey, disguised as a friar, visits Millisent and steals her away. Millisent's excuse to her father, later in the play, is that "Love, thwarted, turns itself to thousand wiles."[15]

The threat of being sent off to a convent had in fact been eliminated in England with the dissolution of the nunneries in the earlier sixteenth century, though until that time convents were fairly common. The chansons were popular because the convents accepted not only those with a vocation but also, as the drama reflects, many girls and women who had entered unwillingly but were nonetheless forced to take the vow of chastity.[16] Thus, Theseus and Egeus, threatening Hermia with the convent, recall not only the blocking agents of Roman drama but also a way of life not long forgotten in England.

Church records, chansons, and stories of nuns suggest further parallels between actual convent life, the cloistered life pictured in Renaissance drama, and the everyday life of young women in Shakespearean comedy. For example, some of the shifts of the imprisoned nuns in the chansons prefigure those of Shakespeare's trapped heroines. Power tells the story of one Agnes de Flixthorpe, a nun of St. Michael's, Stamford, whose history bears "tragic witness to the desperation into which convent life could throw one who was not suited for it."[17] After requesting release several times and being denied, Agnes escaped and was apprehended wearing man's clothes. Her cross-dressing reminds us of the ploys used by the heroines in comedy to hide their own identities and to try to find some of the freedom thought to be associated with male attire. Over and over the chansons complain bitterly about the habit and celebrate nuns who escape with lovers and avoid the convent or simply outwit church officials. Priests are carried to nuns' rooms in chests, and young, handsome men are hired as gardeners in cloisters. Silvia in her high chamber and Valentine with his rope ladder find obvious analogues in *chansons de nonnes* because both songs and play give the victory to love over the sterility of the cloistered life.

The heroine unwillingly sent to an abbey or threatened with living a life like that of a nun is at the heart of comedies like *The Merry Devil of Edmonton, A Midsummer-Night's Dream,* or *The Merchant of Venice* (Lorenzo and Jessica), where the action involves the hero's outwitting his lover's guardians. But there are, of course, Shakespearean heroines who *willingly* enter a convent: Aemilia sequesters herself after losing husband and sons in a shipwreck; Mariana in *Measure for Measure* takes refuge at the "moated grange" (III.i.264) at Saint Luke's, and Isabella chooses life in a convent with "the votarists of Saint Clare" (I.iv.5); and Thaisa becomes a votaress of Diana. Other female characters are willingly professed, though only in a figurative sense. Olivia evades the importunate Orsino by living a life like that of a "cloistress"; Rosalind, Viola, Portia, Helena, and Imogen voluntarily don habits of a sort and immure their personality beneath the folds of disguise. More often it is actions such as these that characterize the typically "Shakespearean" plots than those that feature the nun "unwillingly professed" or the woman who enters a convent in fact. In *The Two Gentlemen of Verona, As You Like It, Twelfth Night, Cymbeline,* and others, it is travail brought about by her relationship with lover or husband that forces the woman to live in some ways as a nun does, simply waiting "like Patience on a monument" (*TN*, II.iv.114), sleeping or "dying" while a surrogate, a friar, duke, or friend, such as Paulina, or a male creation of her own ("Cesario," "Balthazar," "Fidele") works on her behalf. These heroines act out far more complex behaviors than those of women trapped solely by external forces.

Often the same woman who finds herself "unwillingly professed," that is, coerced by father, law, and custom, in act 1, finds herself a willing "Guinevere hiding her sorrows in the silent cloister" in act 3. Imogen is imprisoned by her father but is imprisoned a second time—and in a far more dreadful manner—when Posthumus's rejection of her leads to her dressing as a page, assuming a new identity ("Fidele"), wandering near Milford Haven, and finally collapsing into a death-like state after drinking the queen's potion. Helena limited by her social position as ward at Rossillion is relatively free compared with Helena "dead," or that version of herself who journeys to Saint Jaques le Grand only to assume the place and personality of Diana. Viola is restricted as a vulnerable woman with neither family nor friends when she lands in Illyria but is constricted in a yet more telling manner by the male attire she dons soon after. Far from conferring on her the freedom traditionally associated with a man's clothing, Viola's doublet and hose restrain her even more fully than chamber walls restrain Olivia. Ironically, in these plays the real walls of prison, chamber, or convent usually only encourage lovers' advances, prompting assaults with rope ladders, or midnight escapades through the forest, whereas the woman's wearing male attire stops such assaults entirely. Angelo is aroused by the novice Isabella, and Orsino, who never tires of importuning the "cloistress" Olivia, is oblivious to the disguised Viola. The heroine's male clothes necessitate her acting, at the least modifying language and gesture to accommodate the pretense, and, though unconventional, serve the purposes of convention by restricting— indeed, thwarting—sexual activity, for example, by unsexing Viola into the limbo life of a eunuch.[18] Thus, the real restrictions of act 1, the father's playing the jailer and the patriarchy's laying down the law, are far less forbidding than the metaphorical restrictions of act 3 when the heroine is truly trapped, submerged beneath a covering so complete and effective that who she appears to be has little relation to who she really is. The swaggering young "boys" usually attract all the wrong attention: Phebe falls for Rosalind as Olivia does for Viola, and Guiderius and Arviragus, her own brothers, are Imogen's only real admirers when she is disguised as Fidele.[19]

In Shakespearean comedy, the woman who disguises herself willingly not only is a more typical heroine but is also involved in a far more complex plot than that which characterizes pre-Shakespearean comedy, especially the plays of the Italian Renaissance. Even in Greene's *Friar Bacon and Friar Bungay*, Margaret's reaction to Lacy's spurning her, the announcement that, of her own accord, she "will straight to stately Framingham, / And in the abbey there be shorn a nun, / And yield my loves and liberty to God,"[20] indicates a greater sophistication in plotting and characterization than those plays that simply turn on the conflict between despotic parents and abused daughters forced into convents. Greene, however, misses the psychological depth of Shakespeare's plots by having Margaret's choice be a reaction to Lacy's inscrutable letter of rejection, which he later claims was merely an attempt to try her constancy. Such a trial links this play to patient Griselda literature, where problems are entirely external, rather than to comedies like *All's Well That Ends Well*, where the "pilgrimage" of the heroine is more than merely a retreat and involves instead a splitting of her self into active and passive, male and female personas.

More often than not, it is the men who initiate the action in Shake-speare's comedies, journeying, guessing riddles, but the women who take most of the risks. The men are, after all, separated from their fathers and their homes when they meet women, while the women fall in love under the sharp eye of parents and within the strict boundary of familiar conven-tions and laws. Nonetheless, her love for the man emboldens the woman: for him she defies parents and nation, sacrificing her womanhood and jeopardizing her sense of self. She promises all, gives all, and remains constant to her vows. Though it is most often, and understandably so, the male character who falls in love first—only Rosalind, Olivia, Helena, and Thaisa express their feelings before the man does—it is the woman who, in a sense, creates the love story.

The heroine does all she can, and that is often a great deal, feeling herself, as Portia does, "an unlesson'd girl, unschool'd, unpractic'd" (*MV*, III.ii.159). At the very least Shakespeare's heroines hint and wink to help their lovers, like Portia, who sings a song that perhaps "contains a dis-guised warning to Bassanio not to choose by fancy,"[21] or Bianca, who tries to preserve some semblance of academic propriety during her Latin lesson with "Cambio" (Lucentio) but who nevertheless indulges her passion for him by translating Ovid to her own advantage: "'*Hic ibat Simois,*' I know you not, '*Hic est [Sigeia] tellus,*' I trust you not, '*Hic steterat Priami,*' take heed he hear us not, '*regia,*' presume not, '*celsa senis,*' despair not" (III.i.42-45). The woman's passion, however, usually reveals itself in more direct and daring ways. Rosalind falls in love with Orlando as soon as she sees him and, minutes later, after he defeats Charles the wrestler, gives him a chain from her neck, asking him to "Wear this for me: one out of suits with Fortune, / That could give more, but that her hand lacks means" (I.ii.246-47). Even she is astonished by her openness and generosity and tells Celia, "My pride fell with my fortunes" (252). Julia gives Proteus a ring, Imogen gives her husband, Posthumus, a diamond, and Olivia, after having sent "Cesario" a ring, hands Sebastian a pearl. These gifts are sometimes offered us tokens, tangible symbols of the lovers' vows, as when Portia gives her ring to Bassanio before he leaves her to be with Antonio in Venice. But always, the chains, rings, and jewels are simply gifts flowing generously from the women to the men they love. The heroine's gener-osity is so complete that it betokens at once loyalty, honesty, and uncondi-tional trust. The gift is the woman herself.

The heroine's generosity when she meets and falls in love with the hero is not surprising given cultural imperatives restraining her free movement and inhibiting her choice. However, there is at least a surface contradiction in her situation at the beginning of the play. She seems, and often is, as restrained as a nun in a cloister, but nevertheless has all the power that wealth, position, intelligence, and beauty can confer. Thaisa, Perdita, and the Princess of France are daughters of kings; Rosalind, Celia, Silvia, and Miranda are daughters of dukes; Hero is the daughter of a governor; and Olivia is a countess. Helena is the daughter of a renowned physician and becomes a special interest of the King, as do Isabella and Mariana of the Duke in *Measure for Measure*. Most of the women either run estates or are heiresses to title and fortune and are therefore special to their nations as well as to their fathers.

Occasionally, the combination of a woman's beauty and virtue alone creates a mysterious effect, doubly disarming to suitors when coupled with wealth, as in Portia's case. Marina, Perdita, and Miranda of the romances are especially alluring, and seem to have an otherworldly, almost magical power over men around them. Such is surely the case with Helena, the least obviously powerful of all such women, and with Portia, perhaps the most, and it is to these two characters we now turn. Though the social situations are entirely dissimilar—Portia is an heiress and Helena a ward—the ways in which they interact with men and their apparent effect on men seem identical. Both are enterprising, even forceful, though in different ways. When Helena visits Paris and offers to cure the King, Lafew reminds us that she is the daughter of a legendary physician. He enjoins her to "hold the credit of your father" (I.i.78), and although Helena confides, "I think not on my father (79), all around her do. Lafew announces her to the King of France simply as "Dr. She" (II.i.79), one who "hath amaz'd me" (84). Despite his reluctance to consult physicians yet again, the King is drawn as much by Helena herself as by her description of her father's secret cure. And when the King asks how long it would take him to recover, Helena speaks no longer like a simple girl from the provinces but rather like one of Marlowe's Eastern plenipotentiaries, or a witch from the moors of Scotland:

> The greatest grace lending grace,
> Ere twice the horses of the sun shall bring
> Their fiery torcher his diurnal ring,
> Ere twice in murk and occidental damp
> Moist Hesperus hath quench'd her sleepy lamp,
> Or four and twenty times the pilot's glass
> Hath told the thievish minutes how they pass,
> What is infirm from your sound parts shall fly,
> Health shall live free, and sickness freely die. [160-68]

Helena is no Rappaccini's daughter, ignorant of her effect and her power; she and the cure, her father's "dearest issue" (106), are one and the same.

Helena truly is "Dr. She," and it is little wonder that the King comes to believe that in her "some blessed spirit doth speak" (175).

"Throughout *All's Well That Ends Well*," Arthur Kirsch remarks, "our responses to Helena and to the action that she generates are affected by our awareness of the transcendental force that is working through them."[22] Not only is Helena aware of her power and of her being apprehended by the court of France as "blessed," but she is given by the King yet another kind of power, a more tangible one, when she cures him. In *All's Well That Ends Well*, Helena "hast power to choose" (II.iii.56) among bachelors for a husband, and "they none to forsake" (56); perhaps for that very reason she is at pains to turn her taking Bertram into a form of giving herself. Though Northrop Frye reminds us that the critics "have not yet stopped making faces" at this play for reversing the conventions of the courting rituals,[23] Helena clearly does her best to hand her power, from the King, to Bertram, and to reestablish, if only in her language, the social status quo: "I dare not say I take you, but I give / Me and my service, ever whilst I live, / Into your guiding power.—This is the man" (II.iii.102-4). And in the very next line, the King, who gave her power to choose, echoes her language in commanding Bertram, "Take her, she's thy wife." Out of the idiosyncratic selection process devised for her by the King, Helena has subtly created the conventional—"giving" herself rather than "taking" a man. She tries to assuage Bertram not only by calling him a "man" (others in the play are less charitable) but also by suggesting that he is the active partner and she the passive.[24] Helena, however, is one of Shakespeare's few impoverished heroines, and until the King prefers her she has little to offer a material-minded male such as Bertram claims to be. Much more typical of women in the comedies are Olivia, Hero, or Portia, whose generosity is matched only by her astonishing wealth. Rosalind may temporarily "lack the means" to give a man more than a chain; Portia does not.

The Merchant of Venice is perhaps best remembered for two pivotal scenes, III.ii, when Bassanio wins Portia, and IV.i, when, in a sense, Portia wins Bassanio by saving Antonio from Shylock. The first of these is the focus of the "casket" plot, and the second that of the "bond" plot. The two scenes are related in a number of ways, as several critics have pointed out, and share a common origin in Bassanio's need to court Portia told us in I.i.[25] By borrowing money from Antonio, which he uses to woo her, Bassanio sows the seeds of his eventual separation from Portia when Antonio defaults. Or, to put it another way, the friend on whom he relies to win Portia becomes the reason he must separate from her later. Thus, Bassanio, in effect, engages himself to Antonio before tying himself to Portia as her husband. In this light, the two relationships are contradictory in nature; they pull in opposite directions and threaten to destroy Bassanio's marriage during the trial in IV.i.

Before Shakespeare separates Bassanio from Portia at the end of the "casket" scene, he allows us a very full look at Bassanio winning Portia, undergoing the dangerous ordeal that can end either in his marriage to Portia or in the sterility of single life. In *The Comedy of Errors, Love's Labour's Lost, The Taming of the Shrew,* and *Twelfth Night* we see the complex but abbreviated responses of the young men as they meet women and promptly fall in love. There the men feel lost or confused, hesitant or opposed to marriage. But in *The Merchant of Venice* Shakespeare expands the male response into an entire scene, indeed, rationalizes that response, as Bassanio chooses among the three caskets and vies for Portia. Leo Salingar in part distinguishes Shakespeare from the playwrights of the Italian Renaissance in his showing us young men "falling in love" rather than "already in love,"[26] and this shift in focus allows Shakespeare to concentrate on the change in these characters who, Salingar claims, feel themselves "transformed": "they take a literary language remote from their daily lives (or the daily lives of their audience) to say so. They quote, in effect, from the highest secular literature inculcated by Tudor schoolmasters, but the imagery they draw upon still has an alien colouring. And it is dramatically appropriate for this very reason."[27] The trial is self-consciously compared by both Bassanio and Portia to well-known adventures from mythology, all of which threaten heroes and, through them, heroines, with death. Lucentio's reference to Jove, for example, seems a trifle when compared with the many references in this scene to epic adventures. In fact, III.ii echoes language Bassanio uses in I.i when he first describes Belmont and Portia to Antonio. She is

> nothing undervalu'd
> To Cato's daughter, Brutus' Portia.
> For the four winds blow in from every coast
> Renowned suitors, and her sunny locks
> Hang on her temples like a golden fleece,
> Which makes her seat of Belmont Colchis' strond,
> And many Jasons come in quest of her. [166-72]

Bassanio's description inevitably reminds us of Petruchio's arrival in Padua, blown "from old Verona" (I.ii.49), and of Lucentio's description of Europa on the "Cretan strond" (I.i.170). Here the allusion to Jason and the golden fleece reiterates the imagery of the sea voyage and the archetype of the heroic young man on a perilous adventure risking all for a grand reward.

It is Portia who makes clear the mortal consequences of an incorrect choice as Bassanio stands before the three chests. She pleads with him to postpone the test, and at line 61 ends her lengthy and somewhat confused speech by reminding him, "Live thou, I live." Her insistence on exaggerating the consequences of a wrong choice is thoroughly in keeping with the spirit of romance, whose lovers vow either to marry one another or to die. It was Portia's father who forced the casket ritual upon her as a way of directing her affairs even after his death; thus, in a sense, her father selects the young man whom she will marry and stands between Portia and Bassanio, whom she has clearly chosen prior to the trial. The ritual itself, therefore, suggests on one level that the contest is between the wishes of Portia's dead father and her own living desires. It is difficult to disagree with Kittredge, however, who observes that "throughout the play there is an implication that Portia's father was right in believing that the caskets would make a proper choice for his daughter."[28] Thus, another equally valid opposition seems to exist between Portia and her father on the one hand and Bassanio on the other. Will Bassanio prove to be as shallow and unworthy as previous suitors, or will he be the one young man whose philosophy of life coincides with that of Portia and her father? What the trial seems to be about at this point is whether or not Bassanio merits Portia.

Portia's anxiety is understandable, as is her confidence, which manifests itself in her comparison between Bassanio and Hercules:

> Now he goes,
> With no less presence, but with much more love,
> Than young Alcides, when he did redeem
> The virgin tribute paid by howling Troy
> To the sea-monster. I stand for sacrifice;
> The rest aloof are the Dardanian wives,
> With bleared visages, come forth to view
> The issue of th' exploit. Go, Hercules,
> Live thou, I live; with much, much more dismay
> I view the fight than thou that mak'st the fray. [53-62]

Portia's allusions indicate that her life is in jeopardy, just as she assumes Bassanio's is in his fight with the sea monster to whom Hesione stood as virgin sacrifice. The comparison between Bassanio and Hercules she herself realizes is limited, though it is sufficient to imply that error will mean death, in one form or another, for the two lovers. Much the same is implied in Rosalind's wish for Orlando, "Now Hercules be thy speed, young man!" (I.ii.205) as he turns to battle the Duke's wrestler. Portia's reference to the Hercules/Hesione myth (and perhaps to the death of Orpheus as well)[29] emphasizes the dangers of an incorrect choice and, more importantly, suggests the kind of extraordinary effort required of Bassanio in approaching her as a suitor. Her allusions to mythology imply an obligation on the part of the man to submit himself to the sea and face unknown perils for the woman—when boy meets girl in Shakespearean comedy his chances of drowning are as great as those of his rising on a distant shore. And, as if by way of example, we see the Prince of Morocco, one of many Jasons, travel the seas to marry death, not Portia.

If we strip away the metaphors and allusions embellishing this scene we can more easily see the actual demands Portia's father makes of Bassanio. The casket test asks first of all that the man be courageous enough to accept its rules and consequences (and we learn that several suitors are not). Secondly, it requires a quality of perception that ought to protect marriage from disruption. That is, to avoid the golden chest is to see beyond glittery surfaces, and to cherish things of fundamental value. It suggests the sort of character that can resist temptations of body and mind, resist, in Troilus's phrase, "th' attest of eyes and ears" (V.ii.122) alone. However, when Portia says, of the caskets, "I am lock'd in one of them; / If you do love me, you will find me out" (40-41), she makes the choice more specific than her father had, implying that the test has to do specifically with knowing her rather than with more general principles. To follow her suggestion is to see the chests as symbols of herself: either Portia's beauty is skin-deep, a lure signifying death, or her truest beauty is her virtue.

For Portia the choice seems to be a clever test to determine whether Bassanio's understanding of her is adult and healthy, based on who she really is rather than on what she looks like, or shallow, similar to the ways of preceiving used by the King and his courtiers in *Love's Labour's Lost* when they are tricked merely by changed visors, or by Proteus, for example, in rejecting Julia for Silvia. Bassanio, however, sees the casket test in yet a third way, quite different from Portia's or her father's. For him, the chests are symbolic of kinds of women, the true and the false, rather than representations of general attitudes toward appearance and reality, or emblems of Portia specifically. He interprets the casket ritual as a test to determine whether he can tell one sort of woman from another.

Shakespeare spends a good deal of time here allowing Bassanio to explain his choice of the leaden chest and to lecture Portia and the audience on the danger of being deceived by appearance. Although Bassanio at first reacts to the golden chest by discussing how appearance deceives in law and religion, he reserves the heart of his indignant response to a repudiation of false women in particular. In denouncing such shams, Bassanio draws a comparison between the gold chest and blond hair, a comparison that once again relies on mythology:

> So are those crisped snaky golden locks,
> Which [make] such wanton gambols with the wind
> Upon supposed fairness, often known
> To be the dowry of a second head,
> The skull that bred them in the sepulchre. [92-96]

In this rather macabre reference to the extensive Elizabethan use of hairpieces, Bassanio suggests that not all "fleeces" are genuine.[30] The true hero, so he leads us to believe, must be able to distinguish between reality and mere appearance, for the choice has mortal consequences. In "snaky," an allusion to the Gorgons and Medusa, Bassanio makes clear the awful result of being led by one's eyes alone. He emphatically rejects women who are hollow shells, all embellishment and no substance, for such a golden woman is false, and ultimately evil, we are told, tempting men to live in what sonnet 129 calls "a waste of shame." In other words, the woman who is "good in nothing but in sight" (*Per*, I.i.123) is indeed the enemy of whom the men in Navarre have so much to say. Ornament, Bassanio continues, is like "the beauteous scarf / Veiling an Indian beauty" (98-99), a trick, "The seeming truth which cunning times put on / To entrap the wisest" (100-101). In short, Bassanio skillfully leads us to believe that the casket test and the issue of appearances have mainly to do with women, and that the man who can distinguish the false woman from the true, the evil from the good, is best prepared for marriage. For Bassanio, Portia, as a golden-haired beauty, is, then, symbolic either of the golden fleece or of Medusa.

Bassanio's musing before the chests leads us inexorably to just such a discussion of good and evil women. And yet there is something profoundly unfair and misleading about our evaluating women and discussing female morality at all, for what we witness in this scene is only one sort of woman, the scrupulously loyal Portia. The question we are obliged to ask is why Bassanio lectures Portia, her attendants, and the audience on the dangers of seduction by false women as though he were a city wit, like Jonson's Clerimont in *Epicoene*, who pens ditties about women and cosmetics, "Lady, it is to be presumed, / Though Art's hid cause are not found, / All is not sweet, all is not sound,"[31] or an early version of Bosola in *The Duchess of Malfi*, who calls such painting "scurvy face-physic"[32] and who describes an old woman's closet as "a shop of witchcraft" (II.i.41). Is there not something inappropriate, illogical, and insulting about Bassanio's obsessive reduction of the anemic truism, "All that glisters is not gold" (the legend the Prince of Morocco finds in the golden chest [II.vii.65]), into a lesson for men on how to avoid a world of Medusas? Of whom is he thinking? And what is Portia to make of his pontificating on "supposed fairness"? Like several other male characters in these comedies, Bassanio seems to assume, a priori, that most beautiful women are shams and traps. The chests, then, which Bassanio leads us to interpret as symbols of kinds of women, perhaps function instead as symbols of male attitudes *toward* women, for it is mostly in the hero's psyche, and not in the exterior world of these plays, that good and evil women reside side by side.

Shakespeare calls attention to Bassanio's questionable attitudes toward women in his reaction to the picture of Portia he sees once he does choose correctly and opens the leaden chest. When he suddenly realizes that she is his, he confuses the golden fleece with the false locks of "supposed fairness" and describes Portia in altogether ambiguous terms. He admires the likeness and, feeling himself swept away by the beauty of the picture, suddenly sees Portia as aggressive and dangerous:

> Here in her hairs
> The painter plays the spider, and hath woven
> A golden mesh t'entrap the hearts of men
> Faster than gnats in cobwebs. [120-23]

Earlier Bassanio generalized, and it was false women, the "Indian beauty" behind her "beauteous scarf," who were dangerous; now it is Portia herself whose beauty turns men into trapped insects. Both scenarios describe women as active and predatory and men as passive victims. Though Bassanio intends no more than to pay Portia high compliment, it is not a long stride from "crisped snaky golden locks" to the "golden mesh t' entrap the hearts of men," a phrase that echoes his earlier denunciation of ornament as "seeming truth which cunning times puts on / To entrap the wisest." (100-1)[33] In the context of this scene and of this play, these lines are a gloss on his earlier speech and betray confusion and fear. Bassanio's "cobweb"—like the "snaky locks"—seems reminiscent of Petruchio's "maze" and of Antipholus's "losing" himself. Although we are invited by Bassanio throughout this scene to envision a world of good men choosing between two opposing types of women, the victim Hesione and the violator Medusa, the true and the false, what his images reveal to us as fully as do Navarre's allusions to the military is that Shakespearean comedy, on the contrary, is about good women confronted by men in whom contend contrary ways of apprehending women to whom they are attracted. Although there are faithless or evil women in some of these plays (Cressida, the Princess of Antioch in *Pericles*, the Queen in *Cymbeline*), they are a distinct minority; in general, Shakespearean comedy shows us women whose constancy, in fact, calls into question their taste and judgment. But in delineating heroines whose virtue is generally a given, Shakespeare opts for psychological complexity rather than for a series of cut-and-dried choices made by men between good and evil; in other words, the possibility for happiness or despair resides within the male characters themselves rather than outside them. The audience is often seduced by the thinking of the males into believing that the men are constant and the women changeable partly because literature, like life, still tends to reproduce and validate male views, but also because Shakespearean comedy, in using so many of the trappings of fairy tales, lulls us into assuming that the ethos of the fairy tale, with its black and white characters, is the ethos of the play.

Bassanio's choosing correctly opens a floodgate of giving by Portia, all the more impressive when one remembers that Bassanio is himself insolvent: "when I told you / My state was nothing, I should then have told you / That I was worse than nothing" (258-60). The scroll inside the leaden casket enjoins him to "claim her with a loving kiss" (138). Like Helena, Bassanio finds himself in something of an awkward position. He is asked to "claim" as spouse a person of far greater wealth and higher social standing than he. And like Helena he is reluctant to play the active part, even to believe that he has indeed won her, feeling "doubtful whether what I see be true, / Until confirm'd, sign'd, ratified by you" (147-48). But whereas Bertram is unwilling to take what Helena so graciously gives, Portia is pleased to give what Bassanio seems too diffident to take. When she immediately "confirms" and "ratifies" his victory, Portia sounds like Helena when she chooses Bertram, subtly suggesting that for her their sex roles have not been reversed even if their fortunes seem so, but also declaring her absolute loyalty to Bassanio and trust in herself:

> But the full sum of me
> Is sum of something; which, to term in gross,
> Is an unlesson'd girl, unschool'd, unpractic'd,
> Happy in this, she is not yet so old
> But she may learn; happier than this,
> She is not bred so dull but she can learn;
> Happiest of all, is that her gentle spirit
> Commits itself to yours to be directed,
> As from her lord, her governor, her king.
> Myself, and what is mine, to you and yours
> Is now converted. But now I was the lord
> Of this fair mansion, master of my servants,
> Queen o'er myself; and even now, but now,

This house, these servants, and this same myself
Are yours—my lord's!—I give them with this ring,
Which when you part from, lose, or give away,
Let it presage the ruin of your love,
And be my vantage to exclaim on you. [157-74]

Portia is a lady "richly left" (I.i.161), and herself and all that is hers she gives Bassanio gracefully on the instant that he chooses correctly. Like Rosalind in love with Orlando, Portia seems astonished at the speed of her change in state; from "master" and "Queen" she turns into a subject, "even now, but now." Portia seems liberated by love—as do most of Shakespeare's heroines—though here her freedom expresses itself primarily in giving. Later, after Bassanio surrenders her ring, the question of domestic authority is altogether less clear, Bassanio having been both faithless to his wife and powerless to save his friend, and Portia having saved the day and exposed her husband's weakness.

If Bassanio is like Helena in his poverty, Portia is like Helena in her attempt to place the power in the man's hands. Both women use similar language; Portia "gives" her ring, her mansion, servants, and herself, all of which are now "converted" to Bassanio. She "commits" herself to him to be directed "As from her lord, her governor, her king." When Bassanio chose, Portia stood for "virgin sacrifice" and he, like Hercules, fought with the sea monster. The fable she recalled then, like the vocabulary she uses now, recreates the stereotypical relationship between the sexes out of a situation perhaps as atypical as that in *All's Well That Ends Well*. While Portia must indeed wait, passively, as Bassanio chooses, once he does choose correctly she reveals and immediately transfers to him her considerable authority. In her case, passivity has obviously meant latent power rather than weakness.

Portia's rich gifts include a somewhat surprising description of herself, and one seemingly at odds with conventional imagery used by hero and heroine to describe themselves. Perhaps it is maidenly modesty that restrains her from denoting herself truly, but surely, to say of herself that she is "an unlesson'd girl, unschool'd, unpractic'd," is to say far too little both to Bassanio and to the audience; it is, in fact, "a false representation of her character."[34] If Helena's posture, kneeling before Bertram and giving herself into his "guiding power," toyed with, if not falsified, the social dynamics of that scene, Portia's description of herself can only be called an outright fiction, though indeed the one best designed for the man to whom she will be wed. Bassanio, who is "worse than nothing," indigent and in debt, is a kind of financial equivalent of the rich but impotent Count of Rossillion: Bassanio is free to adventure but has no money (like Fenton in

The Merry Wives of Windsor), while Bertram has title and money but has been barred by the King from adventure, from journeying to the Sienese wars, and kept at home. Both men, for different reasons, are restrained and forced to be passive. Both women, powerful in different ways, create courting scenarios in which their embarrassed men can salvage, should they so choose, more than a measure of dignity. Though the power is the women's, the ladies cautiously and creatively give it all to the men. What remains, however, is "an unresolvable tension in this scene between Portia's manifest authority and her attempt to transfer it to Bassanio."[35]

What happens, then, when man meets woman in Shakespearean comedy is a product not only of the young man's newfound independence with its suggestions of adventure and danger, but also occasionally of the social position of the woman, and of the inevitable contradictions her status, talent, and drive suggest to men accustomed by patriarchal traditions to think of women as the weaker sex. Her apparent helplessness in act 1, her being imprisoned like a nun, or in fact as a nun or votaress in a convent, suggests the sort of impotence that often belies the real power she possesses and the strength she soon reveals. Her wealth and title, her importance to the ruling class, and her boundless generosity serve on occasion to amplify the ambivalence the man feels even before he meets her, as he simply walks about Navarre, Arden, Venice, Paris.

3

"Any Bar, Any Cross, Any Impediment"

However they choose one another, sooner or later the lovers in Shakespearean comedy—indeed, in New Comedy in general—separate. In some plays their division follows hard on the heels of their meeting, as it does in *The Comedy of Errors* when Antipholus of Syracuse tries to book passage out of Ephesus shortly after he falls in love with the "mermaid" (III.ii.45) Luciana; in others it occurs years after their marriage, as when Leontes suddenly accuses Hermione of infidelity in *The Winter's Tale*. What distinguishes Shakespeare's treatment of the lovers' parting is that it is the young man himself, and not an external impediment, who causes the division that in classical New Comedy is caused by paternal figures or other external forces. Hence, in Shakespeare, "The women are the ones who suffer for their love."[1] Although it would seem obvious that his heroes, from Antipholus and Proteus to Claudio and Posthumus are far more responsible for the separations between themselves and the women they love than are storms at sea or angry fathers, criticism persists in seeing external agents, or even "a recalcitrance to human desire built into the universe itself,"[2] as the primary cause of separation between lovers. This misreading of the plays comes about by forcing Shakespeare into the procrustean bed of Plautine and Terentian comedy—where interlopers, especially parents, are indeed responsible for dividing boy and girl—as well as by needing to see the comedies as having evolved from an inept beginning at which time Shakespeare is thought to have been incapable of drawing characters sufficiently deep to motivate themselves.

For Northrop Frye, the union of young man and young woman in New Comedy "is blocked by some kind of opposition, usually paternal.[3] Frye's identification of the parents, especially fathers, as the "blocking agents" is virtually absolute, though he does hedge his bets by stretching the definition to include "father-surrogates": "The opponent to the hero's wishes, when not the father, is generally someone who partakes of the father's closer relation to established society."[4] I am not certain that this description of the plots of Shakespeare's love stories is valid even if we limit our analysis to those few situations where the blocking force is indeed external.

Neither fathers nor surrogates are involved when Pericles loses Thaisa when she dies giving birth to Marina; a shipwreck separates Egeon and Aemilia; and Antonio draws Bassanio from Portia by sending him a letter asking him to travel to Venice. What limits the importance of fathers as impediments is the fact that the hero in Shakespeare, as we have seen, ordinarily separates from his father before he meets and falls in love with a woman. Even in *The Two Gentlemen of Verona*, one of the few plays where love blossoms before the hero leaves home, Proteus's infatuation with Silvia represents a much greater threat to Julia than his father's insistence that he serve the Duke in Milan. Occasionally it is the girl's father who tries to interfere with her plans to marry; however, in almost every instance his troublemaking causes fewer problems than do the suspicions or waywardness of her boyfriend himself. Posthumus's attempted murder of Imogen makes Cymbeline's jailing her earlier in the play seem almost benevolent by comparison, and Egeus does a good deal less harm to his daughter Hermia than Lysander does in the woods at night by spurning her as a "Vile thing" and a "serpent" (III.ii.260, 261).

By making the hero himself his own worst enemy Shakespeare deepens character and enriches plot, and not at the price of jettisoning external impediments any more than he eliminates ghosts from his revenge plays. The comedies have their full complement of angry fathers, fatherly dukes, and a host of "father-surrogates," but Shakespeare relegates them to the play's minor plot or, more especially, uses their interfering as a means of foreshadowing the hero's own ambivalence and anger. Indeed, more often than one might imagine, fathers support lovers, and not only in *The Tempest* where Prospero is at worst curmudgeonly to Miranda and Ferdinand. Compared with Bassanio's own willingness to see Portia as spider, her father's insistence on the casket ritual seems hospitable and forthright. Cressida—and Troilus, too, for that matter,—is far more telling as *senex* than is her father; Kate rejects suitors as fast as her father brings them home. In the problem plays as a whole the older generation usually plays matchmaker and uses its authority to arrange marriages. The Duke in *Measure for Measure* works to bring Mariana and Angelo together, and the Countess of Rossillion and the King of France in *All's Well That Ends Well*, like Leonato in *Much Ado about Nothing* or Pandarus in *Troilus and Cressida*, strive actively to join hero and heroine.

External problems sometimes seem more significant than they really are because Shakespeare's young men are mistakenly apprehended solely as sixteenth-century incarnations of the hollow, one-dimensional characters we find in Roman comedy. In *Anatomy of Criticism*, Frye states what has since become a truism about characterization in comedy: "The technical hero and heroine are not often very interesting people: the *adule-*

scentes of Plautus and Terence are all alike, as hard to tell apart in the dark as Demetrius and Lysander, who may be parodies of them. Generally, the hero's character has the neutrality that enables him to represent a wish-fulfillment." For Frye, the hero and heroine are almost beside the point: "The dramatist tends to play him [the hero] down and make him rather neutral and unformed in character. Next in importance is the heroine, also often played down."[5] Such generalizing has become a common way of discussing any play in the New Comedy tradition, from Menander's *Dyskolos* through Shakespeare to musical comedy. The Roman comedy of Plautus and Terence and its Menandrine ancestors do, after all, rely on interaction between stock types where there is little room for deviation from a clearly recognizable norm. "The rather few types of New Comedy are monotonously repeated in Roman comedy, with only minor individual variations,"[6] observes Madeleine Doran, while for Marvin Herrick, "there is more variety of characterization among the old men of Terence than among his young men. The young men are all pretty much alike, though some are duller than others."[7]

It is when these generalizations, certainly true of Roman comedy, are applied to Shakespeare, or even to Elizabethan drama as a whole, that they become invalid, for "English Renaissance comedy, even realistic bourgeoise comedy, does not strike us as being so thoroughly a comedy of types as Roman comedy or its Italian and French derivatives. The people of Elizabethan comedy more frequently transcend their basic type or lose its outlines in vividly original speech and behavior."[8] Elizabethan critical works, translations of Aristotle's *Poetics*, commentaries on Plautus and Terence, and models provided by the Roman playwrights themselves notwithstanding, Elizabethan dramatic practice simply blurred lines among types and finally, in Shakespeare, erased them altogether. Although Frye would have it otherwise, insisting on simplified characterization in the New Comedy tradition as a whole, Shakespeare's comic characters, especially hero and heroine, are so complex from the start as to obscure any distinctions based upon types and Horatian notions of decorum. Even at the start of his career Shakespeare's characters represent a deepening both of the stock types derived from Roman comedy and of the heroic figures drawn from medieval romance and nondramatic fiction.[9] To say that in his earliest comedies "there is no significant development of the main characters" and that theirs is a "superficial level of characterization"[10] is to ignore the many ways in which Shakespeare had surpassed at the very start of his career the genuinely superficial level of characterization in Roman comedy and in its Italian Renaissance descendants by "drawing out and quickening into life the human significance that lies, sometimes buried, in stock motifs from romance."[11]

Even in his first comedies Shakespeare's heroes reveal the sort of contradictory impulses and complex behaviors indicative of three-dimensionality, and which are completely absent from Roman comedy. We have seen Proteus at least partly willing to leave Julia, and Bassanio describe Portia ambiguously, perhaps indicating a confused response to women and to feelings of attraction. These scenes and others in which the man reveals in one way or another ambivalence about union with a woman, are prefigured in *The Comedy of Errors* in Antipholus's rejection of Luciana. By examining in this chapter *The Comedy of Errors, Much Ado about Nothing, Cymbeline,* and *The Winter's Tale*—representative early, mature, and late comedies—along with two exceptions to Shakespeare's usual treatment of the love story, *The Merry Wives of Windsor* and *Troilus and Cressida*, we shall see the precise ways in which he deepened characterization from the start and motivated heroes who abandon relationships and slander women.

In falling in love with Luciana, Antipholus of Syracuse goes through more than the perfunctory shift from stranger to lover we see, for example, in Lidio, in Bibbiena's *La Calandria*, based, like *The Comedy of Errors*, on the *Menaechmi*.[12] After meeting Luciana, Antipholus behaves in a way that forces us to reject outright any characterization of him as a hero "lacking subtlety and complexity." In doting on her as a "god" (III.ii.39) and then in rejecting her as a witch in the same scene, indeed, in the space of seventy-five lines, Antipholus prefigures in his actions not only the treatment of women in the later comedies and romances but also Hamlet's treatment of Ophelia and Gertrude, Othello's of Desdemona, and Antony's oscillating toward and away from Cleopatra.

Act 3, scene 2, begins *in medias res* with Luciana rejecting Antipholus's advances. She thinks she knows him to be her brother-in-law, Antipholus of Ephesus, and pertinently asks, "may it be that you have quite forgot / A husband's office?" (1-2). Antipholus, awestruck both by her beauty and her knowing his name, can only conclude that she is "more than earth divine" (32). Although he sounds very much the run-of-the-mill Renaissance courtier using hyperbole to win a cruel/fair woman, a Romeo describing Rosaline, he believes he is in fact describing a woman and a situation in literal terms:

> Are you a god? Would you create me new?
> Transform me then, and to your pow'r I'll yield.
> But if that I am I, then well I know
> Your weeping sister is no wife of mine,
> Nor to her bed no homage do I owe:
> Far more, far more, to you do I decline.

> O, train me not, sweet mermaid, with thy note,
> To drown me in thy [sister's] flood of tears.
> Sing, siren, for thyself, and I will dote;
> Spread o'er the silver waves thy golden hairs,
> And as a [bed] I'll take [them], and there lie,
> And in that glorious supposition think
> He gains by death that hath such means to die:
> Let love, being light, be drowned if she sink! [39-52]

And yet in spite of such fulsome praise, when his Dromio returns perhaps five minutes later, Antipholus instructs him to book immediate passage on "any bark" (50): "If every one knows us, and we know none, / 'Tis time, I think, to trudge, pack, and be gone" (152-53). His willingness to leave a woman he loves shows us, in this earliest comedy, how easily ambivalence turns to fear, and fear to flight. It is a response Shakespeare's heroes repeat throughout the comedies, though his rationale for leaving Luciana and Ephesus is yet more instructive:

> There's none but witches do inhabit here,
> And therefore 'tis high time that I were hence.
> She that doth call me husband, even my soul
> Doth for a wife abhor. But her fair sister,
> Possess'd with such a gentle sovereign grace,
> Of such enchanting presence and discourse,
> Hath almost made me traitor to myself;
> But lest myself be guilty to self-wrong,
> I'll stop mine ears against the mermaid's song. [156-64]

The progress from divinity to witch or mermaid is one from good to evil, but no great leap at all for a man misapprehending an innocent and, in Luciana's case, rather painfully tractable and bourgeois woman. On the assumption, however, that she is "more than earth divine" (32), Antipholus easily shifts from one pole of the supernatural to the other. Indeed, his sudden rejection of her is prefigured in large letters in his apostrophe to her quoted above ("Are you a god?"), just as Bassanio's seeing the picture of Portia as a kind of trap is prefigured in his earlier lecture on "crisped snaky golden locks." Astonished by Luciana's apparently superhuman knowledge, Antipholus insists on her divinity and his own innocence, going so far as to call her not simply "a god" but "siren" and "mermaid," compliments in one way, but pejoratives in another, each label suggesting its own best and worst implications for an audience schooled in Ovidian fables and metamorphoses.[13]

Antipholus's misunderstanding is revealed most clearly in the earlier speech's last five lines ("Spread o'er the silver waves thy golden hairs"), an elaborate metaphor that implies both his own sexual fulfillment in Luciana's arms and her concomitant destructive force. In trying to avoid drowning in her sister's "flood of tears," Antipholus finds himself in far deeper water and welcomes "such means to die." Luciana, one would think, might want to know not only why her brother-in-law is behaving so shamefully but also, and more importantly, why, doting on her, he must see her as the instrument of his own death. What had seemed so irresistible a fantasy— lying on the mermaid's hair atop the silver waves—becomes moments later an altogether threatening scene, with supernatural beauty transformed into supernatural evil. Her appealing aspect changes, fear smothers desire, and he flees, as though once seeing her as "more than earth divine" all bets are off. Free to swing from one fantastic depiction of woman to another, he eventually runs the gamut from divinity to siren. "The folded meaning" of her "words' deceit" (36) is seen now as a threat to him from within, as though "incorporation" with a woman were the same as being "traitor" to himself.

It is important that we appreciate Antipholus's vacillation, his contradictory responses to Luciana, but even more important that we recognize that his decision to stay or go depends upon how he thinks he sees, hears, and reads a woman. Antipholus accounts for his confusion, sense of loss, and ambivalence only in terms of who Luciana is, siren or goddess, rather than as the product of his own assumptions. It never occurs to him that it is he who is at least two different people, and not the woman. The audience, who know the source and limits of Luciana's knowledge, understand that it is his error that invests her with an apparently otherworldly power and insight and therefore never examine very closely Antipholus's mood swings. In later plays, although most of the young men insist on valid external reasons for their changes of affection, as Antipholus does, the audience sees the locus of the problem not in the character of the woman but in the prejudices of the man with regard to the woman.

Shakespeare's handling of Claudio in *Much Ado about Nothing* illustrates even more fully the ways in which his locating romantic problems in the young man rather than in external agents tends to deepen characterization and make for psychological complexity. It is Don John, the bastard, who instigates division between Claudio and Hero, but it is impossible to see Don John as the *cause* of Claudio's persistent rejection of Hero. Audiences tend not to forgive Claudio at the end of the play precisely because his excuse, "yet sinn'd I not, / But in mistaking" (V.i.274-75), points the finger at Don John, who serves merely as catalyst, as most villains and interferers in Shakespeare's comedies do.

When Claudio falls in love with Hero in act 1, he describes her to the cynical Benedick as "a modest young lady" (I.i.165), "a jewel" (181), and "the sweetest lady that ever I look'd on" (188). Later he tells Don Pedro that now that the wars are ended and

> war-thoughts
> Have left their places vacant, in their rooms
> Come thronging soft and delicate desires,
> All prompting me how fair young Hero is,
> Saying I lik'd her ere I went to wars. [301-5]

Although I cannot agree with critics who see Claudio as "less the romantic young man in love than the ambitious young soldier primarily concerned with his own advancement,"[14] he does appear at the least stiff and formal, "using only the flowers of rhetoric."[15] Consequently, it comes as no surprise when the diffident Claudio leaps at Don Pedro's suggestion that he assume Claudio's part "in some disguise, / And tell fair Hero I am Claudio" (321-22). It is this wooing by proxy, to which Claudio agrees, that leaves him open to Don John's scheming.

The bastard's insinuations at the dance of II.i and Claudio's sudden agreement with him are as incredible in their way as are other astonishments of comedy. Claudio seems to expect problems between himself and Hero; he is not surprised when Don John tells him that Don Pedro has won Hero for himself, and he generates a philosophy for the occasion:

> *Claud*. Thus answer I in name of Benedick,
> But hear these ill news with the ears of Claudio.
> 'Tis certain so, the Prince woos for himself.
> Friendship is constant in all other things
> Save in the office and affairs of love;
> Therefore all hearts in love use their own tongues.
> Let every eye negotiate for itself,
> And trust no agent; for beauty is a witch
> Against whose charms faith melteth into blood.
> This is an accident of hourly proof,
> Which I mistrusted not. Farewell therefore Hero! [II.i.172-82]

It is preposterous that Claudio should believe the bastard, given his own part in allowing Don Pedro to woo Hero for him, and given Don John's awful reputation, and that ought to tell us how unimportant Don John really is. What we sense is that Claudio's credulousness is less a tribute to the bastard's power to confound than it is an indication of Claudio's a priori assumptions about women.[16] Acting as a catalyst, Don John allows Claudio to release, hurriedly, what seems to be a one-sided and male-oriented philosophy of friendship and romance, and a philosophy at odds with what he and the audience have observed in the behavior of both the Prince and Hero. One can understand that Claudio would feel betrayed should he believe that Don Pedro "woos for himself"; but in concluding that "beauty is a witch / Against whose charms faith melteth into blood," he exonerates his friend and slanders Hero who, not knowing anything about the subterfuge, is entirely innocent. In his absolute and instantaneous understanding that the woman is to blame for the faithlessness of a man and that Hero's supposed enchanting "is an accident of hourly proof" in the lives of women, he echoes Antipholus's accusation that "None but witches do inhabit" Ephesus. In both plays, and with very little instigation, love turns to acrimony, acrimony to misogyny, misogyny to abandonment: "Farewell therefore Hero!"

To this picture of Claudio as predisposed to think the worst of women and inclined to leave them, Shakespeare adds yet another dimension. The scene in which Don John suggests to Claudio and Don Pedro that Hero is a whore, III.ii, opens by showing us a Claudio once again preferring male friend to woman, friendship to marriage, and this well after he has seen the previous error of his ways:

> *D. Pedro.* I do but stay till your marriage be consummate, and then I
> go toward Arragon.
> *Claud.* I'll bring you thither, my lord, if you'll vouchsafe me.
> *D. Pedro.* Nay, that would be as great a soil in the new gloss of your
> marriage as to show a child his new coat and forbid him to wear it. [1-7]

The play establishes a pattern in Claudio's behavior. When he "lik'd" (I.i.299) Hero he left for the wars; loving her, he chooses to woo through the agency of his friend, Don Pedro; seeing Don Pedro converse with her, he concludes that Hero's beauty has enchanted his friend and that all beautiful women are witches; disabused of this notion, he offers to accompany Don Pedro to Arragon after his marriage. At this point it appears fitting that the Prince liken him to a "child." Claudio is opposed to marriage, against uniting himself with a woman in any alliance, and ready to believe the worst of any woman and the best of any man.[17]

As we watch the pattern of Claudio's reluctance develop it seems almost inevitable that he flee from Hero in a yet more drastic and final way. The Claudio Shakespeare has shown us for three acts cannot marry and obviously will not. The tension in these first three acts lies in the way the blocking impulse rises slowly and inexorably from within Claudio himself, and any production of this play that does not capture Claudio's inner delight with the bastard's degrading suggestions in III.ii that Hero is a whore misrepresents the play. Indeed, Claudio's very first response to Don John's hint about Hero is a thinly veiled plea for an excuse to leave her:

> D. John. [To Claudio.] Means your lordship to be married to-morrow?
> D. Pedro. You know he does.
> D. John. I know not that, when he knows what I know.
> Claud. If there be any impediment, I pray you discover it. [88-94]

By way of comparison, notice how, in *Cymbeline*, when Imogen responds to Jachimo's first suggestion that the absent Posthumus has been un-faithful—and it is a strong suggestion here and not merely a hint—Shake-speare echoes some of Claudio's language but with a tone far removed from his:

> Imo. I pray you, sir,
> Deliver with more openness your answers
> To my demands. Why do you pity me?
> Jach. That others do
> (I was about to say) enjoy your—But
> It is an office of the gods to venge it,
> Not mine to speak on't.
> Imo.   You do seem to know
> Something of me, or what concerns me: pray you—
> Since doubting things go ill often hurts more
> Tha to be sure they do; for certainties
> Either are past remedies, or, timely knowing,
> The remedy then born—discover to me
> What both you spur and stop. [I.vi.87-99]

When Jachimo, in his next speech, tells her openly that Posthumus is consorting with women whose lips are "as common as the stairs / That mount the Capitol" (105-6), her response is a simple, "My lord, I fear, / Has forgot Britain" (112-13). One speech later she tells Jachimo, "Let me hear no more" (117).

From what a different world of emotions and attitudes Claudio's reaction comes is all too clear in his meagre responses to suggestions that ought, after all, sadden him as Jachimo's do Imogen. When Don John openly claims, "the lady is disloyal" (III.ii.104), Claudio, apparently stunned, can only ask, "Who, Hero?" (105). His next remark is simply "Disloyal?" (107), and the next after that, the ambiguous "May this be so?" (117), which sounds more like a request than a question. It is left to Don Pedro, not Claudio, to offer some small shred of opposition to Don John's assertions: "I will not think it" (118). Claudio's fullest response comes at line 123: "If I see anything to-night why I should not marry her, to-morrow in the congregation, where I should wed, there will I shame her." I have quoted every one of Claudio's responses to Don John in this scene. At no point does he doubt the bastard or come close to denying or opposing him. Claudio never even approaches what we would expect of the young soldier-hero whose affianced has been slandered. Instead we see a man too ready for slander even to be called "credulous," a hero all too willing to doubt the woman's fidelity and all too willing to punish her, sadistically and publicly. Before he knows her guilty he has dreamed up his rejection. Claudio's final remark in this scene, "O mischief strangely thwarting!" (132), is a con-clusion, not a supposition. He has moved from the conditional mode ("If I see anything to-night") to the indicative in a flash, for Hero's alleged behavior is now accepted as "mischief" and it has "thwarted" the marriage. The audience, which tends to forgive a hero's misdemeanors, can find solace only in the fact that Claudio did not dream up this supposed "impediment" on his own, and in Claudio's stupefaction—the death of his marriage has indeed been "strange." If we are at all disposed to forgive and forget in act 5 perhaps it is because we perceive Claudio here in act 3 as a victim of impulses in himself he simply cannot understand rather than as a victim of the external villainy of Don John. But his readiness to run through a door opened by the bastard, to adopt, in fact, a bastard's view of women, has been meticulously prepared for us by Shakespeare since act 1.

Claudio's rejection of Hero in IV.i is a stunning scene, a collision between an innocent woman and a self-righteous man caught in the grips of a passion he cannot understand and one he seems unable to deny. His denunciation of Hero in the church during their wedding ceremony is extreme; perceiving her as unfaithful, Claudio sees her as Iago might, as an animal, "more intemperate in your blood / Than Venus, or those pamp'red animals / That rage in savage sensuality" (59-61). She is a lie; she blushes like a maid, "But she is none: / She knows the heat of a luxurious bed; / Her blush is guiltiness, not modesty" (40-42). His misapprehension of Hero is described in traditionally Elizabethan terms: she "seems" to be Diana but is in reality Venus. Bassanio's ambivalence, his seeing Portia's golden hair in the painting as a "web," is now Claudio's certainty. Faced with two versions of Hero, the modest woman and the intemperate animal, he can only read her blush as guiltiness. Claudio and, indeed, most of these young men, especially the slanderers, have implicit trust in their eyes, in what they see. For them, the world is a two-dimensional picture, and "vision is pure sensation unencumbered by meaning."[18] In *Love's Labour's Lost* a similar superficial way of seeing trips up the King and his courtiers once they do forsake their academy and advance on the women. When the Princess of France and her ladies secretly change favors at the revels of act 5, the men are confused and each woos the wrong woman: "The ladies did change favors; and then we, / Following the signs, woo'd but the sign of she" (V.ii.468-69). Like those men, Claudio too sees only with his eyes, not with his reason. "If I see anything to-night," he promises Don John, "in the congregation where I should wed, there will I shame her." Having "seen" her room entered, just as he had "seen" Don Pedro betray him at the dance, he concludes that Hero is "but the sign and semblance of her honor" (IV.i.33), a "show of truth" (35) with which "cunning sin" (36) covers itself. Her virtuous appearance is merely part of her deceptive "exterior shows" (40).

In asking Claudio and Hero "if either of you know any inward impediment" (IV.i.12), the Friar begins the marriage ceremony with an echo of Claudio's earlier plea to Don John, "If there be any impediment, I pray you discover it." And while it is important to know that "impediment" was the official term used with regard to problems arising before marriage and implying "certain conditions unknown," the word is etymologically apposite, deriving from *impedire*, "to shackle the feet."[19] Hero's newly revealed condition has become an "impediment" that permits Claudio to "shackle" his own feet. Later in the scene, after he has accused her, he looks back almost regretfully:

> But fare thee well, most foul, most fair! Farewell,
> Thou pure impiety and impious purity!
> For thee I'll lock up all the gates of love,
> And on my eyelids shall conjecture hang,
> To turn all beauty into thoughts of harm,
> And never shall it more be gracious, [103-8]

"But fare thee well, most foul, most fair! Farewell," looks back to Antipholus's leaving the "witches" of Ephesus, "'Tis time, I think, to trudge, pack, and be gone," and is also an echo of Claudio's earlier "Farewell therefore Hero!" in II.i. when he thought beauty a witch. Pretend as he may before Leonato, Hero, and the Friar that his rejection of Hero (and of all women) is the product of her supposed infidelity, the audience knows that rejection has been his tendency all along; Claudio has been saying "farewell" to Hero since he first saw her.

Claudio's jaundiced way of seeing indicates how fully his warring attitudes toward women are projected outward and manifest themselves in images of types of women, "Dian in her orb" and those "pamp'red animals / That rage in savage sensuality." And while these pictures tell us nothing about Hero, nothing about women at all, they do tell us a great deal about the complexity of the male response to beauty and attraction. We can understand how, in a world perceived as a confusing place where goddess and "wanton" (IV.i.44) are like the rind and pulp of a "rotten orange" (32), Claudio would not simply reject Hero, but go as far as one can by rejecting all women and by locking up "all the gates of love." His attitudes and language here repeat those of the courtiers of Navarre who swear to live behind "forbidden gates" and threaten others with "a year's imprisonment" if "taken with a wench."

Like Claudio, Posthumus Leonatus in *Cymbeline* rejects as a whore a faithful woman and, as he does in *Much Ado about Nothing*, Shakespeare takes pains to motivate the rejection. Both men are in some senses tricked by others and seem to be at least partly victims of others' bitter attitudes toward women. Claudio, however, is fertile soil and takes suggestion as the cat laps milk. Posthumus, on the other hand, defends Imogen's honor and is not nearly as quick to believe the worst of her when Jachimo returns from Britain. What Posthumus does do is brag repeatedly about his wife, as though he were either protesting too much or asking to be challenged. We hear that he and a Frenchman, each "with so mortal a purpose" (I.iv.40), argued about female loyalty, "this gentleman [Posthumus] at that time vouching (and upon warrant of bloody affirmation) his to be more fair, virtuous, wise, chaste, constant, qualified, and less attemptable than any the rarest of our ladies in France" (58-61). When he is teased by Jachimo, who picks up the argument where the Frenchman left it, Posthumus responds yet again by rating Imogen at "more than the world enjoys" (79). His public boasting, his exaggerated estimation, and his willingness to wager on her as Petruchio, Lucentio, and Hortensio do on their wives seems not only proprietary but degrading as well.

Posthumus not only bets on Imogen as though she were a horse, he writes a letter of introduction to be presented to Imogen by Jachimo, whom he describes as "'one of the noblest note, to whose kindnesses I am most infinitely tied. Reflect upon him accordingly, as you value your trust—Leonatus'" (I.vi.21-25). The letter seems to us all the more fulsome in its praise of Jachimo for its being a lie, and doubly so; that is, not only is Jachimo *ignoble* (James Nosworthy in the New Arden calls attention to

Jachimo's "ignorance and spiritual poverty" [20]), but Posthumus clearly sees him as such. Instead of rejecting the challenge offered by so untrustworthy a man, Posthumus accepts, exposes his wife to danger and then misleads her, describing Jachimo as "noble" and "kind," asking Imogen to "reflect on him accordingly." [21] Posthumus's repeated boasting, his willingness to wager on her, and his misleading letter to her are indications of an immature attachment, a connection all the more fragile for its absoluteness.

In act 2, scene 4, when Jachimo returns to Rome from his stay at the British court with Imogen, Posthumus is not easily convinced that his wife has been unfaithful, though when Jachimo praises her beauty, Posthumus pontificates, declaring that beauty ought to indicate goodness, else "let her beauty / Look thorough a casement to allure false hearts, / And be false with them" (33-35). The imagery suggests flirtation and prostitution and is familiar to readers of Renaissance drama. In Jonson's *Volpone*, Corvino finds his wife, Celia, at her window smiling at a mountebank. He forbids her to approach the window, commands her to face backwards (i.e., not streetwards) and "be not seen, pain of thy life; / Nor look toward the window," for "A crew of old, unmarried, noted lechers / Stood leering up like satyrs." [22] In *The Merchant of Venice* Shylock commands Jessica,

> Lock up my doors, and when you hear the drum
> And the vile squealing of the wry-neck'd fife,
> Clamber not you up to the casements then,
> Nor thrust your head into the public street
> To gaze on Christian fools with varnish'd faces;
> But stop my house's ears, I mean my casements. [II.v.29-34]

And it is, of course, the sight of Hero talking "with a ruffian at her chamber-window" (*MAdo*, IV.i.91) that drives Claudio to reject her the following day. For Posthumus, if Imogen prove false she is nothing but a prostitute and might as well converse through casements. Though at this point Posthumus believes her true, her looks accurately figuring her virtue (as Portia's picture does hers), he is not far from seeing her beauty as false, like that of women who dally at windows or who wear hair "the dowry of a second head."

Jachimo claims victory at line 45 but is rebuffed by Posthumus who appears confident. Jachimo's description of Imogen's bedchamber, its tapestry, chimney-piece, and roof fails to shake Posthumus who seems emboldened by the weakness of his opponent's evidence. It is only at line 99, when Jachimo shows him Imogen's bracelet that Posthumus quails.

Instantly he is reduced, like Claudio, to a kind of misogynistic philosophizing, and he condemns at once Imogen and all women:

> Let there be no honor
> Where there is beauty; truth, where semblance; love,
> Where there's another man. The vows of women
> Of no more bondage be to where they are made
> Than they are to their virtues, which is nothing.
> O, above measure false! [108-13]

Claudio saw in Hero "the sign and semblance of her honor," just as Posthumus sees Imogen as the "semblance" of truth, outwardly beautiful, inwardly "nothing." For him she has now become as "false" as those who "Look through a casement to allure false hearts."

Philario, older and wiser, restrains Posthumus, asks him to have patience, and does draw him momentarily from his diatribe. Yet, as soon as Jachimo swears—"By Jupiter, I had it from her arm" (121)—Posthumus caves in, or, the sense seems, lets go, giving in to an outpouring of invective that continues, gaining strength, to the end of the scene and beyond, into the polemic against women that comprises II.v. Philario begs patience, Posthumus refuses and grows vulgar, comparing his wife to an animal just as Claudio does Hero: "She hath been colted by him" (133). And again like Claudio, Posthumus luxuriates in vituperation, wanting her to be guilty rather than loyal, threatening Jachimo in strange terms: "If you will swear you have not done't, you lie, / And I will kill thee if thou dost deny / Thou'st made me cuckold" (144-46). These lines are surely among the saddest and most complex in the comedies. As when Othello orders Iago, "Villain, be sure thou prove my love a whore" (III.iii.359), here it is not simply a matter of the magnitude of his emotions, or even of the dubious evidentiary procedure by which he has arrived at his assurance. Rather, it is astonishing because so much passion is spent in affirming so humiliating a position, a self-degradation dependent upon his wife's infidelity. What it implies is that she must be a whore in order for him to be "base," an adjective applied to him repeatedly in act 1 by the King and Cloten. The language and emotion of the statement are stereotypically martial ("I will kill thee"), yet its message is atypically passive, even masochistic ("if thou dost deny / Thou'st made me cuckold"), and the difference between tone and sense jars. Although most commentators argue that Jachimo's testimony is powerful, it is really no different in kind or degree from Don John's (or Iago's). The vigor, the lustfulness with which Posthumus embraces a vision of himself as cuckold and of Imogen as whore simply cannot be accounted for in the paucity of the evidence. Indeed, nowhere in the scene is Philario's reasonable demurrer refuted:

> Have patience, sir,
> And take your ring again, 'tis not yet won.
> It may be probable she lost it; or
> Who knows if one her women, being corrupted,
> Hath stol'n it from her? [113-17]

Posthumus brushes aside these rational explanations (which, in fact, describe what happens in *Othello*), and in his negativism seems more clearly a man in need of seeing her so than one justly incensed by overwhelming evidence. "Like Claudio as well as Othello," Arthur Kirsch points out, "he believes the slander because he is unconsciously disposed to do so, and as in the case of both earlier characters his feverish fantasies of his wife's infidelities are reflections of his own deep ambivalence towards her."[23]

In Posthumus the attitudes of the misogynist lead instantly to the language of violence. He wants "to tear her limb-meal! / I will go there and do't, i' th' court, before / Her father. I'll do something—" (147-49). Like Othello, who wants to "tear" Desdemona "all to pieces" (III.iii.431), to "chop her into messes" (IV.i.200), and like Claudio, who somehow needs to humiliate and destroy Hero "in the congregation," Posthumus hates Imogen in the extreme. The pornographic view of women, which insists upon seeing an animal beneath the trappings of a goddess, whether instigated by Don John, Iago, or Jachimo, or unmotivated, as Leontes' seems to be, moves from hatred of the individual woman, to misogyny in an instant. Such is the logic of Bassanes in *The Broken Heart*, who simply claims, "But all are false. On this truth I am bold: / No woman but can fall, and doth, or would,"[24] and of De Flores in *The Changeling*, who thinks that "if a woman / Fly from one point, from him she makes a husband, / She spreads and mounts then like arithmetic, / One, ten, one hundred, one thousand, ten thousand."[25] And movement from misogyny to violence, to tearing her "limb-meal," for such as Posthumus and Othello, is inevitable. It is this rush to revile one woman, all women, that we see displaced with such terrible force onto the woman herself, onto Antonio's wife in *The Revenger's Tragedy*, who commits suicide rather than continue to live what the male community sees as a dishonored life, and onto Anne Frankford in *A Woman Killed with Kindness*, who pleads, "O to redeem my honour / I would have this hand cut off, these my breasts seared, / Be racked, strappadoed, put to any torment."[26] Distorted views on the part of men, psychological separations, in effect, demand a physical distancing so great they can only be satisfied by the woman's death.

In *The Winter's Tale* there are, of course, two pairs of lovers who are separated, Florizel and Perdita, and Leontes and Hermione. Here (as in *The Merry Wives of Windsor*) it is the younger couple who are harassed from without, in this case by Polixenes, whose pressure, in fact, only serves to drive Florizel and Perdita closer together, and it is the older couple who are threatened from within, by a husband's sudden and murderous insecurities. Shakespeare's fascination with the destructive impulses of males takes a unique turn here, for we ought at least to recognize that Leontes' rejection of Hermione ruptures what had been one of the more durable relationships in the comedies. Perhaps for that reason, most critics find his accusations and his jealousy largely unmotivated and prompted by an "evil passion";[27] "His fit is totally perverse,"[28] "a nervous weakness, a mere hysteria"; in short, "The man is a very drunkard of passion"[29] whose "rage" must be accepted as a given, like "the murderousness of Dionyza and Cymbeline's Queen."[30] We may not know the origin of his jealousy, but we do know the circumstances leading up to his rejection of Hermione and the terms he uses in accusing her.

Leontes has no Iago, Jachimo, or Don John guiding him to accept a poisoned view of women and of other men and needs even less of an excuse to set off what is obviously a predisposition to find women weak and men faithless. In this he is like Antipholus, who shifts from adoring Luciana to hating her almost at will. What is equally unmotivated, however, is Leontes' poor view of himself, and in him more than in most of the other male characters critics have espied a self-loathing almost as strong as his misogyny. Indeed, I.ii, in which he becomes jealous, is structured in a way that forces us first to see Leontes reduce himself and only then to see him attack Hermione. What Leontes becomes in this scene is a child, a version of Claudio or of the "two hours' old" Antipholus, and it is the child who becomes enraged at Hermione and, later, at womankind in general.

The play begins with implicit and explicit references to birth, children, and childhood. Camillo and Archidamus discuss Leontes' and Polixenes' youth, and in I.ii we see a pregnant Hermione and learn that Polixenes has been visiting Sicilia for nine months. In trying to persuade Polixenes to stay, Hermione questions and teases him about his boyhood and Leontes', evoking from her guest fond and perhaps ambiguous recollections of their youth. It is clear that, for Polixenes at least, "to be boy eternal" (65) would have been a sort of perpetual and not unwelcome "innocence" (69), a condition necessarily ended when both young men married. Hermione rightly senses that Polixenes appears to be blaming women for men's loss of innocence, for their having "tripp'd since" (76), and in playful, though sexual, language, chastises and instructs Polixenes:

> Of this make no conclusion, lest you say
> Your queen and I are devils. Yet go on,
> Th' offenses we have made you do we'll answer,
> If you first sinn'd with us, and that with us
> You did continue fault, and that you slipp'd not
> With any but with us. [81-86]

It is shortly after Hermione, speaking for all women, tells the men that praise will do more than criticism, that, in fact, men "may ride 's / With one soft kiss a thousand furlongs ere / With spur we heat an acre" (94-96), that Leontes feels the *"tremor cordis"* (110) and turns to his son, Mamillius, asking, "Art thou my boy?" (120).

J. H. P. Pafford, in the New Arden, calls attention to Alfred Harbage's comparison between Mamillius, Leontes' son, and Hamlet, "since one explanation of his sickening to death is his shame at the supposed sin of his mother and consequent taint upon himself."[31] Though Mamillius may seem a younger version of Hamlet, the comparison would strike us as yet more apt with reference to Leontes than to his son, insofar as Leontes identifies so strongly with his son and seems to be accusing Hermione in the name of his son. When he sees Hermione "Still virginalling / Upon his [Polixenes'] palm" (125-26), he asks Mamillius once again, "Art thou my calf?" (127) and then insists upon their similarities in spite of some differences between them:

> Thou want'st a rough pash and the shoots that I have,
> To be full like me; yet they say we are
> Almost as like as eggs; women say so—
> That will say any thing. But were they false
> As o'er-dy'd blacks, as wind, as waters, false
> As dice are to be wish'd by one that fixes
> No bourn 'twixt his and mine, yet were it true
> To say this boy were like me. [128-35]

These lines are the first part of a speech Mark van Doren calls "the obscurest passage in Shakespeare."[32] Leontes is torn between his identification with Mamillius (and therefore his need to see himself as Mamillius's father), and the jealousy that tells him that women are "false" and that the boy therefore cannot be his:

>   Come, sir page,
> Look on me with your welkin eye. Sweet villain!
> Most dear'st! my collop! Can thy dam?—may't be?—

> Affection! thy intention stabs the centre.
> Thou dost make possible things not so held,
> Communicat'st with dreams (how can this be?)
> With what's unreal thou co-active art,
> And fellow'st nothing. Then 'tis very credent
> Thou mayst co-join with something, and thou dost
> (And that beyond commission), and I find it
> (And that to the infection of my brains
> And hard'ning of my brows). [135-46]

Leontes seems to be saying, "Hermione, your intentions destroy the very core of my being and of goodness in general, and make impossibilities probable. Thus you seem to be like a dream, and like a dream (dreaming being a 'co-active art') are a combination of 'what's unreal' and what is real, and consequently produce no offspring ('fellow'st nothing'). Yet if you can embody the actual and the fantastical, it is possible ('very credent') that you can unite with a living person, and you already have, and I have discovered it, and am a cuckold."[33]

For Leontes, the woman has become a contradiction, a fantastical creature formed of the believable and the unbelievable. It cannot be believed that Mamillius's mother would be faithless, and yet she is, just as Hero seems "Dian in her orb" but in reality is "more intemperate" than Venus. His thinking here reminds us of the disorientation that attends any Shakespearean hero's falling in or out of love, though Leontes' speech has in addition the wild incoherence of a child's semirational ramblings. For him the question is not, "Can my wife?" but rather, "Can thy dam?" suggesting that his tie to Hermione is not as a husband to a wife but rather through their child, Mamillius, as a son to a mother. In fact, Leontes is willing to admit as much to Hermione and Polixenes when they ask him if he is troubled:

>   Looking on the lines
> Of my boy's face, methoughts I did recoil
> Twenty-three years, and saw my self unbreech'd,
> In my green velvet coat, my dagger muzzled,
> Lest it should bite its master, and so prove
> (As [ornament] oft does) too dangerous.
> How like (methought) I then was to this kernel,
> This squash, this gentleman. [153-60]

Like Polixenes, Leontes seems to be yearning throughout for a simpler and more innocent time, for boyhood. The image of himself as a child takes precedence over the image of himself as wronged and angry husband, though it is more likely that the two poses feed one another, Hermione's supposed infidelity making Leontes wish for a more innocent age, and Leontes' identification with Mamillius revealing an inadequate attachment to Hermione. In any case, Leontes is here an angry and confused child, rejecting his wife even as he reduces himself. His surrendering all the responsibilities of a husband is depicted visually as he leaves Hermione and Polixenes alone and walks off with Mamillius. Though he calls his rejection of Hermione "angling" (180), it is clear that he would rather be with his alter ego, Mamillius, than with his wife.[34]

When Polixenes and Camillo flee Sicilia, Leontes believes "All's true that is mistrusted" (II.i.48) and enters fully into a fantastical world where truth and error, the probable and the improbable, change places. Though he had accused Hermione, "Thou . . . / Communicat'st with dreams," she and his counselors and friends know that it is he who has lost "clearer knowledge" (97) and has given in to "weak-hing'd fancy" (iii.119). In act 1 Hermione is undeniably flirtatious, teases Leontes and Polixenes, and peppers her speeches with sexual double entendres, but if her language is often suggestive of the coquette, her meaning is always suggestive of the matron, for Hermione never does stray from the Elizabethan/Jacobean party line on behavior appropriate to her sex. That is, Shakespeare goes to great lengths to direct our attention away from the slandered woman and toward the slanderer, for Hermione describes men and women in utterly traditional terms. For her, women are subservient, "tame things," like horses, and look for nothing so much as grace and the knowledge that they do a "good deed" (I.ii.92). But for Leontes, lost in appearances, the style of Hermione's conversation and the sight of her holding Polixenes' hand have become confused with his notion of who she is in reality, and, like the courtiers in *Love's Labour's Lost*, he reacts only to "the signs of she." His treating appearance as though it were reality allows him to act in accordance with his feelings. "His mind leaps wildly from one fantastic assumption to another"[35] and renders his actions and speeches irrational and incoherent to those around him, especially to the women, rationality in *The Winter's Tale* being presented, Irene Dash observes, "as a sex-linked trait":[36]

> *Her.* Sir,
> You speak a language that I understand not.
> My life stands in the level of your dreams,
> Which I'll lay down.
> *Leon.*   Your actions are my dreams.
> You had a bastard by Polixenes,
> And I but dream'd it. [III.ii.79-84]

In his disorientation and rage Leontes sounds very much like the other misapprehending males in these plays, and Hermione reacts as other women do, Kate, for example, who "Knows not which way to stand, to look, to speak, / And sits as one new risen from a dream" (IV.i.185-86) when Petruchio torments her in his country house. Leontes accuses Hermione of duplicity and rails against her "without-door form" (II.i.69). Leontes is like other Shakespearean heroes in his a priori assumption that most women are corrupt: walking alone with Mamillius, he pretends to take solace in thinking that "There have been / (Or I am much deceiv'd) cuckolds ere now" (I.ii.190-91) and believes "Many a man" (192) lives with a faithless wife. He calculates, "Should all despair / That have revolted wives, the tenth of mankind / Would hang themselves" (198-200), but soon revises his arithmetic and calls the world a "bawdy planet" (201), ending the speech by guessing that "Many thousand on 's / Have the disease, and feel't not" (206-7). Clearly, Hermione's frailty is not particular to her but rather endemic to the sex; like Claudio and Posthumus, Leontes will not hear otherwise.[37] He utterly rejects Camillo's defense of Hermione's honor, insists that she is faithless, "and the expression of it gives him in some perverse way a horrible pleasure."[38] Perhaps Camillo, Paulina, and Antigonus cannot talk him out of his insistence that he is a cuckold and that it is a "bawdy planet" because his "heart dances" (I.ii.110) when he thinks it.

What we must remember is that Leontes lives in absolute certainty of the rectitude of his opinions. He and Antipholus, Claudio, Posthumus, are to be distinguished from the true villains in these plays (as we shall see more fully in Chapter 4) by their emotional honesty; that is, they act on what they feel, and although each at times is faithless, untrusting, even vengeful, each feels he is morally correct in taking extreme actions. There is no sense anywhere in Leontes' speeches that he is posing or adopting a stance for ulterior reasons. What we do feel is that Leontes cannot contain his rage, and that his rage itself is partly a product of his feeling so right and so clearly abused by his wife. Thus, he sends emissaries to the Oracle and determines to "Proceed in justice, which shall have due course, / Even to the guilt or the purgation" (III.ii.6-7). But the certainty that compels him to send agents to the Oracle allows him to condemn his daughter to death on a deserted shore before they return. He lives in the child's world of untempered emotions; Hermione's is the "sorry plight of the wife of the lover whose sentiments instead of maturing remain locked in the romance of the nursery."[39]

The separations between man and woman caused by the hero's faulty reasoning and impulsiveness are treated far less seriously in *The Merry Wives of Windsor.* However, in spite of Shakespeare's handling Master

Ford, the jealous husband, more as Jonson would, Ford's scheming and his reasoning are identical to those of the more elevated personages in *Much Ado about Nothing*, *Cymbeline*, and *The Winter's Tale*. Ford loses his wife in exactly the same way the majority of Shakespeare's male characters do, in his fantasies.

Ford's ill-founded suspicions of his wife and his jealous temperament lead him to disguise himself as "Brook," a man supposedly trying to seduce Mistress Ford, and to convince Falstaff to try his own wife's virtue, a version of Posthumus's loosing Jachimo on Imogen and of Claudio's peeping outside Hero's chamber. He pays Falstaff, provides him with sack, and encourages him to "win her to consent to you" (II.ii.236). Falstaff quite logically tells "Brook," "Methinks you prescribe to yourself very preposterously" (240-41), a judgment that can be leveled against Claudio and Posthumus as easily. Ford's explanation, that Falstaff will pave the way for him to seduce her, is a more comic version, and therefore an easier one to apprehend, than Posthumus's outfitting Jachimo in the latter's attempt to seduce Imogen.

Where Ford is most like other male characters we have seen is not only in his suspicions—his willingness to believe the worst—but especially in his hair-trigger response to evidence the audience considers inadequate or imaginary. Mere moments after Ford encourages Falstaff to seduce his wife, he concludes that she and, so the implication goes, all women are false:

> What a damn'd Epicurean rascal is this! My heart is ready to crack with impatience. Who says this is improvident jealousy? My wife hath sent to him, the hour is fix'd, the match is made. Would any man have thought this? See the hell of having a false woman! My bed shall be abus'd, my coffers ransack'd, my reputation gnawn at, and I shall not only receive this villainous wrong, but stand under the adoption of abominable terms, and by him that does me wrong. . . . I will rather trust a Fleming with my butter, Parson Hugh the Welshman with my cheese, an Irishman with my aqua-vitae bottle, or a thief to walk my ambling gelding, than my wife with herself. Then she plots, then she ruminates, then she devises; and what they think in their hearts they may effect, they will break their hearts but they will effect. . . . Fie, fie, fie! cuckold, cuckold, cuckold! [287-314]

Thought of his wife's infidelity makes his heart "ready to crack," not with sadness but with "impatience." His predictions ("my bed shall be abus'd") have already come true, for he has done all he could do to besmirch his own reputation and to make himself a cuckold. What else are we to say of a man who pays others to seduce his own wife, declares her "false" before he knows her to be so, is impatient in not knowing her unfaithful, and seems positively buoyant at the prospect of his own cuckolding? It is clear that he would rather have her faithless than faithful and joys in reviling women in general. By an almost imperceptible shift in pronoun, Ford makes that grand leap from one woman's supposed infidelity to castigation of the entire sex. He moves from "my wife" and "she plots" to "and what they think in their hearts they may effect, they will break their hearts but they will effect." "She" becomes "they," and the audience can relax in the familiar stereotype of the slippery wife. "Would any man have thought this?" The men in Shakespearean comedy frequently do.

In *The Merry Wives of Windsor* the young lovers, Fenton and Anne Page, are separated by external problems, while the older folks, Master and Mistress Ford, are separated by those that are internal. In *Troilus and Cressida* both sorts of divisions can be seen in one relationship. Calchas's demand that Cressida be exchanged for Antenor brings about a physical distancing between lovers, but Cressida's liaison with Diomedes represents, of course, the real separation between her and Troilus. To say as much is to indicate at the start the anomalous position this play holds in the canon. The stereotypical roles each sex plays are reversed, for here it is the woman who leaves the man, and the man who is confined, literally, within walls and behind gates. That sense of physical restriction is quite strong and leads rather subtly to our understanding that geographical freedom, which traditionally belongs to the male, often enough implies the sort of sexual freedom that here is Cressida's. It is the man who must have faith in the absent woman and not vice versa as in, say, *The Two Gentlemen of Verona* or *Cymbeline*.

The woman's leaving the man is just one of many atypical elements in Shakespeare's handling of the love story in *Troilus and Cressida*. This is the only Shakespearean comedy in which man and woman sleep together before they marry (Claudio and Juliet in *Measure for Measure* are betrothed), and the only play in which a woman is in fact unfaithful (Titania in *A Midsummer-Night's Dream* excepted). Of course, in the writing of *Troilus and Cressida* Shakespeare was constrained by history and literary tradition; perhaps because of their demands Troilus's reaction to a faithless woman is so different from the reactions of his counterparts in other comedies. Nonetheless, it is astounding that only here, where the woman is in fact disloyal, is the man reluctant to believe what he sees, patient, loathe to blame all women for the faults of one, and sad at what is lost rather than joyful at the opportunity to condemn all women. In her introduction to the Riverside edition of the play, Anne Barton writes that Shakespeare's "approach to the three principals was far less indulgent than Chaucer's,"[40] but in terms of Troilus's attitudes Shakespeare is indeed "indulgent" while Chaucer seems always to reach for the larger point, reminding his reader that Cressida is a woman, "Biseeching every lady bright of hewe, / And every gentil womman what she be, / That al be that Criseide was untrewe, / That for that gilt she not be wroth with me."[41]

In Shakespeare when Troilus sees Cressida with Diomedes the audience sees them as well. Troilus has "ocular proof" of the first degree, not the sort of refracted vision of secondhand accounts in *The Merry Wives of Windsor*, *Much Ado about Nothing*, and *Cymbeline*, nor the absolute misapprehension of *The Comedy of Errors* and *The Winter's Tale*. What Troilus sees is incontrovertible, and, although he is angered and saddened throughout the scene, he continually forces himself to be "patient." Four times, even while Cressida "strokes" (V.ii.51) Diomedes' cheek, Troilus contains himself: "I will not be myself, nor have cognition / Of what I feel; I am all patience" (63-64). Though the virtue of being patient was recommended for men and women alike in the Middle Ages and Renaissance, patience was always personified as a woman (as when Viola speaks of her "sister's" sitting like "Patience on a monument" [*TN*, II.iv.114]), and Troilus's passion here expresses itself as a submission and passivity ordinarily associated with women. And while, as we have seen, other young men in Shakespeare's comedies adopt a passive posture, a "look what she has done to me" attitude, that pose works in the service of their anger with women as a way of expressing misogynistic views and of defining themselves as innocent victims. Their passivity allows them to detest and frees them for vengeance. Troilus's passivity serves a far different purpose; he is submissive as he watches Cressida betray him with Diomedes in order that he *not* believe her false, and this in the face of the strongest sort of evidence, substantiated by Ulysses. Immediately after Cressida admits her "turpitude" (112), Troilus admits to "a credence in my heart, / An esperance so obstinately strong, / That doth invert th' attest of eyes and ears" (120-22). He refuses to believe what he sees in contradistinction to all those men who refuse not to believe "th' attest" of stories, rumors, staged shows, vivid imagery, handkerchiefs and "paddling palms" (*WT*, I.ii.115). With a sort of consummate irony Shakespeare presents us with a Cressida maligning her sex, "Ah, poor our sex! this fault in us I find, / The error of our eye directs our minds" (109-10), and a Troilus defending women:

> Let it not be believ'd for womanhood!
> Think we had mothers, do not give advantage
> To stubborn critics, apt without a theme
> For depravation, to square the general sex
> By Cressid's rule. Rather think this not Cressid. [129-33]

Troilus's anger is not directed at Cressida but at Diomedes, again opposite to the attitude of Claudio, Ford, and Posthumus who are ready to "tear" the women rather than the men: "as much [as] I do Cressid love, / So much by weight hate I her Diomed" (167-68). How different from Claudio, who trusts only men, or Antipholus who flees with his Dromio, or Ford who hires Falstaff, or Posthumus who will kill Jachimo only if he denies that he is a cuckold.

Troilus's response to Cressida's infidelity is in every way anomalous, not least in his self-conscious attempt to be fair to women and in his general anemia of expression. Shakespeare seems much more at home in writing vituperative young men than one who seems the very model of patience and suffering. Perhaps because of Chaucer's conclusion, in which he implicitly compares Troilus with Christ, or because of a tradition that would not allow Troilus to respond viciously, Shakespeare was forced to present his hero a ponderous ruminator:

> This is, and is not, Cressid!
> Within my soul there doth conduce a fight
> Of this strange nature, that a thing inseparate
> Divides more wider than the sky and earth,
> And yet the spacious breadth of this division
> Admits no orifex for a point as subtle
> As Ariachne's broken woof to enter. [146-52]

This passion, which spends itself in thinking rather than in acting, results in a clipped and awkward line, inappropriate and reminiscent of earlier writing, *The Comedy of Errors* and *Titus Andronicus*. E.M.W. Tillyard praises this entire scene for its "richness of content,"[42] though other critics are less charitable. Derek Traversi finds in this speech "all the characteristics of the love poetry of Troilus," including "its tenuous and unnaturally refined expression" and "its sensuous thinness"; "Troilus's passion, for all its surface intensity, has an inadequate foundation, is vitiated by the strained self-pity."[43] Hazlitt dismisses Troilus in one sentence as "no character" at all,[44] and Dr. Johnson declares the play as a whole "more correctly written than most of Shakespeare's compositions, but it is not one of those in which either the extent of his views or elevation of his fancy is fully displayed."[45] Dr. Johnson's famous observation in the Preface to his edition of the plays that Shakespeare's tragedy "seems to be skill, his comedy to be instinct,"[46] is a distinction we feel when we compare Troilus to the other males heroes; Troilus seems all "skill," they all "instinct." Shakespeare's natural bent took him in an entirely different direction from that foisted upon him by the Troy story. Troilus represents an excursion away from the psychological complexity and illogic of the typical male heroes of his comedies and is an experiment he was never to repeat. The wicked woman and the loyal man were types he was drawn to in the sonnets and some of the tragedies but not in the comedies.

4

"We Are All Bastards"

In *A Midsummer-Night's Dream* Lysander tells us that "The course of true love never did run smooth" (I.i.134), that it is perturbed by threats of forced marriage to another or by "War, death, or sickness" (142). Watching *A Midsummer-Night's Dream*, which begins with an angry father separating his daughter from her true love, Shakespeare's audience could hardly be faulted for assuming that the play would simply illustrate how lovers overcome parents and other, greater vexations. As it turns out, of course, the real problems for Lysander and Hermia, as for Demetrius and Helena, have a good deal less to do with the external impediments of "War, death, or sickness" than with the fickleness of the men themselves. Lysander's catalog, however, is a fairly accurate description of trials that await lovers in most romantic comedies of the sixteenth century. In *Mucedorus*, the most popular of all such plays in Elizabethan England, the hero, disguised as a shepherd, is exiled by the King and must leave the woman he loves, Amadine, the Princess. Away from the court he disguises himself yet again, as a hermit, accustoms himself to the solitary life, and takes solace in the thought that Amadine will be his "one day."[1] When she is captured by the wild man, Bremo, Mucedorus bides his time and at an opportune moment slays the ogre. He and Amadine return to court where he reveals that he is the son of a King, and plans are made for their marriage. Mucedorus has indeed "passed many troubles near to death" (V.ii.63), as he tells the King, though he and Amadine are not plagued by the typical impediments Shakespeare's lovers face: the young man's wandering eye or his suspicion that his true love has been faithless.

In George Wilkins's *The Miseries of Enforced Marriage*, the proto-typical tale of patriarchal restraints on young love, William Scarborrow's pre-contract to Clare Harcop is broken when his guardian—violently opposed to the union—threatens to withhold his patrimony unless he marry his niece. Scarborrow obeys, Clare commits suicide, and his "enforced marriage" is tortured as the guilt-ridden groom turns into a vicious prodigal. Though all ends well enough, both in terms of Scarborrow's marriage and his inheritance, *The Miseries of Enforced Marriage* reinforced popular notions that the problems encountered by young lovers in comedy were entirely external. Scarborrow's enemies, he lets us know early on, are others: "For I have heard those matches have cost blood, / Where love is once begun and then withstood. . . ."2

Killing a wild man, changing a king's mind, or wresting a patrimony from a guardian can bring about a tolerably happy ending in plays like *Mucedorus* and *The Miseries of Enforced Marriage* precisely because such problems are entirely external. Mucedorus need only trust that sooner or later he will find himself in the right place at the right time and be in a position to release his beloved. Scarborrow's marriage to Katherine will survive because he has his money and is no longer an adulterer—thanks to Clare's suicide. In addition to effecting similar external changes, however, Shakespeare's heroes need to undergo internal changes—metamorphoses is probably a better word—so as to see their society anew and to apprehend women more clearly. For this reason, what happens while the male characters are separated from wives and lovers has far less to do with killing ogres, like Cloten, than with transforming themselves in such a way that they see the world afresh, either recognizing their true love for who she is or becoming less suspicious and less susceptible to the machinations of villains. Admittedly, these internal changes are sometimes given short shrift by Shakespeare, as when Proteus simply comes to his senses, so to speak, and agrees to love Julia, or when Lysander and Demetrius awake to discover that their affections, happily, have changed yet again. The problems of Shakespeare's more complex characters, however, cannot be dismissed so summarily, and what happens to them from the time they reject women to their reunions in act 5 involves more than a simple rearranging of the furniture.

In choosing to believe Jachimo, Posthumus Leonatus turns Imogen and himself into whore and cuckold and *Cymbeline* into a love story threatened from within. Mucedorus can win Amadine by clubbing the ogre Bremo, but in order for Posthumus to win Imogen he needs to turn a club of sorts on himself. Yet self-recrimination is the furthest thing from his mind when he rushes from Jachimo and Philario in act 2, for at this point in the play Posthumus seems to have become a combination of Mucedorus and Bremo, hero and "wild man," Imogen's true love and her only real enemy. His soliloquy at II.v is clearly a continuation of II.iv, when he came to believe Jachimo, with Posthumus reentering after the other men have left. In fact, the First Folio does not indicate a new scene here, and the sense of an emotional continuation is quite strong, for Posthumus picks up where he had left off minutes earlier when he insisted on being called "cuckold" and when he threatened to "tear" Imogen "limb-meal." This speech is remarkable, not only for the depth of its anger but for the logic of Post-humus's illogic; the speech is a watershed for most nuances of classical, Renaissance, and Shakespearean misogyny:

> Is there no way for men to be, but women
> Must be half-workers? We are all bastards,
> And that most venerable man which I
> Did call my father, was I know not where
> When I was stamp'd. Some coiner with his tools
> Made me a counterfeit; yet my mother seem'd
> The Dian of that time. So doth my wife
> The nonpareil of this. O vengeance, vengeance!
> Me of my lawful pleasure she restrain'd,
> And pray'd me oft forbearance; did it with
> A pudency so rosy the sweet view on't
> Might well have warm'd old Saturn; that I thought her
> As chaste as unsunn'd snow. O, all the devils!
> This yellow Jachimo, in an hour—was't not?—
> Or less—at first? Perchance he spoke not, but
> Like a full-acorn'd boar, a German [one],
> Cried "O!" and mounted; found no opposition
> But what he look'd for should oppose and she
> Should from encounter guard. Could I find out
> The woman's part in me—for there's no motion
> That tends to vice in man, but I affirm
> It is the woman's part. . . .
> .   .   .   .
>   I'll write against them,
> Detest them, curse them; yet 'tis greater skill
> In a true hate, to pray they have their will:
> The very devils cannot plague them better. [1-35]

As outlandish as parts of this soliloquy may sound, its attitudes find clear antecedents in the literature of the period. Posthumus begins with a philosophical statement indicating his abhorrence of womankind, not simply Imogen, and calling for procreation without women. Nosworthy, who calls this issue "a question fairly often asked in medieval literature," refers to Renaissance analogs in Lodge's *Rosalynde* and in Marston's *The Fawne*.[3] In Shakespeare, the idea of procreation without women seems a logical, if bizarre, extension of attitudes expressed earlier, by Claudio, for example, who vows to "look up all the gates of love," "To turn all beauty into thoughts of harm," and the idea is implicit later in Leontes' revulsion at the thought of Mamillius's having some of Hermione's blood and at Perdita's supposed bastardy. Indeed, Posthumus's "We are all bastards" strikes what by now seems a familiar chord: if Imogen is false, then all women are false; if all women are false then his mother was false, and "we are all bastards." Thus, his father was "I know not where" even though his "mother seem'd / The Dian of that time." To Posthumus, such reasoning has an irrefutable logic. If the best is corrupt, what of the others? Yet his logic serves not only to debase women but to debase himself as well. If Imogen is a whore, he must be a bastard.

Posthumus continues as well the bestializing of Imogen. Earlier, he had described her as having been "colted," and now Jachimo is "a full-acorn'd boar" that "cried 'O!' and mounted."[4] The woman's passivity, suggested by the boar's mounting, leads Posthumus to the military analogy that follows, "She should from encounter guard" herself, but Jachimo "found not opposition." This female passivity then drives Posthumus to want to find and, presumably, expunge, "the woman's part in me," with which he associates "All the faults that name, nay, that hell knows" (27). The emphasis is on the total perversity and evil of women and, by implication, on the complete purity and goodness of men, a far more sweeping accusation than that implied in Leontes' calculation that "Should all despair / That have revolted wives, the tenth of mankind / Would hang themselves" (I.ii.200). Posthumus will become a sort of pamphleteer, writing "against them," as Claudio had threatened to do, though Posthumus's first missive, read to us by Pisanio at III.ii, not only accuses Imogen of adultery but enjoins his servant to kill her. Posthumus, not at all satisfied merely with writing or to "Detest them, curse them," longs to purify the world by excising the malignant female.[5]

It is perhaps fitting that Posthumus think himself a bastard, for he has been without father and family since birth. Meredith Skura quite correctly suggests that "Posthumus' trouble at the beginning of the play is that he does not know who he is—and this is partly because he does not know who his family is."[6] In act 1 we learn that no one can "delve him to the root" (i.28); that is, although his father and mother are known, his family line is not. We also learn that his father had

> Two other sons, who in the wars o' th' time
> Died with their swords in hand; for which their father,
> Then old and fond of issue, took such sorrow
> That he quit being, and his gentle lady,
> Big of this gentleman, our theme, deceas'd
> As he was born. [35-40]

Shakespeare slurs over the puzzling contradiction of Sicilius's dying "fond of issue" while his wife is pregnant,[7] in favor of indicating Posthumus's unimportance from his birth. His name, too, denotes clearly to what extent he remains unformed and underdeveloped in society's eyes.[8] In a sense, he has no name, and is simply "he who was born after Leonatus died." In difficult circumstances from birth, Posthumus is perceived by those around him as diminished even further in comparison with his father, who was given the name "Leonatus" as a "sur-addition" (I.i.33) for his valor. Posthumus is exiled by Cymbeline, his King and erstwhile guardian, because he is base and yet has married Imogen, heir to the throne in the absense of the King's two kidnapped sons. Shakespeare seems to have stacked the deck against Posthumus, whom he would have us apprehend as the base son of a great father respected and loved by the King. The contradiction is doubly damning.

Cymbeline's readiness to call Posthumus "base" stems from the conjunction of his apparently obscure lineage and his present poverty. The King chastises Imogen for having married him and calls Posthumus a "basest thing" (i.125) and a "beggar" (141) who would have helped his daughter make his throne a "seat for baseness" (142). Cloten, like Cymbeline, attacks Posthumus for being poor and unattached, a "base wretch, / One bred of alms and foster'd with cold dishes, / With scraps o' th' court" (II.iii.113-15). Posthumus is known abroad, too, as an indigent, for even Jachimo thinks Imogen open to criticism "for taking a beggar" (I.iv.23).

"Base" was, of course, a synonym for "bastard," and one definition of "base" in the OED is "illegitimate, bastard," now obsolete except in "base-born." For Edmund in *King Lear*, there is absolutely no difference at all between "bastard" and "base":

> Why bastard? Wherefore base?
> When my dimensions are as well compact,
> My mind as generous, and my shape as true,
> As honest madam's issue? Why brand they us
> With base? with baseness? bastardy? base, base? [I.ii.6-10][9]

"Base" was used as a synonym for "bastard" in legal documents as well as in conversation and literature. The Act Books kept by the ecclestiastical or so-called "bawdy court" in Stratford uses "notha," "spuria," "bastard," and "base" as synonyms for illegitimate, as, for example, in an entry in 1624: "Isabella Hall: for incontinence: she appeared: 'she confesseth that she had a bastard or base child by Thomas West and that he and none but he had the use of her body and was the father of the base child.'"[10]

The emphasis on Posthumus's baseness, that is, on his being like a bastard, is the negative way of saying what we learned earlier: Posthumus cannot be delved "to the root" and is poor. After all, two of the hallmarks of illegitimacy then as now are namelessness and poverty. Unlike those sons who inherit title (e.g., Bertram and Pericles), or others left money by testament (Orlando and Petruchio), or those helped by generous fathers (Lucentio and Proteus), Posthumus is the son of a national hero, yet has nothing of substance with which to further himself. Because he has lost his association with his father and has inherited neither title nor goods, the King's argument seems to run, he is unfit for alliance with a daughter of the royal family. To Pisanio, who is commanded to kill Imogen, it is clear that Posthumus's "mind to her is now as low as were / Thy fortunes" (III.ii.10-11). A young man who has been called base by all and sundry—as if he were a bastard in fact—whose father has died "fond of issue," whom none can "delve to the root," in other words, one whose outward circumstances have all along suggested those of a bastard, has now developed in his misogyny, his rejection of his father, and his suspicion of his mother the perspective of a bastard and, consequently, in II.v, declares himself one: my father "was I know not where / When I was stamp'd."

Bastardy was of particular interest to the sixteenth century, partly because Elizabeth I was unmarried and childless—questions relating to succession necessarily involved questions of legitimacy—but also because, as Marilyn Williamson notes, "The rate of illegitimacy had doubled during Shakespeare's lifetime, peaking in 1604."[11] Economic hardship led to postponed marriages, which, in turn, increased the incidence of pregnancy outside wedlock. Then, too, Williamson notes, the Poor Law of 1601 "made a bastard the charge of the parish in which the child was born" and thus placed the financial burden of illegitimate children on the community as a whole.[12] Unmarried pregnant women were often punished in a variety of ways—social and physical—for their condition, as were their offspring. On both were visited social opprobrium and devastating legal restrictions. In the Renaissance, bastardy in fact implied a constellation of attitudes. To be a bastard was, in the first place, not to know one's father, and thus not to have a family name, often to have no name at all. Bastardy certainly meant impoverishment as well, for it was not until the French Revolution that some of the economic sanctions against bastards were lifted, and then only briefly.[13] Separated from his father and indigent, a bastard was stigmatized yet again, for his mother was, by definition, a whore and he "the issue of the defiled bed," as William Clerke describes it in *The Triall of Bastardie*,[14] or, more simply, a "whoreson," as Gloucester jovially describes Edmund to Kent (I.i.24).

Edgar's progress in *King Lear* from legitimate son and heir to outcast, as the reverse of Edmund's progress from "baseness" to earldom, describes for us the sort of bastardizing Posthumus undergoes and indicates popular attitudes toward illegitimacy. Edgar loses his connection with his father and consequently his name ("Edgar I nothing am" [II.iii.21]), becoming "Poor Tom o' Bedlam," while Edmund fills his place and eventually steals what would have been his title. Edgar's ragged clothing in particular helps to define him as an impoverished outcast, as does the wildly fictitious account he tells Lear of his past, when he was "A servingman! proud in heart and mind; that curl'd my hair; wore gloves in my cap; serv'd the lust of my mistress' heart, and did the act of darkness with her" (III.iv.85-88), suggesting as it does materialism, lechery, and the lustfulness of women. Fatherless, with a new name, impoverished, and slandering women, Edgar's position and attitudes are not only those of Edmund but also those of Don John in *Much Ado about Nothing* and of most such bastards in the drama. Caliban has, of course, been construed as the epitome of this type for years: his physical deformities have been read as the outward sign of a primitive and, therefore, degenerate mind. His birth out of wedlock is told to us by Prospero in his act 1 narrative to Miranda. Sycorax, his mother, was banished from Argier pregnant with Caliban, whom she "did litter here," a child "hag-born," "not honor'd with / A human shape" (I.ii.282-84). Caliban's attempted rape of Miranda and murder of Prospero are actions fully consonant with the philosophies of most of Shakespeare's bastards, Don John, Edmund, and Thersites, and consonant as well with actions described in official accounts of illegitimate children.[15]

With his denunciation of Imogen at II.v and his letter to Pisanio at III.ii ordering Imogen's death, Posthumus adds to his poverty, mean clothing, and separation from father the perverse sexual attitudes of bastards: the assumption that all women are whores and all men cuckolds and whoresons. Having said as much, however, I am aware that although Posthumus's attitudes toward women are exactly those of a Don John or an Edmund, there is a world of difference between him and them. Posthumus adopts a bastard's philosophy but none of the bastard's self-conscious immorality. For him, rejection of women is not an attitude used in the service of mischievousness or malice but rather the only stance possible for a good man in a bad world, and it is ironic that in trying to live a good life he winds up in the company of the real bastards of Elizabethan and Jacobean literature.

Because he has none of the self-conscious maliciousness characteristic of the bastards, the bastardy Posthumus embraces in his declaration, "we are all bastards," is not that of Thersites, who boasts, "I love bastards. I am bastard begot, bastard instructed, bastard in mind, bastard in valor, in every thing illegitimate" (*TC*, V.vii.16-18), or of Edmund, who brags of his "composition, and fierce quality" (I. ii. 12). Posthumus is reminiscent rather of Euripides' Hippolytus, the bastard son of Theseus and Antiopa (Hippolyta), one of very few bastards in Western literature who are admirable or are presented as capable of achieving tragic stature. It is primarily in Hippolytus' righteous withdrawal from women, in his use of bastardy as a reasonable moral stance, that he suggests the heroes of Shakespearean comedy.

That Shakespeare knew some plays by Euripides is probable, for Euripides was, Madeleine Doran points out, "the most translated and imitated by continental authors; in England, the few translations of Greek drama that were made are of him."[16] However, there is no record of a translation of his *Hippolytus,* though it is certain that Shakespeare knew Seneca's *Hippolytus,* perhaps in Latin, but surely in the landmark edition, *Seneca His Tenne Tragedies,* published in 1581. *Hippolytus,* translated by John Studley for that edition, is, of course, a far cry from Euripides' play, though the central facts of the story, including Hippolytus's bastardy, are abundantly clear in both. Then, too, a synopsis of the Hippolytus story appears in Golding's translation of Ovid's *Metamorphoses,* where we are told by Hippolytus that "The daughter of *Pasyphae,*" "for feare I should her wickednesse bewray, / Or else for spyght bycause I had so often sayd her nay . . . chardgd mee with her owne offence."[17]

It is very likely not only that Shakespeare knew Seneca's *Hippolytus* but that he was influenced by it. Hippolytus sounds like Posthumus, or Claudio, or the King of Navarre when he establishes his academy, or Antipholus fleeing from Ephesus, or Bertram refusing to "bed" Helena, or Leontes condemning women. There is an innocence about him, in Euripides, Ovid, and Seneca, rather than the citified sophistication that seems a badge of bastards in sixteenth- and seventeenth-century literature. Hippolytus is chaste and avoids women and sexuality for fear of defilement. He is a misogynist of the very first order and is depicted so in Seneca where, as in Euripides, Hippolytus's woman-hating is simply presented as a given. Unlike Posthumus, however, Hippolytus does not appear to change or develop into a misogynist as the result of a traumatic experience as an adult. From act 1 to his death in act 4, Hippolytus remains faithful to an ideal he seems to have had since birth—life without women. In Euripides, in fact, his misogyny is clearly the product of his bastardy and he is destroyed by Aphrodite precisely for that misogyny. Like Posthumus, Hippolytus chides,

> Why hast thou given a home beneath the sun,
> Zeus, unto woman, specious curse to man?
> For, were thy will to raise a mortal seed,

This ought they not of women to have gotten,
But in thy temples should they lay its price,
Or gold, or iron, or a weight of bronze,
And so buy seed of children, every man
After the worth of that his gift, and dwell
Free in free homes unvexed of womankind.[18]

Though he is equally misogynistic in Studley's Seneca, Hippolytus seems less clearly motivated in his rejection of women, merely two-dimensional, much more "the man who hates women," a sort of Senecan humour character without much psychological depth but nonetheless cut from the same cloth as Euripides' character:

Yet who can move Hippolytus most stony stubborne mynd?
He wil abhorre the very name detesting womankind,
And faring franticly, wil gyve himselfe to single life,
And shunne the hated spousall bedde of every marride
    wife. . . .[19]

Elsewhere, he is "cruell child Hippolitus" (151) who, with "his stubborne hardned hart" and "brutish breast" (152), refuses all women and rails against them.

Hippolytus's misogyny in Greek and Roman versions is thorough-going, and he is implacable. Like Posthumus, Seneca's Hippolytus thinks "womankinde in mischiefe is ringleader" (156), the source of all the world's evils. "I hate, detest, abhore, I loth, I curse them from my heart. / Bee 't reason, right, or Nature's law, or vengeance fury fell, / It likes me to abhorre them still" (156). The similarity here with *Cymbeline* is not contextual alone; Hippolytus and Posthumus speak the same language. If we compare the lines just quoted with Posthumus's "I'll write against them, / Detest them, curse them; yet 'tis greater skill / In a true hate, to pray they have their will," we see Shakespeare using "detest," "curse," and "hate," three of the five verbs in Seneca and, again, immediately after the accusation that women are the source of all evil. Furthermore, like Posthumus, Hippolytus debases his mother: "This onely comfort of my Mother must I keepe behinde, / That leeful [lawful] unto me it is to hate all Womankinde" (157).

Once Phaedra tells Hippolytus of her love he couples misogyny with self-righteous protestations of his own purity and is appalled and incensed that his virtue should even have been attempted: "Doe not with shamelesse fawning Pawes my spotlesse body staine. / What meaneth this? with hawsing [praising] mee t' imbrace she doth begin: / Draw, draw my sword"

(161). He is revulsed by her. She touches his sword and he refuses to take it up, calling it "filed" (162), that is, "defiled": "What bathing lukewarme Tanais may I defilde obtaine, / Whose clensing watry Channell pure may washe mee cleane again?" (162). Posthumus feels doubly betrayed by Imogen's supposed infidelity, for "Me of my lawful pleasure she restrain'd, / And prayed me oft forbearance" (II.v.9-10). Claudio does not wish to "knit" his "soul to an approved wanton" (IV.i.44), and he never tempted Hero "with word too large, / But as a brother to his sister, show'd / Bashful sincerity and comely love" (52-54).

However, once Theseus is informed that Hippolytus has tried to rape Phaedra, the King describes his son as just the sort of bastard we recognize in Edmund, Don John, or Caliban, and the young man who has avoided women in order to remain pure is now, ironically, described as a villain whose bastardy leads him to rape and revel in lust. Misreading his son, Theseus now sees Hippolytus's misogyny not as the abstinence of a man trying to be good but rather as a sign of his being the vicious bastard so familiar as the stereotype of literature: "Cat after kinde hee is, and will th' unkindly Bastard blood / Returne unto his kindreds course, whence first his ligne he claims" (169). He owns a "filthy minde" and is a hypocrite, a "brainsicke beast who liv'd in chast estate / An undefyled Bachiler" (169). Theseus calls his son "Vagabond" (169) and can only hope he will "rawnge, rawnge, about to finde / Straunge forraine soyles, and outcast landes aloofe at world his end" (169-70). This version of Hippolytus is precisely the sort of character Posthumus becomes after ordering Imogen's death, a "brainsicke" "vagabond."

For Shakespeare, bastardy was a convenient and familiar metaphor by which he was able to suggest much about a young man's social position and attitudes. Posthumus, of course, is not a bastard, but he develops the attitudes of stereotypical bastards, and perhaps exemplifies the principle Tristram Shandy's father refers to when he maintains "all misogynists to be bastards."[20] In his soliloquy at II.v Posthumus clearly professes the views of Don John, or of Thersites, or of the Hippolytus described by the angry Theseus when he believes his son has attempted his wife's virtue. When he rejects Imogen, Posthumus is separated from his father, family, and wife; he is a dangerous misogynist, an indigent vagabond. He turns himself into a mad Tom o' Bedlam and becomes the very worst that the King and Cloten have expected him to become, as though he were bent on living down to their expectations. *Hippolytus* provided Shakespeare with just such a model of the well-intentioned and high-minded bastard who came to be thought of as a "brainsicke beast."

In her excellent study of illegitimacy Jenny Teichman draws a useful distinction between bastardy and attitudes we associate with bastardy in her discussion of Dickens's *Oliver Twist*:

> The hero of *Oliver Twist* is technically illegitimate but, as it were, ideologically legitimate. He is the innocent victim of family greed—which forced his father to marry a woman he did not love—and of the machinations of a scoundrelly half-brother who wishes to destroy him. The half-brother, Edward Leeford, alias Monks, is technically legitimate but, as it were, ideologically illegitimate. Like a real bastard, he is a person about whose surname there is some doubt; furthermore, he is archetypally degenerate, diseased in body and in will. At the end of the story Edward Leeford is expelled from the family and Oliver, the hero, is welcomed into it. Dickens thus reverses the traditional roles of legitimate and illegitimate characters in his story—with the clear intention of attacking the ancient dictum that tells us all bastards are bad.[21]

Shakespeare's intentions in *Cymbeline* are far different, for although Posthumus is treated as if he were "technically illegitimate," he is not, in fact, a bastard. Shakespeare does, however, self-consciously parallel his hero with the "ideologically illegitimate" Cloten, and in so doing emphasizes the ways in which illegitimacy—technical and ideological—affects attitudes and behaviors in a romantic comedy.

The portrait of Posthumus as "bastard" is immeasurably strengthened by Shakespeare's depiction of Cloten, for in *Cymbeline* we find the descent of the hero coupled with the rise of a villain. Such is the case as well in *Much Ado about Nothing,* where the bastard Don John precipitates Claudio's downfall and finds his views of women and male friendship prevailing with Claudio and Don Pedro. Such warped views achieve currency in plays without bastards through the bastardizing of the hero as he loses social status, and are emphasized by the parallel rise of any villain. Shakespeare indicated its wider implications in his pairing not only of Claudio and Don John (whom one critic calls Claudio's "double"[22]) but of Ford and Falstaff, Orlando and Oliver, Duke Senior and Duke Frederick, Bertram and Parolles, Claudio and Angelo, Troilus and Diomedes. The possibility of such villainy is strongly suggested in *The Winter's Tale* in Florizel's changing clothes with the thief Autolycus, as the Prince tries to flee Bohemia and his father's wrath. Similarly, in *The Tempest* the suggestion that Ferdinand's descent will be paralleled by Caliban's rise is never made explicit, although Ferdinand fetches logs while Caliban, the only other creature to show an amorous interest in Miranda, plots rape and murder with Stephano and Trinculo. There is a sense in all the plays matching a hero with his opposite that the world is confused and on a disastrous course. Nations are certainly threatened with destruction in the possibility of Cloten's ascent, and in these plays the personal trials of hero and heroine are magnified in the upheaval in the macrocosm of the state. The evil men, often bastards, gain the upper hand, while the hero falls, languishing in poverty or the moral morass the bastard helped create.

From the very beginning of *Cymbeline*, Shakespeare seems to be asking the audience to contrast Posthumus with Cloten. Before we meet either of them we are told that they are reverse images of one another:

> *1. Gent.*   He that hath miss'd the Princess is a thing
> Too bad for bad report; and he that hath her
> (I mean, that married her, alack, good man!
> And therefore banish'd) is a creature such
> As, to seek through the regions of the earth
> For one his like, there would be something failing
> In him that should compare. [I.i.16-22]

Cloten is an excellent example of the "ideologically illegitimate," perhaps even better than Richard III or Iago. Cloten is highly placed but lowly minded; his hatred of other men, for whom he never has a good word, and his plan to rape Imogen are characteristic of bastards (when Belarius urges that Cloten he buried as befits a prince, Guiderius remarks, "Thersites' body is as good as Ajax'" [IV.ii.252]). It is the great irony and tragedy of this play that Posthumus, who is lowly placed but highly minded, should come to sound, think, and act as Cloten does, to become, in fact, "a version of Cloten,"[23] and that Cloten should become "a parodic surrogate for Posthumus."[24]

The point that Posthumus has become a kind of Cloten is brought home very effectively through Shakespeare's use of clothing images and of clothes themselves, for Cloten, decapitated and in Posthumus's clothing in act 4, is mistaken by Imogen for Posthumus himself. Shakespeare had used clothes in earlier comedies as a means of bringing about mistakes of identity, but he had also used them to make moral and psychological points, as when the men of Navarre are fooled by the ladies from France simply because the latter have put on masks, or when Petruchio summarizes his relationship with Kate by saying, "To me she's married, not unto my clothes" (III.ii.117). In *Cymbeline* Shakespeare uses clothes both to create confusion over identity and to suggest, almost subliminally, that the attitudes of the hero and the villain have become almost identical.[25]

Clothes are a significant target in this play because raggedness implied baseness; in fact, there was a kind of coarse cloth "of inferior or mixed quality" known as "bastard."[26] In *King John* it is suggested that bastards not only dressed more humbly but perhaps distinctively so, for the Bastard, Faulconbridge, describes himself as "a bastard to the time" (I.i.207), "And not alone in habit and device, / Exterior form, outward accoutrement" (210-11). From the start Cloten attacks Posthumus exclusively on the basis of his poverty, especially as it evidences itself in his clothing. For Cloten, Posthumus is "a base slave, / A hilding for a livery, a squire's cloth, / A pantler—not so eminent" (II.iii.122-24). For the "ideological" bastard like Cloten, fine clothes confer a kind of legitimacy, though, as M.C. Bradbrook reminds us, "There was a firm tradition that gaudy clothes were the sign of a fop or gull, and that plain attire indicated honest worth."[27] The more base Posthumus appears and the more grand Cloten dresses, the more assured of his station a snob like Cloten feels. Elizabethan and Jacobean playwrights often emphasized a bastard's evil by satisfying what had become known to audiences as his insatiable craving for the material signs of affluence. To John Danby, the bastard is simply a Hobbesian "New Man" in a world of commodity and gain.[28] Edmund seeks "land" (I.ii.16); Spurio, the bastard in *The Revenger's Tragedy,* is pleased to be seen on the arm of the Duchess and to shame his betters (Ambitioso asks, "Must she needs choose such an unequal sinner . . . ?")[29] and Faulconbridge talks of "the footsteps of my rising" (I.i.216). Thus, when Imogen defends Posthumus, calling Cloten "too base / To be his groom" (II.iii.126-27), and tells him that her husband's "mean'st garment / That ever hath but clipt his body, is dearer / In my respect than all the hairs above thee, / Were they all made such men" (133-36), Cloten is moved to violence. Cloten's sense of who Posthumus is and of who he himself is rests solely on "exterior form, outward accoutrement"; without his props Cloten falls and Posthumus must inevitably rise. Apparently stupefied, four times Cloten repeats variations on Imogen's words, "'His mean'st garment'?"

If Posthumus and Cloten are moral opposites who gradually come to think and act alike (one critic finds an "ironic parallel" between the two in the fact that "Posthumus' experience seems to confirm Cloten's vulgar opinion of love-making"[30]), it is clear from the start that they are physical doubles. No less than three times we are told that they look alike, twice by Cloten and once by Imogen. Indeed, in order for Imogen to believe that Posthumus is dead she must be convinced that Cloten's body is Posthumus's. Shakespeare prepares the audience to accept Imogen's error as reasonable by having Cloten enter in act 4 wearing Posthumus's clothes as easily as if they were made for him: "How fit his garments serve me!" (i.2-3). His plan is to kill Posthumus, ravish Imogen, and then cut the garments "to pieces before [her] face" (18). The audience, of course, thoroughly steeped in stories from romance and religion, knows almost instinctively that while Posthumus will eventually shed his "mean garments," they are precisely Cloten's due. When he meets Guiderius, who is dressed in rustic clothing, Cloten, apparently forgetting that he is wearing Posthumus's clothes, asks, "Thou villain base, / Know'st me not by my clothes?" (IV.ii.80-81). For Guiderius, as for the audience, Cloten's apparel is now an accurate reflection of his temper of mind: "At fools I laugh, not fear them" (96).[31]

The psychological changes Posthumus undergoes are much more easily discerned because he and Cloten look alike and come to occupy the same moral terrain. But Posthumus, who has been absent from the stage for some time, reappears in V.i. lamenting Imogen's death even though he still thinks she has betrayed him with Jachimo. This spectacular change in view, which has perplexed critics for some time, and which I will discuss more fully in Chapter 6, is prepared for by Imogen's lamenting Posthumus's supposed death here in act 4. In a sense, it is only when she and the audience see Cloten dead that we can begin to understand that a version of Posthumus is dead, that Posthumus is now ready to be reborn and to assume that natural dignity and nobility we were told he had in the first twenty lines of the play.

When Imogen awakens and finds the corpse, she forces the audience to reaffirm its understanding of Posthumus's essential goodness:

> A headless man? The garments of Posthumus?
> I know the shape of 's leg; this is his hand,
> His foot Mercurial, his Martial thigh,
> The brawns of Hercules; but his Jovial face—
> Murther in heaven? How? 'Tis gone. [ii.308-12]

And so Posthumus begins to rise in our estimation as Imogen revives our sense of his heroic qualities. It is as though he sloughs off the bastard in him, that part of his nature that has turned him into a kind of Cloten, and is gradually reborn as the best he could have been had he been reared more legitimately, so to speak, with a firm and clear connection to his family in name and fact, that is, in a manner more fitting his natural dignity of spirit. When Lucius and the Roman army find Imogen and ask who her dead master is, she tells them, "Richard du Champ" (377). It seems likely that Shakespeare is here alluding to Richard Field, the publisher of "Venus and Adonis" and "The Rape of Lucrece," a friend who was married to a Frenchwoman and who often styled himself "Ricardo Campo." In any case, it is clear that Shakespeare is complimenting Posthumus.[32] Our appreciation of Posthumus's transformation in V.i (some one hundred lines later), is almost assured when Imogen insists on burying "Posthumus" and strewing his grave with "wild wood-leaves and weeds" and saying "a century of prayers" (390, 391). As the scene ends, Lucius commands his men to "Find out the prettiest daisied plot we can" (398) and tacitly instructs Imogen and the audience to prepare for a new Posthumus:

> Boy, he's preferr'd
> By thee to us, and he shall be interr'd
> As soldiers can. Be cheerful; wipe thine eyes:
> Some falls are means the happier to arise. [400-403]

Our sense that the play is turning about, resolving the problems between Imogen and Posthumus, is unmistakable. Michael Taylor puts it very well when he writes, "In structural and emotional terms Imogen's degradation in act 4, scene 2 marks a watershed in the play's action; after it, with almost every wink of the eye some new grace will be born."[33]

Though Posthumus is the only one of Shakespeare's comic heroes to call himself a bastard, his situation and attitudes differ very little from those of the other males, most of whom, to a greater or lesser degree, move toward his circumstances and viewpoints. The paradigm is indeed bastardy, and it is that constellation of attitudes and social relations the heroic young men in the comedies begin to approximate as soon as they separate from their fathers. It is as if separation from father leads inexorably to disguise, loss of name, impoverishment, and, all too often, misogyny and distrust of men.

We have seen some of Posthumus's attitudes and actions even as early as *The Comedy of Errors* in Antipholus's confusion of "god" and "witch," and later in Claudio's assumption that "Beauty is a witch" and in his rejection of Hero as a woman who only "seems" a kind of Diana. In *The Winter's Tale* bastardy is a crucial issue, though one not often associated with Leontes himself. However, it is Leontes who becomes "ideologically illegitimate"; his suspicion that Hermione is faithless is best seen in his insistence that the infant Perdita is a bastard and in his occasionally doubting the legitimacy of his son Mamillius. His identifying himself with his son suggests obliquely that Leontes thinks he himself stands on slippery ground, an inference that can be drawn from his believing that it is a "bawdy planet" (I.ii.201). Indeed, his belief that "Many thousand on 's / Have the disease, and feel't not" (206-7) is an opinion we associate with the likes of Don John, Thersites, and the other bastards, as we do his notion that men cannot be trusted, that a neighbor is "Sir Smile" (196) and a friend from childhood, such as Polixenes, merely disloyal. His condition during the first two and a half acts suggests that of a bastard, as much in his luxuriating in what he feels to be his corrupt situation as in his refusal to be disabused of his ugly notions. He tortures Camillo in terms familiar to us from *Cymbeline*:

> If thou wilt confess,
> Or else be impudently negative,
> To have nor eyes nor ears nor thought, then say
> My wife's a [hobby]-horse, deserves a name
> As rank as any flax-wench that puts to
> Before her troth-plight: say't and justify't! [273-78]

For Leontes it is a world of whores, cuckolds, bastards, and smiling neighbors, and this viewpoint, characteristic of the "ideologically illegitimate," is opposed by Antigonus, who argues not simply against Leontes' particular claim that Hermione "puts to" and Perdita is a bastard, but against the larger position from which the King argues: that it is a "bawdy planet." Antigonus can only guess that "some putter-on" (II.i.141), an instigator, has been at work, and will not believe that Leontes has played the part of villain to himself. If the King is right about Hermione then bastardy achieves currency and women must be neutered. Leontes has turned the world upside down, branded his wife a whore and his children bastards; he has given "scandal to the blood o' th' Prince" (I.ii.330) and caused a rift in his family so deep that sixteen years are barely enough time to reestablish a legitimate family history: "the King shall live without an heir, if that which is lost be not found" (III.ii.134-36). What is lost is not simply Perdita, but rather all that Perdita stands for: a view of the planet as wholesome and an acceptance, Derek Traversi remarks, "of a right sexual relationship, of natural fertility consecrated, given its proper spiritual context in the bond of marriage."[34] In short, a view of life antithetical to that of a bastard, one which presupposes the best of friends and neighbors, husbands and wives.

In *Pericles* Shakespeare presents what is on the surface a very different scenario from that in other comedies, for the daughter of Antiochus, involved in an incestuous relationship with her father, the King, is genuinely corrupt. But while the unsuspecting young man in this play is confronted in fact with a woman "good in nothing but in sight" (I.i.123), the pattern of male approach-avoidance is familiar, as are the attitudes of the hero. Pericles finds the young lady a "celestial tree" (21) "apparelled like the spring" (12). She is, according to her incestuous father, "clothed like a bride / For embracements even of Jove himself" (6-7), and is a "fair

Hesperides, / With golden fruit" (27-28) and a face "like heaven" (30). Pericles is, then, reminiscent of earlier heroes partly because he is described as godlike, but also because the scene in which he tries to answer the King's riddle is itself a version of earlier scenes in which young men are asked to make crucial choices, as, for example, when Lucentio falls in love with Bianca and tosses his education to the wind, or when Sebastian walks off with Olivia, but especially when Bassanio chooses among the caskets in *The Merchant of Venice*.

Like Bassanio, Pericles too must risk all for a woman. Both scenes in these two plays are described in terms taken from classical mythology and romantic fiction. The daughter of Antiochus suggests "golden fruit" (28) and is a "glorious casket" (77); Portia is a "golden fleece" (I.i.170) and is symbolized by a casket. Pericles is like "Jove" (7), Bassanio "Hercules" (III.ii.60). Pericles is threatened by "death-like dragons" (29), Bassanio by a "sea-monster" (57); and Pericles must interpret a riddle, while Bassanio interprets three legends. Pericles concludes that the King's daughter is "stor'd with ill" (77) and rejects her by fleeing from Antioch and trumpeting her sinfulness. We are told that Pericles is correct, and so he seems fundamentally different from Antipholus, Claudio, Posthumus, or even Bassanio—who saw in Portia's picture hair that seemed a web to "entrap the hearts of men" (122)—and more like, indeed, even identical to, the virtuous Hippolytus, when he flees from Phaedra's incestuous advances.[35]

Pericles is like other Shakespearean heroes, however, in his apprehending a woman as celestial, rejecting her as evil, and then fleeing from her. He is like them, too, in his essential goodness, but instead of misapprehending one woman and seeing in her antipodal characteristics, he simply moves from the daughter of Antiochus to Thaisa, her opposite, one who is famous for her virtue. Shakespeare splits the misapprehended heroine of other comedies—Hero, or Imogen, for example—into two women and thus validates Pericles' reaction. Thaisa's goodness is confirmed externally by her subsequent death, resurrection, and service to Diana, no less clearly than Antiochus's daughter's evil is confirmed by Gower and by her death by lightning. Later in the play the two halves, the Princess of Antioch and Thaisa, seem reunited in Marina, a virgin in a brothel, a more familiar Shakespearean type, the misapprehended woman who appears to be Venus but who is, in fact, virtue personified.

Pericles' similarity to other heroes, especially Posthumus, is clear not only in his separation from a good and famous father to whom he feels inferior and in his rejection of a woman as a serpent (I.i.132) but also in his vagabondage and poverty. After fleeing from Antioch and then Tyre, he becomes a prince living like a beggar. His ship is wrecked and he is washed ashore in Pentapolis, in a condition worse than Antipholus's or Sebastian's in degree though not in kind:

> What I have been I have forgot to know,
> But what I am, want teaches me to think on:
> A man throng'd up with cold, my veins are chill,
> And have no more of life than may suffice
> To give my tongue that heat to ask your help;
> Which if you shall refuse, when I am dead,
> For that I am a man, pray you see me buried. [II.i.71-77]

The separation from his dead father and his flight from the evil woman have led to poverty and an even greater separation from father ("What I have been I have forgot to know"), a sense of loss that approaches death, shared by Antipholus and by Proteus as he leaves Verona and Julia. Like Posthumus, Pericles has become a wanderer, at others' mercy, reminiscent of Hippolytus, but also of Edgar.

In flight from the King of Antioch and his agents, separated from his father and close to death, Pericles is in those circumstances that often suggest bastardy. Pericles, however, has what Antipholus and Posthumus do not, that is, a sure and ineradicable sense of who he is and, more to the point, of who his forebears were. He avoids "ideological illegitimacy" by the fortuitous discovery of his dead father's armor and by repeating almost catechistically his connection with father and heritage:

> An armor, friends? I pray you let me see it.
> Thanks, Fortune, yet, that after all [thy] crosses,
> Thou givest me somewhat to repair myself;
> And though it was mine own, part of my heritage,
> Which my dead father did bequeath to me. . . .
> . . . .
> My shipwrack now's no ill,
> Since I have here my father gave in his will. [II.i.120-34]

Though the armor is rusty, Pericles considers it a "coat of worth" (136) and feels "cloth'd in steel" (154), ready for the tournament at Pentapolis, ready to win and marry Thaisa. His misfortunes are now "no ill" simply because his connection with his father has been reaffirmed.

Outfitted with his father's armor, Pericles enters the tournament at Pentapolis in hopes of winning Thaisa. The emblem on his shield depicts a "withered branch, that's only green at top" (II.ii.43), bearing the motto "*In hac spe vivo*" (44), "In this hope I live." The device on his shield, suggesting new growth from barrenness, is thus an appropriate emblem for a Prince who begins his ascent from death and despair when he discovers his patrimony. Over and again in scenes 2 and 3 of act 2 Shakespeare seems to make the point that nobility and strength of character may reside beneath an unassuming exterior and that it is one's own sure understanding of who he is that allows him to become as great a man as his father was. It is in fact the knight in "the dejected state" (ii.46) who wins the day and who has performed "better than his outward show / Can any way speak in his just commend" (48-49).

Though Pericles feels like a "glow-worm in the night" (iii.43) compared with his father, Thaisa's father, Simonides, at once recognizes his heroic attributes. Later, in scene 5, when Simonides teases Pericles and calls him traitor, Pericles responds instantly, "My actions are as noble as my thoughts, / That never relish'd of a base descent" (59-60). In allowing Pericles to marry his daughter, Simonides concludes that Pericles "May be (nor can I think the contrary) / As great in blood as I myself" (79-80). The circumstances of the hero in *Pericles* closely resemble those in *Cymbeline*, but with the crucial difference that Posthumus cannot be delved to the root, and Pericles, although lost and impoverished, is always firmly rooted in a clear family line. His "heritage" and his father's "will" provide the confidence that helps him past dangerous encounters. It is this difference that accounts for Pericles' ability to resist the temptation of thinking himself a bastard and an outcast even though his outward circumstances suggest those of an illegitimate; it is Posthumus's failure that he cannot.

Orlando, like Pericles, is a hero whose outward circumstances are similar to those of the typical bastard but whose inner qualities are those of the gentleman and hero and remain so, especially with regard to Rosalind, whom he never leaves in any real sense of the word. *As You Like It* begins with Orlando's lamenting his condition and deploring his brother's refusal to treat him in the manner indicated by their father's will. Oliver refuses to educate him and treats him as he does "his hinds" (I.i.19) and his farm animals, "for call you that keeping for a gentleman of my birth, that differs not from the stalling of an ox?" (9-11). It is clear, however, that even if Oliver were to give him the money left Orlando by their father, he would not be much better off. After all, Orlando is the youngest son and was bequeathed "but poor a thousand crowns" (2-3). When Oliver finally agrees to give Orlando his due, it is apparent to the older brother that the younger has few choices: "And what wilt thou do? beg, when that is spent?" (75).

If Orlando's situation is bad in I.i, it is worse in I.ii, for after he defeats the wrestler, he is exiled by the Duke and must "from the smoke into the smother" (287). Though his fortunes can go no lower, his attitudes can. Like

Pericles, however, Orlando resists the state of mind his circumstances suggest. He does not become a misogynist and spares us the spectacle of his contriving against Rosalind or of coming to believe all men cuckolds and schemers. Indeed, he does not become the sort of man Oliver describes to Charles as he slanders his youngest brother in hopes that the wrestler will kill him:

> I'll tell thee, Charles, it is the stubbornest young fellow of France, full of ambition, an envious emulator of every man's good parts, a secret and villainous contriver against me his natural brother; therefore use thy discretion—I had as lief thou didst break his neck as his finger. And thou wert best look to't; for if thou dost him any slight disgrace, or if he do not mightily grace himself on thee, he will practice against thee by poison, entrap thee by some treacherous device, and never leave thee till he hath ta'en thy life by some indirect means or other; for I assure thee (and almost with tears I speak it) there is not one so young and so villainous this day living. [I.i.141-55]

The "brother" Oliver creates is Cloten or Iago, but especially Edmund, who is indeed a "secret and villainous contriver" against his own brother. Oliver's creation is, in fact, the prototypical bastard of Elizabethan fiction, a Don John, who describes himself as a "plain-dealing villain" (*MAdo*, I.iii.32) whose "blood" it better suits "to be disdain'd of all than to fashion a carriage to rob love from any" (28, 29-30). The audience, of course, recognizes his speech as confession, as simple self-description. Oliver does, after all, contrive against Orlando by slandering him, and he admits as much at the end of the scene when he tells us in soliloquy that he hates Orlando simply because he is good: "Yet he's gentle, never school'd and yet learned, full of noble device, of all sorts enchantingly belov'd, and indeed so much in the heart of the world, and especially of my own people, who best know him, that I am altogether mispris'd" (I.i.166-71). Orlando remains wholesome throughout and does not adopt the ideology of the bastard and come to suspect Rosalind, and the reason lies in his unquestioned sense of being "the youngest son of Sir Rowland de Boys" (I.i.56-57). His connection with his father leads him past the trials imposed by impoverishment, degradation, and exile, and enables him to cherish Rosalind and to trust in her fidelity and love for him. Three times in the play's first eighty lines Orlando refers to his sense that he is the embodiment of all that his father was. In fact, *As You Like It* begins at the point when Orlando is capable of becoming what his father was: "This is it, Adam, that grieves me, and the spirit of my father, which I think is within me, begins to mutiny against this servitude" (I.i.21-24). He reminds Oliver that his being last born "takes not away my blood" (48), for "I have as much of my father in me as you" (49). What we witness in act 1 is Orlando's standing up for himself with the aid of his dead father: "The spirit of my father grows strong in me" (70-71). Just as Pericles rises from the waters and with his father's armor wins Thaisa, so Orlando rises from his "stall," throttles Oliver, defeats Charles, and wins Rosalind.

Adam, his father's servant, confirms Orlando's sense of himself and simply calls him, "you memory / Of old Sir Rowland!" (II.iii.3-4). As his name suggests, Adam is a link with the past, and with a better past, when Sir Rowland lived and Duke Senior ruled. He is a link in a material sense, too, for it is the money he saved while working for Sir Rowland that enables Orlando to flee from Duke Frederick's court and take to the woods rather than "beg" for food "Or with a base and boist'rous sword enforce / A thievish living on the common road" (32-33). With Adam's aid and his own clear sense of self, Orlando avoids baseness and the mentality of a bastard. It is his brother, the eldest and therefore the "nearer to his reverence" (I.i.51) who, ironically, approaches the ideology of the bastard and represents "diverted blood" (II.iii.37). And, at the end of act 2, Duke Senior tells us what we have known all along, that Orlando is the only real son of Sir Rowland, his only son in both blood and spirit:

> If that you were the good Sir Rowland's son,
> As you have whisper'd faithfully you were,
> And as mine eye doth his effigies witness
> Most truly limn'd and living in your face,
> Be truly welcome hither. I am the Duke
> That lov'd your father. [191-96]

Romantic love stories such as Orlando's in *As You Like It* were extraordinarily popular in the late sixteenth century. For the most part, plays of this sort usually show the lengths to which true lovers must go before they can live happily ever after. In *Mucedorus* a bear chases the heroine through the woods, the hero adopts lowly disguises to win his love, and an ogre threatens before the final act's revelation that the shepherd is really a prince. But what we do not find in these plays, in *Mucedorus* or in *The Merry Devil of Edmonton*, another popular romance, is any sense that the father is anything more than a reason why "the course of true love never did run smooth." In *As You Like It*, however, Sir Rowland de Boys, deceased when the play starts, lives on in Orlando, and seems as important a presence as Hamlet's father does in that play.

There are other significant differences between Shakespeare's version of the love story and that of his predecessors and contemporaries. In

Shakespeare, disguise is usually more than simple stratagem; it becomes one manifestation of a coherent psychological pattern that often indicates the bastardization of the hero, as in *Cymbeline*. In *Mucedorus*, when the hero has good reason to think the heroine has tried to have him exiled, the worst he does is call her "churlish"; mostly, he laments—just before he is to leave, Mucedorus asks the "goodly groves" to "wail awhile with me."[36] What he does not do is threaten Amadine, call her a whore, slander his mother and declare his father a cuckold. In *The Merry Devil of Edmonton*, when the lovers are separated by a greedy father they remain constant to one another, and, though they are sad, they are faithless in neither thought nor deed. In these plays, "Love, thwarted, turns itself to thousand wiles,"[37] to the deceptions described in the chansons or to the she-nanigans typical of Roman drama but not to the suspicions of Posthumus and Leontes. To turn from Shakespeare to the romantic comedy of his contemporaries is to move to a simpler and far less psychologically complex universe, one in which social situation and family history play little part, one inhabited by characters whose development is slight and who seem close to the stock figures of antiquity. There are no shades of gray in these plays, and perhaps they were popular because they allowed the audience to experience the easy pleasures of a world of absolutes.

It is ironic that the disconnection from his father, the destitution and separation from wife that Posthumus laments, is precisely the condition toward which all young men in Shakespearean comedy, even those more fortunate in their family histories, eventually move. The young heroes of these plays, by conscious design or by accident, sooner or later find themselves dressed in humble attire, impoverished or assuming indigence for one reason or another, and separated from their fathers and family name. These conditions vary from play to play, as we might expect, though the general movement toward the disenfranchisement of the hero, whether real or feigned, can be traced in early, middle, and late comedies, in "happy" comedies, problem plays, and romances. For example, from most vantage points Lucentio and Posthumus are about as different as any two characters in Shakespeare, the former a robust and jovial boy whose only goal is to outwit his generous and very much living father, and Posthumus an outcast seemingly rejected by his family even at birth. However, in the changes brought about by his jolly pursuit of Bianca, Lucentio clearly prefigures Posthumus's more awful decline. Rather than study moral philosophy, Lucentio trades places with Tranio, becomes a sham tutor, disassociates himself from the Bentivolii by changing his name to "Cambio" (which itself translates as "change"), appears "in the habit of a mean man" (s.d. II.i.38), and, finally, in act 4, creates a new father out of the hapless pedant, a parent more suitable to his needs as a lover. Lucentio becomes what Posthumus is—poor and estranged from his father. When Vincentio, his real father, arrives in Padua, the old man finds that familiar topsy-turvy world we associate with the temporary mania of comedy. In this mad world Vincentio soon hears that his son has disappeared, perhaps been murdered, and that an imposter has usurped the family name. In rejecting a father who, apparently, refused to reject him, Lucentio has approximated the disenfranchisement of Posthumus.

Lucentio's progress toward complete separation from father and family and toward the lower rungs of the social ladder is by no means an atypical descent. In the very same play Petruchio, in spite of his "crowns" and his air of self-confidence, dresses in "mad attire" (III.ii.124) and rides a pitiful nag into town on his wedding day. Shakespeare's direction with both men can be seen in his treatment of the Lord in the play's Induction, who, in elevating Christopher Sly, reduces himself: "Then take him up, and manage well the jest. / Carry him gently to my fairest chamber, / And hang it round with all my wanton pictures" (Ind.i.45-47). In relinquishing his rooms to Sly, the Lord prefigures the descents of the more fully developed young men of this comedy. Though the reversal of social position in this play strikes us as good fun, its pattern is a general feature of Shakespearean comedy. As a rule, men separated from their fathers drive, knowingly or unknowingly, for the furthest limit of separation, bastardy, the condition Posthumus so willingly and explicitly accepts in II.v when he thinks he discovers that Imogen has been unfaithful.

The hero's inexorable movement toward the circumstances or attitudes of a bastard as a part of comedy's march to the altar is suggested in *The Taming of the Shrew* by a device used in comic plots for two thousand years. Tranio declares to his master,

> I see no reason but suppos'd Lucentio
> Must get a father, call'd suppos'd Vincentio;
> And that's a wonder. Fathers commonly
> Do get their children; but in this case of wooing,
> A child shall get a sire, if I fail not of my cunning. [II.i.407-11]

To "get" a new father is to reject an old one, to assert independence by denying past history in a family.[38] The pitiful condition of Posthumus Leonatus is, strangely enough, the self-conscious goal of Lucentio.

Like Lucentio and Posthumus, other lovers in Shakespearean comedy undergo significant change, but change always tending toward estrangement from father and from society, governance, or simply power insofar as these suggest the paternal, that which a legitimate son would inherit or use. As the legitimate sons fall from positions of power and authority, willingly or not, the bastards and villains gravitate toward them. *King Lear* is outside our balliwick, but it is clear that, as John Danby writes, the "two poles of the play, from one point of view, are Edmund and Edgar," and that Edgar is a kind of bastard in reverse: "Edgar at the end of the play is the national champion of the Faulconbridge tradition."[39] As Edmund rises in society and becomes Duke of Gloucester, Edgar falls from his family name into the anonymity of mad, half-naked Tom. Edmund and Edgar reverse positions, and then reverse them yet again as the play finally restores name, rank, and appropriate dress to Edgar, who could pass for the young man of Shakespearean comedy. Perhaps for this reason Nahum Tate revised the ending of the play not only by having Lear live but by having Edgar marry Cordelia.

To varying degrees, Shakespeare's comic heroes partake of the condition of Edgar and share the attitudes of Hippolytus. The King of Navarre in *Love's Labour's Lost*, for example, promises the Princess of France in act 5 to undergo a one-year constitutional, leaving what is presumably his inherited right to title and kingdom for a "forlorn and naked hermitage" (V.ii.795). The play ends before we see Navarre's voluntary disenfranchisement and his separation from power and woman, but in *All's Well That Ends Well* Bertram's divestiture is given prominence and occurs while he is separated from Helena. Bertram slips effortlessly into the strange world of the base-born. In his rejection of Helena and his seducing of Diana, the young Count couples separation from father, family, and name with movement toward a woman who he will later suggest is a whore.

The aptly named Diana is, of course, yet another of Shakespeare's misapprehended women. Like Luciana, Hero, Imogen, and Marina, Diana is the chaste woman thought to be corruptible. Bertram has tried to seduce her with "tokens and letters" (III.vi.115) and "with musics of all sorts" (III.vii.40), but he has found her "wondrous cold" (III.vi.113). When Helena tells Diana her own sad story, Diana pities her and agrees to become her accomplice and to trick Bertram by demanding his family ring. Other Shakespearean heroes (Bassanio, Proteus) give away rings that are tokens from a woman, but Bertram will give to Diana a token from his father, a ring passed down in his house from father to son for generations. In this way, he is unfaithful to his family even as he is unfaithful to his wife. Helena tells Diana,

> A ring the County wears,
> That downward hath succeeded in his house
> From son to son, some four or five descents,
> Since the first father wore it. This ring he holds
> In most rich choice; yet in his idle fire,

To buy his will, it would not seem too dear,
Howe'er repented after. [III.vii.22-28]

Bertram can be delved to the root by name, title, and ring, all of which identify him as his father's son, as the last son in a long, clear line, and there is something puzzling, even contradictory, about Helena's assuming that he will hand over to Diana so important a symbol of his connection with past generations. Bertram has called Diana a "lass" (III.vi.111) and a "fair creature" (116), but there is no sign that she means more to him than did any of the other women whom we are told he has seduced in Florence. Helena's intuition, however, is correct, and Bertram does give Diana the ring, though there remains a contradiction between the speed with which he sheds the ring and the remarkable estimation in which he holds it, the same contradiction we find in Helena's promising that Bertram will part with the ring and her knowing that he holds it "In most rich choice":

> *Ber.* It is an honor 'longing to our house,
> Bequeathed down from many ancestors,
> Which were the greatest obloquy i' th' world
> In me to lose.
>   *Dia.* Mine honor's such a ring. . . .
> . . . .
>   *Ber.*   Here, take my ring!
> My house, mine honor, yea, my life, be thine,
> And I'll be bid by thee. [IV.ii.42-53]

Bertram is aware of the ring's significance and its symbolic value, and it is difficult to reconcile his actions with his words. What is clear is that by giving her the ring he breaks faith with his family, especially with his father and paternal ancestors, no less fully than Bassanio and Proteus break faith with Portia and Julia by giving away their rings, or Cressida with Troilus by giving to Diomedes her lover's token. What these men do and what Bertram does is generally regarded as a mistake in judgment; ironically, however, Bertram's giving away the ring turns out to be a healthful step, for it is only by virtue of his willingness to break faith with his father that he and Helena finally agree to live as man and wife.[40] Indeed, it is only when he agrees to part company with his father that he tacitly agrees to "bed" his wife, and in this play rejection of the father is thus a prerequisite for union with a woman. The prerequisite, moreover, had been established by Bertram himself when he wrote to Helena as he left Paris. That letter, which reads like a set of instructions, explicitly tells his wife how to win him, and his first requirement is that she separate him from all connection with his father and family: "When thou canst get the ring" (III.ii.57).

In *The Winter's Tale* Florizel, too, approximates the conditions of a bastard, loss of father and family name, in order to win a woman. His wooing of Perdita in IV.iv necessitates his disguising himself in order that his father not find him; he obscures himself "With a swain's wearing" (9) and is "Vildly bound up" (22) when we first see him. Although he compares himself to Jupiter, Neptune, and Apollo, his transformation leads him down the social scale, toward Posthumus's condition, from prince to shepherd and, at the same time, from son to bastard, for in disguising himself he explicitly chooses Perdita over his father:

> Or I'll be thine, my fair,
> Or not my father's; for I cannot be
> Mine own, nor any thing to any, if
> I be not thine. To this I am most constant,
> Though destiny say no. [42-46]

Earlier, in Chapter 1, I quoted from this scene, when Florizel vows to marry Perdita and her "father," the shepherd, promises to make her portion equal his. Polixenes, in disguise, asks Florizel, "Have you a father?" (392) and Florizel, confirmed in his rejection of father, answers, "I have; but what of him?" Polixenes then argues that

> a father
> Is at the nuptial of his son a guest
> That best becomes the table. Pray you once more,
> Is not your father grown incapable
> Of reasonable affairs? is he not stupid
> With age and alt'ring rheums? Can he speak? hear?
> Know man from man? dispute his own estate?
> Lies he not bed-rid? and again does nothing
> But what he did being childish? [394-402]

Polixenes implies not only the appropriateness of a father's presence at a son's wedding but also the father's right to "dispute his own estate," for Florizel had promised the shepherd "more than you can dream of yet" (388) as his dower. He implies as well a kind of reversal of customary roles in Florizel's speaking for himself, as if his father were dead, or sick, or "childish." Polixenes sees in his son's presumption "a wrong / Something unfilial" (405-6). When Florizel persists in contracting himself and in disregarding his father, Polixenes unmasks and sarcastically calls his son's lineage into question, echoing Florizel's earlier rejection of him ("or I'll be thine, my fair, / Or not my father's"), and ironically threatens the very condition his son has already chosen:

> Mark your divorce, young sir,
> Whom son I dare not call. Thou art too base
> To be [acknowledg'd]. Thou, a sceptre's heir,
> That thus affects a sheep-hook! [417-20]

The accusation of baseness suggests illegitimacy, and suggests as well that the real "divorce" is between father and son. And with Polixenes' rejection of Florizel comes the parallel denunciation of Perdita, a slandering appropriate for the woman coupled with the disinherited son:

> And thou, fresh piece
> Of excellent witchcraft, whom of force must know
> The royal fool thou cop'st with—
> *Shep.*   O, my heart!
> *Pol.*   I'll have thy beauty scratch'd with briers
>   and made
> More homely than thy state. [422-26]

The situation here quickly degenerates into the familiar one of bastard boy and bewitching girl, Polixenes driving home his displeasure with Florizel by emphasizing the connection between "base" actions and loss of "blood" relations:

> we'll bar thee from succession,
> Not hold thee of our blood, no, not our kin,
> Farre than Deucalion off. [429-31]

The threat, of course, is to turn Florizel into Edgar by denying kinship, to force him into the situation of a nameless vagabond who must live in the limbo imposed by bastardy and experienced by the real bastards in Shakespeare but also by Antipholus, Pericles, Posthumus, Bertram, and others. In rejecting his son, however, Polixenes does nothing more than Florizel himself had done in disguising himself and speaking for his father at his own betrothal.

However favored by fortune in his birth, Florizel insists upon choosing Perdita over his father even though it means anonymity, poverty, and wandering, becoming a kind of Pericles, always on the run. He rejects as well his father's misogyny, his "devaluation of Perdita,"[41] which echoes

Leontes' attack on Hermione. When Polixenes leaves, Florizel remarks, yet again, on his willingness to separate himself from his father:

> From my succession wipe me, father, I
> Am heir to my affection. [480-81]

As if to confirm himself his own and not his father's, a bastard divorced from kin and from rights of inheritance, Florizel accepts Camillo's advice and lowers himself yet again, from shepherd to beggar, by exchanging clothes with the thief Autolycus, representative of the play's lowest social level. And with that change the transformation is complete; the Prince has become something other than Jupiter, Neptune, or Apollo, and he is quite right in concluding, "Should I now meet my father, / He would not call me son" (657-58).

Ferdinand, in *The Tempest*, is yet another favored son brought close to bastardy by the action or structure of Shakespeare's love story. His separation from his father and his subsequent descent into orphanhood and servitude are sudden and traumatic. Ashore after the shipwreck, Ferdinand sits by himself lamenting "the King my father's wrack" (I.ii.391). When he is approached by Prospero and Miranda and describes himself as "the best of them that speak this speech" (430), Prospero tells him, "thou dost here usurp / The name thou ow'st not" (454-55). Ferdinand is accused of being an "imposter" (478) and "traitor" (461), and the suggestion is that he is a patricide (and regicide), a convenient excuse for Prospero to imprison him and riffle the waters of romance. But what is fascinating here is how deeply Ferdinand descends, and how quickly and willingly. Prospero in fact treats him as he does Caliban, and the "effect of these charms is to reduce him in the social hierarchy to the status of a menial, bearing logs in humble service to his new-found mistress":[42]

> Come,
> I'll manacle thy neck and feet together.
> Sea-water shalt thou drink; thy food shall be
> The fresh-brook mussels, wither'd roots, and husks
> Wherein the acorn cradled. Follow. [461-65]

But unlike Caliban, Ferdinand does not chafe against slavery:

> My father's loss, the weakness which I feel,
> The wrack of all my friends, nor this man's threats
> To whom I am subdu'd, are but light to me,

> Might I but through my prison once a day
> Behold this maid. [488-92]

Here Ferdinand rationalizes that life in prison is not too great a price for
Miranda and treats "lightly," as Florizel does, not only the loss of his father
but also his descent from prince and heir to drudge, as well as the
possibility of his living as an imprisoned slave on Prospero's island. It is the
same sort of devil-may-care attitude we see the men adopt in other plays as
they travel and scatter after their fathers die. Later, in act 3, Ferdinand
tells us in soliloquy that "some kinds of baseness / Are nobly undergone"
(i.2-3), and that his "mean task" (4) is made pleasurable by Miranda.

Ferdinand's stance is that of the King of Navarre and of such well-to-do
gentlemen as Lucentio and Petruchio, the latter a harried new husband
who repeatedly declares that his "poor accoutrements" (III.ii.119) are part
of a grand scheme to retrain Kate. As a young beneficiary Petruchio
undergoes a variety of degrading experiences as he travels from son to
husband. In addition to changing his wardrobe for the worse, he rides an
old and diseased horse through foul weather to his cold country house, eats
scraps and loses sleep in keeping Kate hungry and awake. These inconve-
niences are, of course, in addition to his forfeiting consummation of the
marriage on his wedding night, and thus his humiliation of Kate is a self-
humiliation as well, echoing both the Lord's treatment of Sly, as I suggested earlier, and Lucentio's transformation into "Cambio." Florizel's
excuse for dressing like a beggar is that he must hide himself from his
father's search, while it is the storm and shipwreck that deprive Pericles of
his father's shield and rust the dead King's armor. His dress is not unlike
that of Petruchio on his wedding day, for Pericles' subsequent appearance
in Pentapolis during the "triumph" that determines who will marry Thaisa,
prompts a spectator to remark, "He had need mean better than his
outward show / Can any way speak in his just commend; / For by his rusty
outside he appears / To have practic'd more the whipstock than the lance"
(II.ii.48-51).

Thus poverty, real or feigned, consciously sought after or not, seems to
be a common denominator among the male characters who have lost their
connections with fathers and family. It is curious, indeed, that the young
men of comedy who are moneyed when the play begins should drop so
willingly into such embarrassing and disabling poverty. Posthumus is
simply born into very different circumstances from those of his father;
Orlando's patrimony is withheld by his brother; Fenton in *The Merry
Wives of Windsor* and Bassanio in *The Merchant of Venice* slip into poverty
through prodigality; and Florizel and Ferdinand willingly accept impoverishment as the price for happiness with a woman. In terms of their

development as romantic heroes, most of these men undergo similar trials and come to look, if not sound, like illegitimate sons, Petruchio starving himself in his cold country house, Ferdinand rapturously carrying logs for Prospero, and Posthumus a self-declared bastard, exiled and reviling women. In one way or another, the young heroes of Shakespearean comedy are brought into a kind of bastardy: poverty and separation from their fathers and family name.

Just as any excuse will do to separate father and son, as we saw earlier, so any excuse will serve to bring the son to impoverishment, to Orlando's or Bassanio's penury, the latter's a more serious predicament given the stress placed upon solvency in *The Merchant of Venice*. Bassanio tells Antonio in act 1, "I have disabled mine estate, / By something showing a more swelling port / Than my faint means would grant continuance" (i.123-25), and borrows money in order "To hold a rival place" (174) with Portia's many suitors. Fenton, in *The Merry Wives of Windsor*, like Bassanio, has run through his estate and is disliked by Master Page who describes him as a gentleman "of no having" (III.ii.72) and who suspects him of loving Anne "but as a property" (iv.10). Florizel simply surrenders all for Perdita after his contract is discovered. Indeed, the speed and determination with which Shakespeare's young lovers relinquish all material wealth is one of the strong links between Shakespearean comedy and its Plautine sources, where young men "want the girl, not the gold."[43] Yet, while in Plautus "*connubium* always takes precedence over *commercium*," and while his *adulescentes* dream of "parricide and bankruptcy"—the money going from their dead fathers to the girl—in Shakespeare money is simply irrelevant and has no useful purpose at all.[44] Then too, the drive for *connubium* in Plautus's young men seems as superficial as their filial attachment, and separation from their fathers occasions no more deep a psychological repercussion than does a Plautine father's separation from his nagging wife. The son's attachments to a girl and to his father seem equally trivial in Roman comedy. Thus, while "the departure of father or wife is always the occasion for a Plautine party,"[45] in Shakespeare such separation leads ultimately to a sense of loss, doubt, and the hero's feeling or acting more like a bastard than a secure and legitimate son.

Charinus in *Mercator* is typical of Plautus's sons. He tells us in act 1 that "after I had come of age and lost my zest for childish things, I became completely captivated by a courtesan here; forthwith my father's property quietly went into exile to her."[46] Renouncing his love for her, he persuades his father to finance a trading venture that takes him to Rhodes where, we are told, he falls in love with a maid sent to his room one night by his obliging host. All his business profits go to buying this girl, and he and she return to Athens as the play begins. In Shakespeare, winning the girl has to do with discovering self, moving out of the mazes and mists of ambivalence and into the clear air of self-knowledge. But in Plautus there is no sense at all of an emotional or psychological estrangement between father and son. The cause of the rift in the first place is financial, and these plays use the love story as an excuse to raise the economic issue.

In Plautus's *Pseudolus* the young man again needs money to buy a courtesan, whom he loves, and once the need for money and for the girl are identified with one another, the play devotes itself to schemes for cash. The romance between boy and girl and the relationship between father and son are conventional associations, perfunctorily treated and soon dismissed in favor of the cunning servant's attempts to swindle the young man's father. In Plautus, the love interest itself, like the familial bond between father and son, is treated far less seriously than are the schemes for getting the father's money, in part, perhaps, because Plautus's goal was more generally a satirizing of Roman institutions and values. It is as though the characters have no feelings that go beyond their sex drive or their joy in scheming and trickery. In Shakespeare, however, the division between father and son is most complex in origin and in consequences, and the son's impoverishment can only be read as one significant element in a full relationship. It is not unusual in Roman comedy for young men to do as Charinus does, that is, return to home and father, but such is rare in Shakespeare, where sons who have sought estrangement are reunited with their fathers either through an accidental meeting or because the father himself, or an agent of his, seeks it out. Thus, the break with the father seems deeper and more lasting in Shakespeare, a necessary step in the son's establishing a relationship with a woman, and the impoverishment of the hero a significant event in his development as a man.

5

"Patience on a Monument"

In the fourth act of *Othello,* Desdemona sings the "Willow" song as she waits for her husband in her bedchamber. The sad song describes a relationship gone bad, and a "poor soul" who "sat [sighing] by a sycamore tree," "Her hand on her bosom, her head on her knee" (iii.40-42). Desdemona learned the song from Barbary, her mother's maid, a woman whose lover "prov'd mad, / And did forsake her" (27-28) and who "died singing it" (30). Barbary's sad song will not go from Desdemona's head on the night Othello kills her.

Shakespeare uses the "Willow" song to suggest the pathos of a world where men will lose faith and women will die. We associate this scenario with tragedy, though in Shakespeare it is more typical of the comedies, where men seem predestined to reject the women they love. In play after play the separations caused by the men threaten to become the permanent losses of tragedy; the action of comedy can therefore be characterized as the successful attempt to avert the disasters described in the song.

Though villains tend to be faithhearted in the comedies and a high percentage of the characters well-intentioned, even brave, in these plays it is especially the women whose attitudes and actions lead to the comedy's happy (or, at worst, bittersweet) conclusion. While the men roam like Hippolytus, declaiming the virtues of misogyny and the joys of bastardy, or simply sink into the lethargy of impoverishment, the heroines react in one of two extraordinary ways. Either they accept the situation as a challenge and a call to action or they retreat into passivity, almost hibernation, and wait patiently for the separation to end.

Those women who are outwardly patient seem to assume that time will correct all problems, and their passivity is optimistic, implying hope, not despair. Although sequestration and the passive life of the convent was a real option for women in England in the earlier sixteenth century, in Shakespeare the passivity of the conventual way of life, literally or figuratively, is never hopeless or despairing. Between Adriana's efforts to be patient and Hermione's becoming a statue lie a variety of female descents and responses to the loss of a man. Separated from Egeon by shipwreck,

Aemilia in *The Comedy of Errors* has, inexplicably, done nothing to help unite herself with her husband. Although she has neither remarried nor become a Cressida, she has remained chaste and outside the hurly-burly of everyday life, living, in effect, as Portia falsely announces she will during Bassanio's absence, at a monastery. Thaisa's becoming a votaress of Diana when she is miraculously brought back to life by Cerimon after having died and been buried at sea is even less understandable, for Shakespeare takes no pains at all to explain why Thaisa chooses not to seek Pericles: "But since King Pericles, / My wedded lord, I ne'er shall see again, / A vestal livery will I take me to, / And never more have joy" (III.iv.8-11). Gower opens the following act by boldly stating, "His woeful queen we leave at Ephesus, / Unto Diana there 's a votaress" (IV.i.3-4). Except for the fact that Thaisa knows her husband to be living, the votaress in Ephesus could be Aemilia from the comedy written twenty years earlier. In these cases patience seems to be its own reward, and there is a sense in *The Comedy of Errors* as in *Pericles* that waiting is a kind of activity, and not at all a desparate gesture.

Biblical patience "implies not only physical and spiritual endurance but an expectation for someone to help or for something to happen,"[1] and it is this biblical interpretation of patience that informs medieval and Renaissance notions of the virtue, most obviously expressed in Shakespeare's pairing less active heroines, such as Hero, Mariana, and Hermione, with those who are more active and work energetically and imaginatively on their behalf. The two often seem halves of one integrated personality, one persona waiting patiently, like Mariana, the other arguing and threatening the errant male, like Isabella with Angelo. Hero may be gone and forgotten by the men of Messina but Beatrice acts for her in commanding Benedick to "Kill Claudio" (IV.i.289). Hermione is turned into stone, yet Paulina lashes Leontes for sixteen years. Helena, who can by no means be described as inactive, nonetheless obtains Bertram's ring and becomes pregnant with his child even though she is "dead" and on her circuitous way to the abbey of St. Jaques le Grand, thanks to Diana's efforts in negotiating with Bertram on her behalf. In *All's Well That Ends Well*, especially, there is a sense that women must stick together. In act 3, scene 5, when the Widow and her daughter, Diana, accompanied by their female friends, meet the disguised Helena, the women are as one in lamenting the sad condition of the young Count's wife and in counseling Diana against succumbing to Bertram's proposition. Diana herself simply says, "I would he lov'd his wife" (79).

The willingness of women to work for and support women, the active aiding the passive or, rather, those who can aiding those who cannot, is an important element in bringing about a happy ending. Carol Thomas

Neely, it seems to me, is quite right in believing that "Intimacy, mutual aid, and instinctive sympathy are characteristic of most female relationships delineated by Shakespeare."[2] Women in the comedies are best friends in a way the men are not, and it is women, loyal to other women, who help each other to overcome social restrictions inhibiting their free movement.[3] For example, in *Love's Labour's Lost* the Princess of France and her ladies cohere in a way that makes Navarre and his courtiers seem even more adolescent, sniping at one another, secretive, impulsive. Here the women appear as a group, though elsewhere they are simply paired off: Adriana and Luciana, Hermia and Helena, Portia and Nerissa, Rosalind and Celia, Helena and Diana, Hero and Beatrice, Isabella and Mariana, Hermione and Paulina. Even Viola, in love with Orsino, pleads his case with Olivia, working not only according to the Duke's wishes, but for what she assumes to be Olivia's good too, just as Silvia argues for Julia and against Proteus in *The Two Gentlemen of Verona*, upbraiding him, "Return, return, and make thy love amends" (IV.ii.99).

In contrast, the great friendships between men in these comedies seem strained and unnatural. It is not just that the men are unfaithful to one another—and they are disloyal—but that their fidelities are self-conscious; they seem always to be protesting how much they love one another while the women are simply loyal, friendly, and familiar. There is a coldness about the male relationships that has left critics scrambling to define them in terms of sixteenth-century essays on the love of man for man, or as examples of repressed homosexuality. The strained and shallow friendships are many: Bertram and Parolles, Benedick and Claudio, Orlando and Oliver, Duke Senior and Duke Frederick, Prospero and Antonio, Posthumus and his foreign acquaintances. Other pairs, such as Proteus and Valentine, Antonio and Bassanio, Leontes and Polixenes, seem constitutionally different and are, in fact, often at odds. W. Thomas MacCary, who thinks that "the essential problem in Shakespearean comedy" is that "men must first define themselves in terms of themselves before they can commit themselves to women," accounts in part for the young heroes' fascination with women as a realization that "unlike their male companions, these young women need not always be their adversaries, their rivals in military, intellectual, and other endeavors."[4] The strong bond between women seems an even more effective force in repairing relationships and in responding to distress compared with the weak bond between men.

The women who have come to be known as Shakespeare's great heroines—Portia, Rosalind, Viola, Helena, Imogen, among others—do not, however, rely very fully on female surrogates when the going gets rough and tend by nature toward the active, responding to separation as though a gauntlet had been tossed at their feet. Instead of depending on others to represent them while they wait patiently at home for time to change the feelings of errant men, these women don disguises and often journey far from home, usually with no other motive than the desire to be with or to protect the men they love. And yet their disguising, usually as boys, is not to be explained simply as their becoming more active, or as pantomime, a playing of the knave, to borrow Rosalind's phrase (III.ii.296). Though the idea of a woman's pretending to be a boy does, on the one hand, suggest androgyny, at least today if not in Shakespeare's time (where the boy actor dressed as a boy would suggest only the male), the female character is likely to be apprehended by the audience as two distinct personalities. In most of Shakespeare's disguised heroines—in Helena, disguised as a (female) pilgrim no less than in those women who disguise as males—we are aware of two personas, the patient and the impatient, the passive and the active, which we see represented in some plays in two women, for example, in Mariana and Isabella, Hero and Beatrice, or in Hermione and Paulina. Because the audience sees both the woman and the disguise, it sees something other than purely and simply an "active" woman or a woman's version of a man. Dramatic irony is the prevailing mode of perception.

But the disguises of these more active women are often still more complex. Portia, for example, does not simply metamorphose into a man, disguise herself and travel to Venice when Bassanio leaves her in response to Antonio's letter. Her first act is to invent one "Portia," a fictitious woman who dutifully goes on retreat when her husband leaves Belmont:

> For mine own part,
> I have toward heaven breath'd a secret vow
> To live in prayer and contemplation,
> Only attended by Nerissa here,
> Until her husband and my lord's return.
> There is a monast'ry two miles off,
> And there we will abide. [III.iv.26-32]

Her next act, of course, is to create a second fiction, "Balthazar," "a young doctor of Rome" (IV.i.153), and it is as Balthazar that Portia travels to Venice and argues law. Balthazar himself is a complex personality, composed as he is both of a male exterior and of Portia who animates him. Thus, Portia's response to Bassanio's absence is very much more complicated than it would be were it simply a matter of her pretending to be a man.

Portia's activity when Bassanio leaves her is perfectly illustrative of the complexity of the female response to separation in the comedies. Three points, I think, need to be highlighted. First, both aspects of her personality ("Portia" and "Balthazar") are in some manner disguised, one as a woman and the prototypically submissive wife and the other as a man. Second, both personas are equally fictitious, for in reality there is neither a "Portia" at the monastery nor a man named Balthazar.[5] Because Portia is not at the monastery Lorenzo is deceived; and because Balthazar is not a man, Bassanio, Antonio, and the male world of Venice are deceived. Portia tells the truth only to Nerissa, her closest friend—and a woman—and so it goes in Shakespearean comedy.[6]

Third, and perhaps most important, the active woman must be construed as in some senses passive, too, not only in the fact of her having created a passive, or patient, persona—at the "monast'ry"—but in the constriction her male disguise demands. Balthazar is free, free to travel, to debate, to command men, to be heroic, "to range the passions and the world,"[7] but Portia, the woman, is as restrained in her male clothes as she was when she was "locked" in her father's leaden chest, and perhaps more so, for then, at least, she was free to be herself, that is, to use her own name, wear her own clothes, in short, retain a direct relation to herself, no matter how confined. Her male disguise, therefore, confers freedom of action only at the price of holding her familiar self hostage. The female persona at the monastery is an outright fiction, and the male in the Venetian courtroom a disguised lie; both delimit and bind. Much the same can be said of Viola, who first invents a male persona, "Cesario," who then, in turn, constructs an elaborate fiction about a "sister" who sat "like Patience on a monument," pining for love, a second-level fiction Viola herself uses as the only way open—disguised as she is—to represent herself to Orsino. Similarly, Rosalind creates Ganymede, who then invents "Rosalind," the male version of the woman Orlando loves, and the persona whom he playfully courts. Helena invents the pilgrim, who then, in a sense, creates Diana, through whom she contacts Bertram and as whom she consummates her marriage. In these cases, as in Portia's, the disguises are seen as complex ploys, many-layered and faceted versions of self created by women as a means of reviving unhealthy and stagnant relationships. In each case, and of necessity, the woman is apprehended by the audience as both active and passive.

In order to bide her time "in prayer and contemplation" at the monastery, and to express herself through the artificial construct she calls "Balthazar," Portia needs patience, a virtue made familiar to Shakespeare by literary and artistic traditions. For the Middle Ages and the Renaissance patience was an active virtue that exemplified the major tenets of Christianity. Patience called for fortitude as well as hope; it required strength, not neglect or apathy, and in this was perceived as fundamentally different from stoicism. Patience was the hallmark of the great martyrs, was associated with Hope and Fortitude in handbooks on vice and virtue and in exemplum books and emblem books, and "was seen as an active virtue and a positive response to God's will in time of suffering."[8] And, interestingly, "Despite the legendary patience of Job, Tobias, and the other biblical figures, Patience in the arts is most often personified as a woman."[9]

That Shakespeare's heroines as a group embody just such an active patience is clear not only because when most distressed they seem to combine sadness and fortitude, but also because they describe themselves in terms that bear striking resemblance to popular visual representations of patience in emblem books and engravings. Perhaps the most well-known of such illustrations is the 1557 engraving, *Patientia*, from a drawing by Peter Bruegel the Elder. Beneath the engraving is the caption, "*Patientia est malorvm quae avt infervntvr avt accidvnt, cvm aeqvanimitate perlatio*" ("Patience is the tranquil endurance of evils that assail you through malice or through accident").[10] The picture itself is a typically sixteenth-century Flemish phantasmogoria, characteristic of Bruegel, but perhaps more familiarly associated with Bosch as, for example, in "The Garden of Earthly Delights." What seems at first an endless jumble of nightmarish creatures—outsized insects, reptiles, freaks, automata—slowly resolves itself into a scene depicting the deadly vices (which Bruegel had also engraved) at work on sea and land. Apparently oblivious to this apocalyptic vision is Patience herself, in the center foreground, dwarfed by the figures and details surrounding her. She wears a flowing gown and sits on a block of stone, her hands holding a cross and prayerfully clasped as she looks heavenward. Bruegel has chosen to depict Patience in a typical way, near the sea, often taken in these pictures to represent the uncertainty of our daily life, to which patience was thought to be a useful response. Gerald J. Schiffhorst tells us that stone is "a common attribute of virtues associated with endurance," signifying "both physical and spiritual solidity: *terra firma*."[11] Such an image of solidity can be contrasted with typical representations of Fortune who often stands on a sphere or poses atop her wheel. In George Wither's emblem, *Constante Fiducia*, a crowned Patience stands on a block of stone, holds a cross, and looks upward rather than into a distant landscape dotted with crucifixes.[12]

Many of these depictions remind us of traditional representations of women in literature, and therefore of Shakespeare's heroines, measuring their time in male disguise, locked in rooms, sealed in coffins, limited by moats, or as fictions pining for love, lost in prayer. Patterns of imagery in many of these plays suggest that women are stone, the "monumental alabaster" (V.ii.5) to which Othello likens Desdemona's skin minutes before he murders her. Because she will not comply with his wishes, Bertram calls Diana "no maiden, but a monument" (IV.ii.6), that is, a statue of a woman in stone. Jachimo wishes the sleeping Imogen to be a stone effigy, "a monument, / Thus in a chapel lying!" (II.ii.32-33); Mariana threatens to remain a "marble monument" (V.i.233) at Duke Vincentio's feet until her story is accepted as truth; and Leontes and the audience are asked to believe that Hermione has been transformed into a statue in fact.[13] In the sixteenth and seventeenth centuries "monument" signified as well a tomb, as when Romeo refers to the "monument" of the Capulets, and thus for Shakespeare's audience a woman likened to stone or to a monument suggested the kind of petrification often associated with death.

Viola is a typical example of the actively patient heroine in Shakespearean comedy—patient in her willingness to wait for Orsino and to live the life of an unrequited, anonymous lover. Ashore in Illyria in act 1, Viola asks the Captain, "Conceal me what I am, and be my aid / For such disguise as haply shall become / The form of my intent" (ii.53-55). Hidden beneath a kind of double disguise, as man and then again as eunuch, Viola represents herself as "Cesario." In I.iv we are told that in the space of three days Orsino has shown Cesario great regard and "unclasp'd" (13) his soul to her. Later in the scene Viola tells us in an aside that she herself "would be his wife" (42), and we can begin to appreciate how difficult her situation has become and how it has evolved in ways she could not imagine when she guessed Orsino a bachelor (I.ii.29). She is herself absolutely convinced of the dangers of disguise later when she learns that Olivia has fallen in love with her, a "poor monster" (II.ii.34), deprived of love, or at least of the freedom to act more directly on her own behalf, by her lies and the verbal shifts they demand. It is little wonder, then, that she should compare herself, obliquely, to "Patience on a monument" in a passage that evokes, if anything, a sense of the restriction conferred on her by her having chosen to "conceal" herself. Viola is, after all, thrice removed from Orsino, for she has created Cesario, who in turn creates a sister:

> *Duke.*   And what's her history?
> *Vio.* A blank, my lord; she never told her love,
> But let concealment like a worm i' th' bud
> Feed on her damask cheek; she pin'd in thought,
> And with a green and yellow melancholy
> She sate like Patience on a monument,
> Smiling at grief. [II.iv.109-15]

This stereotypically sedate and patient sister, this melancholic who could only pine and smile at her own grief, is a sort of emblem, as I suggested earlier, for the woman whom Viola sees herself becoming as she languishes behind "Cesario," a male voice used to deliver messages to Orsino from a Viola "concealed" from view. Then, too, the very artfulness of the speech reinforces our sense of the artificiality of the persona she has chosen to present to Orsino.

Viola, of course, is in reality far freer than "Patience," just as Portia is not to be identified exclusively with "Portia" at the monastery. What we must not forget is that the audience sees and hears a most active *woman*, frequently frustrated in her attempts to relate directly to a man, but free enough to hint, and certainly free enough to tell *us* how she feels. These disguised heroines, in fact, sometimes positively enjoy reading themselves as fiction, as interesting but misleading texts or emblems, "signs," to use Berowne's word in *Love's Labour's Lost* (V.ii.469), and their observations—Portia's, Rosalind's, Viola's playful asides or Helena's and Imogen's more serious self-revelations—make it likely that the audience will perceive the love story's happy ending as the accomplishment of a woman. But the text, the fiction she creates out of her personal distress, is a valid enough expression, not of what these heroines are, but rather of what they seem to be or fear becoming, and for that reason must be taken as comedy's worst-case scenario. To be "Patience on a monument" or to live one's life on perpetual retreat, is to be constant and loyal but also restricted, indeed pertrified. To be a block of stone itself is to be a work of art; hence, women in Shakespeare's comedies often are described not simply as "monuments" or monuments in the sense of tombs, but as statues and artworks of all sorts. Women have, of course, been described as artworks for millenia, though we tend to associate the notion especially with the Victorians. The idea was, however, a commonplace way of describing women throughout the sixteenth and seventeenth centuries. In *A Woman Killed with Kindness*, for example, Frankford is complimented on his wife Anne, who is compared to "a well-made suit / In which the tailor hath used all his art," and to "a chain of gold to adorn your neck."[14] Though the Victorians were indeed preoccupied with women as works of art, as in Browning's "My Last Duchess," James's *The Portrait of a Lady*, and Edith Wharton's *The House of Mirth*, the emphasis in Shakespearean comedy is less on woman as possession—silent, decorative, and valuable—than on woman as inanimate and frozen in time, sterile or dead.

When *Twelfth Night* begins, Olivia has not only immured and enwrapped herself like a cloistress, in a sense she has become art itself. When "Cesario" asks to see her face, Olivia agrees to remove the veil, to "draw the curtain, and show you the picture" (I.v.233); "Is't not well done?" (235) she proudly asks. In rejecting love and devoting herself to seven years of mourning, Olivia, Feste's "good madonna" (57), is not simply the useless decorative head of an English country house, she is the Bergsonian paralytic no less fully immobile than Hermione transformed by Julio Romano into "a piece many years in doing" (V.ii.95-96) ensconced in Paulina's art gallery. Until Olivia drops the pretense and pursues Cesario, *Twelfth Night* is one of Shakespeare's more "artful" plays, with Viola a disguised eunuch sitting like a statue of Patience on a tomb, and Olivia a painting herself, meting "divers schedules" (I.v.245) of her beauty and self-portraits bedecked with jewels.

Similar representations of heroines as artworks are used in other comedies. In *Pericles*, the harpy-like Dionyza, thinking she has killed "absolute Marina" (IV.ch.31), builds "Her monument / . . . and her epitaphs / In glitt'ring golden characters" (IV.iii.42-44). Similarly, Portia, though free to love where her heart directs, is circumscribed by her dead father's wish that suitors choose among the three caskets, and then again by her incarnation as "Balthazar." Like Imogen, who is imprisoned in fact when her father banishes Posthumus, Portia is imprisoned and tells Bassanio that she is "lock'd" in one of the caskets: "If you do love me, you will find me out" (III.ii.40-41). When Bassanio opens the leaden casket it is "fair Portia's counterfeit" (115), a painting, which signals this chest as the correct one. A painting locked in a chest at "Belmont," an estate itself a work of art, under "the floor of heaven / . . . thick inlaid with patens of bright gold" (V.i.58-59)—Portia and her world consist of one treasured art work within another, and she at the center, the "golden fleece."

To be a work of art or a stone monument is to be inanimate, and in these plays "Patience" is often the starting point for a woman's descent into the immobility of death, a descent that parallels, and occurs as a response to, the hero's more awful psychosocial decline. In *The Comedy of Errors* Shakespeare presents his first example of an impatient woman adopting patience as a stratagem, and one endorsed by the community and presented as morally correct. Having lost her husband, Antipholus of Ephesus, to a courtesan, Adriana reacts realistically: she bemoans her loss, is angry, and argues strenuously against his defection:

> My decayed fair
> A sunny look of his would soon repair.
> But, too unruly deer, he breaks the pale,
> And feeds from home; poor I am but his stale.
>> *Luc.* Self-harming jealousy—fie, beat it hence!
>> *Adr.* Unfeeling fools can with such wrongs dispense:
> I know his eye doth homage otherwhere,
> Or else what lets it but he would be here? [II.i.98-105]

Her sister Luciana counsels against jealousy and anger throughout the play: "Fie, how impatience low'reth in your face!" (86), she chides, but Adriana counters that Antipholus's "unkindness" blunts her discourse "more than marble hard" (93). Earlier in the scene, in a more general debate on how a wife ought to treat her husband, Adriana argues that a husband's liberty ought not be denied a wife, and hers is the position espoused later in Shakespeare by Emilia in *Othello*, by Paulina, and, implicitly, by all those heroines who choose an active response. In Adriana's argument we hear not just an intellectual position but the real frustration of a woman who lacks the means to effect a change. This play, of course, is structured in a way that precludes Shakespeare's allowing Adriana the opportunity to follow her husband "otherwhere," that is, to the courtesan's house, and chide him home. Instead, following Plautus, Shakespeare devises at least a temporary domestic tranquility by bringing to her an idealized version of her husband, a needful man entirely willing to come home and to be fed. Later heroines, however, do exercise an option to leave home, paying whatever price is necessary, and therefore allow us to see on stage the sort of woman Adriana can only hope to be. In *The Comedy of Errors* it is, of course, Luciana's view, one more in keeping with the hierarchical traditions touted by Renaissance propagandists, that is destined to prevail. Her position is mocked by Adriana as "Patience unmov'd!" (32) and "fool-begg'd patience" (41), though Adriana herself is chastised by Aemilia, the Abbess, in act 5 and cautioned so fully against nagging a husband that even Luciana is prompted to ask her, "Why bear you these rebukes, and answer not?" (V.i.89). But the victory of patience in this play is complete and Adriana can only reply that the Abbess "did betray me to my own reproof" (90).

While in Shakespeare it is Luciana and Aemilia who berate Adriana for her jealousy and impatience, in Shakespeare's source, the *Menaechmi*, that role belongs to the father of the wife of Menaechmus of Epidamnus. In assigning that role to women in *The Comedy of Errors* (it is a woman who controls other women in *The Taming of the Shrew* as well), Shakespeare reveals how completely attitudes that serve the best interests of males have been accepted by women as appropriate indeed. (It is Grissil herself in Dekker's play who comes to embody the patriarchal view that patience is a rare and precious virtue. She chides her father, "let true patience cure all woe, / you bid me be content, oh, be you so."[15]) What Luciana and Aemilia advocate, as unwitting spokeswomen for a patriarchal version of marriage, is a relationship based on a double standard demanding that the husband rule and the wife obey. This system was advocated with the authority of the religious and political communities in England and was said to be based on the very ordered world of nature itself. It is a view that, of course, prevailed in the drama for many years. In George Farquhar's *The Beaux' Stratagem* Dorinda and Mrs. Sullen, two sisters surprisingly like Luciana and Adriana, argue in a way that recalls *The Comedy of Errors*. Married to a "country blockhead," Mrs. Sullen laments,

> I must bear the Punishment,—'Tis hard Sister.
> *Dor.*   I own it—but you must have Patience.
> *Mrs. Sullen.*   Patience! the Cant of Custom.—Providence sends no
> Evil without a Remedy—shou'd I lie groaning under a Yoke I can
> shake off, I were accessory to my Ruin, and my Patience were no
> better than self-Murder.[16]

Today, Dorinda's position, or the Abbess's at V.i.68 ("The venom clamors of a jealous woman / Poisons more deadly than a mad dog's tooth"), or Kate's lecture on wifely duty at the end of *The Taming of the Shrew*, ring false, untrue to character, and tell us how these eras liked to think of themselves rather than how they were or we ought to be. But such views prevail among Shakespeare's men, and constrain his women, who acknowledge this social code not so much in what they say as in how they behave. The "liberty"—to think, to talk, to act—that Adriana craves is achieved by others, first of all, as we shall soon see, by Julia in *The Two Gentlemen of Verona*, but only at the price of sacrificing identity, that is, of beginning a descent from self that finally implies, and occasionally includes, death itself.

In Shakespeare, lovely lady always stoops to conquer, though never quite as self-consciously or innocuously as in Goldsmith. When her mother announces Paris's marriage offer to Juliet, the garrulous Nurse recounts the story of Juliet's falling and hitting her head as a child. Her husband,

> 'A was a merry man—took up the child.
> 'Yea,' quoth he, 'dost thou fall upon thy face?
> Thou wilt fall backward when thou hast more wit,
> Wilt thou not, Jule?' and by my holidam,
> The pretty wretch left crying and said 'Ay.' [I.iii.40-44]

The tragedy in Shakespearean comedy is that the women fall upon their faces, appearing to die, before they can "fall backward" into the bridal bed. When a woman "stoops" in Shakespeare, she often falls much further than merely into a lower social class.

It is in *The Two Gentlemen of Verona* that Shakespeare first introduces not only the motif of the disguised woman, but also the notion of the woman's dying as a reaction to the loss of her lover. When Proteus is ordered to follow Valentine to Milan, Julia's comfort must be "patience":

> Pro. Have patience, gentle Julia.
> Jul. I must, where is no remedy.
> Pro. When possibly I can, I will return.
> Jul. If you turn not, you will return the sooner.
> Keep this remembrance for thy Julia's sake.
> [Giving a ring] [II.ii.1-5]

Many of the familiar plot elements of Shakespearean comedy are encapsulated in these five lines. The man leaves; the woman stays. He counsels patience and promises to see her often. She is threatened by his impending absence, fears he will "turn," that is, be lost to another woman, and offers a token, here, a ring. In addition, we notice that Julia puns—"turn" and "return"—displaying the sort of verbal skill frequently seen in Shakespeare's heroines, in Beatrice, but also in Portia (both when she argues law and, later, when she produces the "lawyer's" ring), Rosalind, Viola (Feste's only equal in this regard in *Twelfth Night*), Isabella (who wins even Lucio's grudging respect as she fences with Angelo), Hermione (persuading Polixenes to stay in Sicilia and defending herself during her trial), and so on. Lisa Jardine has written insightfully about the negative connotations of a woman's proverbial ability to speak, to use her tongue, which she sees as "the symbol of impotence and inaction," the female weapon that will always be less adequate than the man's physical strength.[17] More often than not Julia's ability to speak establishes an ironic tone; here it tends both to downplay the seriousness of Proteus's leaving and to define her as more aware of the possible consequences of such a move. And yet, in spite of her insight and ability (neither revealed very fully here), she is incapable of stopping Proteus or, for that matter, of making him understand that distance sometimes determines morality.

When we see Julia next, in II.vii, she has decided to leave Verona and find Proteus, and her haste ought to show us to what extent she realizes mere words are insufficient. She likens herself, predictably, to "A true-devoted pilgrim" (9) searching for "divine perfection" (13) and justifies her journey by suggesting that if she is impeded she will "impatiently" (26) rage, but if she follows him unhindered she will "be as patient as a gentle stream, / And make a pastime of each weary step" (34-35). Hers is precisely that active patience of which Schiffhorst writes, for she will be patient only if she can be active and follow Proteus.

In Milan, when she learns that her lover woos Silvia, Julia is patient yet again, though her range of responses is now limited by her disguise. When she hears Proteus tell Silvia, "I did love a lady; / But she is dead" (IV.ii.105-6), Julia becomes the first of Shakespeare's heroines to "die." She has, in fact, journeyed farther than from Verona to Milan: she has descended from Proteus's love to patient "pilgrim," to male page, to dead lady. Julia has learned that in Proteus's eyes and, in a sense, in reality, she is a living paradox, at one and the same time a page in Milan and a dead woman in Verona, and that her life, consequently, has become a double lie, for she is neither dead nor a page, but rather a sort of monstrous creature (Viola, we remember, calls herself "poor monster" [II.ii.34]) capable of being both sexes at once and in two places at the same time.

In her complex response to her difficult situation, Julia prefigures Shakespeare's later heroines and especially Viola. For example, in IV.iv, when she speaks up in her own defense to Silvia, Julia is asked to describe this "Julia" whom Proteus has forsaken, and in doing so she shows all of Viola's inventiveness:

> *Sil.*   How tall was she?
> *Jul.*   About my stature; for at Pentecost,
> When all our pageants of delight were play'd,
> Our youth got me to play the woman's part,
> And I was trimm'd in Madam Julia's gown,
> Which served me as fit, by all men's judgments,
> As if the garment had been made for me;
> Therefore I know she is about my height.
> And at that time I made her weep agood,
> For I did play a lamentable part.
> Madam, 'twas Ariadne passioning
> For Theseus' perjury and unjust flight;
> Which I so lively acted with my tears
> That my poor mistress, moved therewithal,
> Wept bitterly; and would I might be dead
> If I in thought felt not her very sorrow. [157-72]

Just as Viola creates a sister, Julia indulges in the creation of an alter ego, a woman named "Julia," a feeling woman who cries at the suffering of forlorn women everywhere, a woman like Barbary, or Desdemona, or the maid of the "Willow" song herself. Like Viola's patient "sister" or "Portia" at the monastery, the "Julia" who "Wept bitterly" at the pageant seems to us the sort of feeling woman Julia herself must be, one who relates to other women, as Neely puts it, with "Intimacy, mutual aid, and instinctive sympathy."[18] Thus this fictitious version of herself, this text she creates, is in some senses truer to her nature than the real woman in the misleading page's clothes. And Julia's story, interestingly, creates a story within a story, for the page tells us of "Julia" watching a play about Ariadne. This scenario not only lifts the Julia/Proteus romance to the level of myth, traditional in Renaissance stories of young lovers, but increases our sense of the artifice that has become Julia's life. She too is a character in a play, a woman acting the part of a man at the price of leaving a complete version of herself stranded somewhere, concealed beneath disguise like Ariadne marooned on Naxos.

The last step Julia takes in her descent occurs in the woods after Valentine preposterously offers Silvia to Proteus. At this point Julia swoons, and it is here, when she is in reality closest to death, that Proteus suddenly realizes her true worth. In falling to the ground as the disguised page, Julia, assumed dead back in Verona, begins to languish in earnest. Her decline, which adumbrates those of Hero, Imogen, and Hermione, entirely befits a woman who has been falling throughout the play, who has been progressively atrophying and becoming more and more a fiction. It is, therefore, quintessentially appropriate that, separated from the faithless Proteus, Julia invent a pageant in which she played "a lamentable part," "Ariadne passioning / for Theseus' perjury and unjust flight," and tell us that her acting was "so lively." The story of Ariadne's pining when Theseus deserts her illustrates precisely Julia's supposed passive response to Proteus's leaving—remaining in Verona and "dying"—as well as her true sequestration in her disguise as the page. Shakespeare knew the story of Ariadne from many sources but probably best from Golding's translation of Ovid's *Metamorphoses*, where the tale of Theseus's leaving her "post alone / Upon the shore" is summarized:

> Thus desolate and making dolefull mone
> God *Bacchus* did both comfort hir and take hir to his bed.
> And with an everlasting starre the more hir fame to spred,
> He tooke the Chaplet from hir head, and up to Heaven it threw.
> The Chaplet thirled through the Aire: and as it gliding flew,
> The precious stones were turnd to starres which blased cleare and bright,
> And tooke their place (continuing like a Chaplet still to sight)
> Amid betweene the kneeler downe and him that gripes the Snake.[19]

The emphasis here is on Ariadne's loneliness, her victimization, and her becoming precious artwork, for her diadem tossed heavenward is transformed into a constellation, itself "continuing like a Chaplet still to sight."

Julia's plight, her falling both from her self and to the ground, is also Hero's ("Why, how now, cousin, wherefore sink you down?" [IV.i.110], asks Beatrice, while Leonato thinks his daughter has "fall'n / Into a pit of ink [139-40]) and Rosalind's too ("Many will swoon when they do look on blood," Celia comments after her friend faints [IV.iii.158]). Thaisa dies and is buried at sea, and later faints when she meets Pericles in the Temple of Diana; Imogen drinks the potion given her by Pisanio and descends so fully into a state resembling death that her obsequies are sung by Guiderius and Arviragus, though she falls yet again when Posthumus strikes her in the fifth act, in a scene clearly reminiscent of Julia's collapse in the last act of *The Two Gentlemen of Verona*.

Hermione's fall in *The Winter's Tale* is more pronounced than that of her counterparts in other comedies, for she moves in clearly discernible stages from a position of relative freedom to one increasingly more restricted. In act 1 she is free to walk and talk as she chooses; her marriage seems to confer upon her a kind of freedom she would surely be without were she single. Accused of infidelity by Leontes, she is placed under guard and imprisoned, losing her physical freedom; it is in jail, too, that she learns to restrain herself psychologically: "There's some ill planet reigns; / I must be patient, till the heavens look / With an aspect more favorable" (II.i.105-7). And again, in III.ii, during her trial, she defends herself by telling her accuser,

> But thus, if pow'rs divine
> Behold our human actions (as they do),
> I doubt not then but innocence shall make
> False accusation blush, and tyranny
> Tremble at patience. [28-32]

During the trial when she hears that her son has died of grief, we actually see her fall, for she swoons; Paulina tells the court, "This news is mortal to the Queen. Look down / And see what death is doing" (III.ii.148-49). Hermione is immediately carried off and Paulina returns minutes later with the news that the Queen is dead. Her progress, or rather, regress, from freedom to restriction, from life to death, involves her slowly becoming more and more bound, physically and psychologically, and forces her to become that patient type symbolized for us in her appearance later in the play as a statue, perhaps a statue of Patience herself.

Most of the women in Shakespearean comedy are brought "down" in one way or another as a result of their interactions with men. While some fall literally and die, others feign death, and still others are thought to be dead. In addition, many of the women fall in less obvious, though telling, ways, and are compared, for example, to animals. Thus the taming metaphor is often used as a description of the heroine's descent. Keith Thomas writes in *Man and the Natural World* that in sixteenth- and seventeenth-century England, many viewed American Indians, Africans, the Irish, and infants as "inferior humans" and that "women were also near the animal state."[20] Thomas tells us that for several centuries "theologians had debated, half frivolously, half seriously, whether or not the female sex had souls, a discussion which closely paralleled the debate about animals" and that "Jane Austen was in a long tradition when she described her sex as 'poor animals,' worn out by annual childbearing."[21] Imogen adopts the pseudonym "Fidele," not far from "Fido," the traditional name for "man's best friend." In *A Midsummer-Night's Dream,* just before Helena complains that women "should be woo'd, and were not made to woo" (II.i.242), she turns herself into an animal:

> I am your spaniel; and, Demetrius,
> The more you beat me, I will fawn on you.
> Use me but as your spaniel; spurn me, strike me,
> Neglect me, lose me; only give me leave,
> Unworthy as I am, to follow you.
> What worser place can I beg in your love
> (And yet a place of high respect with me)
> Than to be used as you use your dog? [203-10]

Kate refers to Petruchio as her "keeper" (V.ii.146), and it is clear that taming, which, of course, assumes a woman's animality, is one manifestation of that dehumanizing that ends in and, in some senses, makes possible the idea of a woman's death. In act 5, Kate takes pride in telling Bianca and the Widow, "place your hands below your husband's foot" (177); Titania is forced to lie with Bottom; Viola, of course, becomes "Patience on a monument" and then, in act 5, tells Orsino that she "a thousand deaths would die" (V.i.133) for him when he offers to "sacrifice the lamb" (130) he loves. Cressida lowers herself by becoming Diomedes' concubine, and Helena takes the place of Diana and sleeps with a man who loathes her. Isabella argues for her brother's life in a cause she detests; Mariana sleeps with a man who had spurned her, and then in act 5 pleads for him on bended knee. Later in the same scene, Isabella kneels before the Duke to beg that Angelo not be put to death for his crimes.

Literally and figuratively, the heroines lower themselves in a process that ends for so many female characters in Elizabethan and Jacobean tragedy and tragicomedy at the grave. In George Wilkins's *The Miseries of Enforced Marriage* Clare Harcop kills herself when William Scarborrow breaks his pre-contract. When her father finds her body, he says, "Thou hast no tung to answere no, or I, / But in red letters writes: For him I die."[22] The dramatic literature of the period is rife with tales of fallen women, suicides, sacrifices, victims all, like the unhappy Penthea in *The Broken Heart*. Forced by a cruel brother to marry a man she dislikes and to forsake Orgilus, her true love, Penthea repairs the ruins of her honor by starving herself (the answer for so many beleaguered women in these plays is often anorectic and passive in the extreme). Her brother begs, "Be not, my sister / A murd'ress to thyself."[23] Catherine Belsey suggests that in general "the stability of the family requires the subjugation of women to the point were thy must be willing to efface themselves finally in order to preserve it."[24]

However, what saves the women of Shakespearean comedy and permits the happier ending is their astonishing ability to move from the passive victimhood of Clare Harcop, Penthea, or—quintessentially—Ariadne, to a more active mode. Ariadne, left by Theseus, is the archetypal victim, restricted to an island and finally transmuted into an ethereal work of art. Her life does not stand as an example of the active patience characterized by Shakespeare's heroines. Rather, her descendants seem to be the female characters of tragedy, or at least those whom we identify as the stereotypically good women, Lavinia in *Titus Andronicus*, Virgilia in *Coriolanus*, Ophelia and Desdemona, or even Anne in *Richard III*.

If Ariadne is useful as a symbol of the stereotypically trapped and victimized woman, then Alcestis is equally useful as a model of the woman whose patience and passivity are, in fact, active virtues. Euripides' *Alcestis* provides one of the earliest and clearest examples of a woman who willingly dies for her husband as an active sacrifice, almost a "masculine" gesture. Although Euripides' play was not known to Shakespeare, Alcestis's journey is in many important respects similar to that undertaken by Shakespeare's heroines, and how Euripides' play discusses Alcestis and her husband, Admetus, is helpful in our reading the actions of Shakespeare's women vis-à-vis their men. Although popular tradition has it that men ought to be sacrificed for "women and children," Western literature would have it otherwise. The story of a woman dying for or because of a man is pervasive in Shakespeare, and Rosalind may indeed be correct when she debunks the stereotypes and tells Orlando, "there was not any man died in his own person, *videlicet*, in a love-cause" (IV.i.96-97). Just as Euripides' *Hippolytus* describes a pattern that prefigures the descent of the male in Shakespearean comedy, his *Alcestis* describes the fall of the heroine.

Alcestis is the earliest extant tragedy by Euripides though it appears to have been written in the middle of his career. To a Shakespearean, the

story seems decidedly comedic, describing as it does the separation
between Alcestis and Admetus and their subsequent miraculous reunion.
Gilbert Norwood argues that "it deals poignantly with the most solemn
interests of humanity" and that the story of husband and wife is handled
with "dignity" and "pathos."[25] Solemnity, however, is not at all inconso-
nant with the tone of a good deal of Shakespearean comedy, and one need
not be a Jan Kott to appreciate the suffering Shakespeare's characters,
particularly his heroines, undergo. At any rate, it is clear that Euripides'
subjects, his focus on familial relationships, personal reactions, and recognition scenes, place him closer to the world of New Comedy than to that of
the Greek tragedians before him.[26]

Euripides' play begins on the day Alcestis is to die as a replacement for
her husband, the Fates having agreed to spare Admetus on condition that
he provide them with a surrogate. None but Alcestis would agree to die in
his place. Her handmaiden, claiming that "she liveth, and is dead,"[27]
extols her as the best of women, as does Admetus who laments her leaving
and begs that she stay but who refuses to die himself and thereby prevent
her death. Alcestis makes it clear that she is dying for her husband, to
honor and save him, and Admetus in return praises her while reviling his
father who refused to die to save his own son. When she is dead, Admetus
will honor Alcestis by having a craftsman create a likeness of her, which he
will stretch out on their bed:

> Fashioned by craftsmen's cunning hands, thy form
> Imaged, shall lie as sleeping on a bed,
> Falling whereon, and clasping with mine hands,
> Calling thy name, in fancy shall mine arms
> Hold my beloved, though I hold her not:—
> A drear delight, I wot: yet shall I lift
> The burden from my soul. In dreams shalt thou
> Haunt me and gladden: sweet to see the loved,
> Though but as fleeting phantoms of the night. [349-57]

After Admetus engages in a rancorous exchange with his father, Hercules
saves the day by promising to return Alcestis from the netherworld because Admetus had proven himself a gracious host. Hercules soon enters
with a veiled woman, whom Admetus rejects, wanting to remain faithful to
the dead Alcestis. However, when the veil is lifted, Admetus rejoices in the
return of his wife, a holiday is proclaimed, and the Chorus declares the
event, "this marvellous thing" (1163).

In *Alcestis* a woman acts, takes all the chances, and in fact undertakes a
terrible journey for her husband's sake. It is the man, Admetus, who is

passive and she who is active. Furthermore, her activity only highlights his
weaknesses and his willingness to live without her and with a figure merely
representing her. Were Admetus to have accepted his fate and died,
Alcestis would have become a version of Ariadne, or of Penelope, heroic in
her passivity and loyalty, though a loyalty not much different from that of
Ulysses' dog. Ironically, it is because she volunteers to die in his stead that
the man of the house is turned into a kind of patient female, lamenting his
loss and bewailing his inaction. It is largely because the heroines of
Shakespeare's comedies move beyond the female stereotype suggested by
Ariadne and toward the model suggested by Alcestis that the plays escape
the despair chronicled in the "Willow" song. Bold enough to lie, create
new versions of themselves, adopt disguises, act for other women and for
themselves, be both active and passive, impatient and patient, Shakespeare's heroines rough-hew destinies that go beyond the limitations
imposed by the fears and ambivalence of the males. And that tendency
toward the active and the heroic, toward Alcestis's response rather than
Ariadne's, toward a sacrifice and descent which is both heroic and active,
develops very little as Shakespeare's career progresses, for it is present at
the start in Adriana's impatience and is shown us full-blown in Julia's
refusal to wait in Verona and in her subsequent fall, the final collapse as a
disguised page in the forest and far from home.

When her husband or lover leaves her, Shakespeare's heroine—patient, loyal, and solid as monumental stone—dies. That is, she either dies,
comes near to death, is thought to be dead, or is wished dead. Her
confrontation with death, furthermore, is occasionally signified by her
assuming religious orders, by serving as a votaress, or at the least by her
residing at a convent or temple. It is interesting to note that Alcestis's dying
leads the Chorus to predict that travelers will worship her:

> Unto her let the wayfarer pray.
> As he treadeth the pathway that trendeth
> Aside from the highway, and bendeth
>   At her shrine, he shall say:
> 'Her life for her lord's was given;
>   With the Blest now abides she on high.
> Hail, Queen, show us grace from thine heaven!'
>   Even so shall they cry. [999-1005]

In Alcestis's death, beatification, and resurrection we can see in which
ways Shakespeare's heroines suggest redeemers. Northrop Frye, in fact,
has called attention to the parallel between Christ's sacrifice and that of the
heroine of comedy and romance, particularly Alcestis, whom he labels a

"redemptive female."[28] Shakespeare's women too can be said to "die" for men, to sacrifice themselves in a variety of ways, as Alcestis does for Admetus. In Euripides as in Shakespeare the woman dies as a result of, indeed, as part of, her relationship with a man, and that death leads both to his redemption and to the revival of their union. Her disappearance allows the man to experience her differently, to interact with her in quite unusual, almost surreal, ways, to learn about her loyalty and patience, and to value her true worth.

The descent of Shakespeare's heroine, then, parallels the descent of the hero, and in some ways the two movements are comparable. Like the man, the woman falls socially, ordinarily from a position of power and importance to the station of a menial, and her dress, like his, changes for the worse. But their regression socially leads the two to very different places. The hero, as we have seen, drops into an ideology approximating that of the bastard, becoming a vagabond and holding mistaken and, at times, criminal views. The heroine, however, retains her essential goodness, and though her dress, as his, usually suggests the lower classes, her attitudes have nothing in common with those of a bastard. Her way of thinking remains untainted, and most would agree with Julia that "It is the lesser blot, modesty finds, / Women to change their shapes than men their minds" (V.iv.108-9). The hero becomes a failed version of Theseus, Jupiter, or Hercules, while the woman usually becomes a male servant or page, choosing names that suggest youth or servitude. "Fidele" is simply fidelity itself; "Ganymede," Jove's cup-bearer, is a child, and "Cesario" is reminiscent of Caesarion, Cleopatra's young son in *Antony and Cleopatra*. "Balthazar" is a name Shakespeare used for a merchant in *The Comedy of Errors*, a servant in *Romeo and Juliet*, and an attendant of Don Pedro in *Much Ado about Nothing*. If the young man thinks himself a kind of god, it is fitting and ironic that the woman create a version of herself who serves this hero. But the ways in which the fallen lovers relate are never quite as simple in Shakespeare as we might expect and are never simply a matter of two waifs meeting in the woods and following breadcrumbs out of a forest of suspicion and insecurity. The irony in Rosalind's playing "Ganymede" to Orlando's Jove is light, but Portia's choosing to become "Balthazar," a name that seems to be associated by Shakespeare with servants, and then saving a husband whose financial status is "worse than nothing," is perhaps a comment on the man's and woman's inverted positions in the play, and a hint at the complex social issues raised as both agree to marry.

6

"Th' Idea of Her Life"

When Claudio spurns Hero as a whore in IV.i of *Much Ado about Nothing* and Hero swoons under the weight of public humiliation, Friar Francis devises a plan to "Change slander to remorse" (211) and rescue lost love. He suggests to her father, Leonato, that they lie and "publish it that she is dead indeed" (204). His stratagem will gain time for the beleaguered Hero, but from "this travail" he looks "for greater birth" (213):

> So will it fare with Claudio:
> When he shall hear she died upon his words,
> Th' idea of her life shall sweetly creep
> Into his study of imagination,
> And every lovely organ of her life
> Shall come apparell'd in more precious habit,
> More moving, delicate, and full of life,
> Into the eye and prospect of his soul,
> Than when she liv'd indeed. Then shall he mourn. . . . [222-30]

Although Shakespeare devotes thirty-three lines to the Friar's idea, it is clear that the plan simply does not work. It is, in fact, a spectacular failure, and partly responsible for making the ending of the play so difficult to accept. As it turns out, Claudio is entirely unaffected by Hero's death, and his smugness and lack of compassion make it difficult for most audiences to understand Hero's willingness to forgive him and start anew as the play ends. Set against the Friar's high hopes, Claudio's behavior seems doubly cold.

The Friar's optimism about the possibility of a man's spontaneously changing accurately predicts what happens in *Cymbeline* and, perhaps, in *The Winter's Tale* as well. But the fact of the matter is that the reunion of the man and woman in Shakespearean comedy often defies logic and common sense, even the most basic sort of assumptions about cause and effect such as those Friar Francis makes. Leo Salingar reminds us that "between the wonderful and the probable for an ending to his comedies, Shakespeare evidently preferred the wonderful."[1] It is difficult to account for the reconciliations of act five, coming as they do after often painful separations and humiliating descents into versions of bastardy and death. Unless we lapse into an attack on actors and staging, or rely on tired assumptions that the hero *is* changed and *does* appreciate her, or that "love was different in the sixteenth century," we risk being dumbfounded by the pairings these plays finally affirm. Most audiences, faced with the baffling reconciliations between Shakespeare's lovers, do exactly what Puck recommends, that is, think "this weak and idle theme, / No more yielding but a dream" (V.i.427-28). We must assume that Antipholus of Ephesus and his wife Adriana will live happily now that she has learned the value of patience; Antipholus of Syracuse and Luciana love each other; Kate has been tamed and really is pleased with her "governor," Petruchio; the King of Navarre and his courtiers will be changed for good a year after *Love's Labour's Lost* ends; Proteus does love Julia and snaps back to his senses when he rushes to her aid as she swoons; Valentine does love Silvia even though he has just offered her up on the altar of his friendship; Claudio sinned not "But in mistaking" (V.i. 275); Bertram will love Helena "dearly, ever, ever dearly" (V.iii.316); Angelo has a "quick'ning" (V.i.495) in his eye and will love the same Mariana whom he jilted years earlier; and Lysimachus loves Marina in spite of his having discovered her at a brothel where he is treated as an honored client. And all this, of course, is in addition to our accepting reconciliations brought about through miraculous resuscitations, love potions, and visions.

The usual argument around the illogic of the reconciliations in the fifth act stresses the difference between life and art, especially the art of romantic fictions, and cautions that we ought not come to a Shakespearean comedy with the same set of assumptions we bring to life. The danger in such a critical posture, however, is that it regards the plays merely as "comedies," that is, fluff, a day at the amusement park, entertaining but only as a diversion. This is a position, in fact, critics have often taken, Hazlitt, for example, remarking that "a comedy is not so serious a thing as a tragedy."[2] Not only does this stance reduce Shakespeare's plays, and comedies of all sorts, but it also implies a certain silliness in any serious study of what, precisely, is happening in comedy. Tragedy, on the other hand, in spite of its main action being far outside the audience's normal range of experience, seems in comparison so much more serious, that is, real. But tragedies of love gone bad owe their apparently realistic endings in part to their never having to deal with the reconciliation of lovers that comedy demands: Hamlet consigns Ophelia to the hinterland of his imagination, and there she stays; Othello murders Desdemona, and the audience is spared her forgiving him and the spectacle of their setting up house in Venice.

The problem with the ending in these comedies is that Shakespeare rewrites New Comedy so that it is the lover who causes the divisions between himself and the woman, and then insists that these couples, wounded in a variety of ways, nonetheless love each other "dearly, ever, ever dearly." In *Love's Labour's Lost*, the reconciliation is less romantically satisfying than in other plays, but it is a good deal more realistic and logical. Though *Love's Labour's Lost* is often dismissed as dated folderol, it presents four rather intelligent, perceptive, and quick-witted ladies, all with "an air of reality about them," [3] and has the common sense to suggest that they would not leap at the chance "To make a world-without-end bargain" (V.ii.789) with four confused young men who alternately adore and fear them. The Princess of France and her companions defer any plans for marriage until such time as the men mature enough to know their own minds. By swearing "not to see a woman" (I.i.37) for three years, indeed, not to allow a woman to come "within a mile" (120) of court (and this in a land where "It was proclaim'd a year's imprisonment to be taken with a wench" [287]), and then by reversing their field—wooing their guests and bumbling the wooing as well as the studying—the men reveal not simply their flightiness and inconsistency but those two very opposite views of women that characterize male thinking in Shakespearean comedy. Is woman the enemy, to be lodged "in the field, / Like one that comes here to besiege his court" (II.i.85-86), or is she "queen of queens" (IV.iii.39), whose eyes "sparkle still the right Promethean fire" (348)?

By sending Berowne to "converse / With groaning wretches" (V.ii.851-52) for a year and the King to a "forlorn and naked hermitage" (795) for twelve months, the women treat the men's "perjury" (394) as seriously as life might; thus, Irene Dash suggests, "What makes the play unusual is that its ending confirms the women's skepticism." [4] In *The Comedy of Errors* Shakespeare resolves the ambiguities in the relationship between Antipholus of Syracuse and Luciana in the same way he resolves problems in *Love's Labour's Lost*—by deferring their marriage at least until some time after the curtain drops. Shakespeare simply does not allow Luciana to respond to Antipholus's offer of marriage in act 5, just as he was to get around the difficulty of having the novice Isabella respond to the Duke's marriage proposal in *Measure for Measure*. The silence of the women in *The Comedy of Errors* and *Measure for Measure*, like the stalling tactics of the women in *Love's Labour's Lost*, is a commonsensical response to the problems attendant on comedy's insisting that Jill say yes to every mistaking and confused Jack.

Generally, however, the reconciliations in these plays are not mature and prudent and make little sense to an audience that prefers, after all, the apparent illogic of reunited lovers to the realism of deferred marriages. To the women, however, like Mariana in *Measure for Measure*, who plead for men we find either worthless or repulsive ("O my dear lord, / I crave no other, nor no better man" [V.i.425-26]), the conclusions do seem to make a great deal of sense. Julia, Viola, Mariana, Helena, Imogen, and others want men who not only ignore or flee from them but often despise them and occasionally wish them dead, or try to kill them and then celebrate their freedom. What man can be said to be worthy of a woman who does so much for him, and at her own psyche's expense, and ordinarily after such bad behavior on his part? Frye asks, quite appropriately, "Is getting Bertram of *All's Well* worth the skill, devotion, and elaborate deceptions of Helena?"[5] Thus, the central question we face when we try to understand, rather than simply accept, the reconciliation, is what has happened in these plays that allows otherwise sensible, loving, and intelligent women to behave in ways the audience often considers against their own best interests. Why, in Catherine Belsey's phrase, do Shakespeare's women believe so strongly in "the infinite redeemability of men"?[6] Will Angelo make a better husband than he has a fiancé? Can Lysander and Demetrius be trusted in the woods at night or, for that matter, in Athens by day? Who would forgive Claudio and Bertram, and what sort of women would want to marry those two?

Perhaps the answer lies in Shakespeare's handling of hero and heroine during the time when they are separated from one another, that is, physically apart or together but disguised. The young impoverished hero, separated from his father and to a certain extent in the circumstances of a bastard, makes contact with the women for whose fall he is often at least partly responsible. The contact itself is often sexual, explicitly so in the bed-tricks of *All's Well That Ends Well* and *Measure for Measure*, implicitly so in the majority of plays, for example, in *The Merchant of Venice* or *As You Like It* where sexual relations and especially infidelity are important topics. The woman is "fallen" in the sense that she may be thought of as dead but also "fallen" in her having humbled herself by adopting a disguise, hiding her femininity, and waiting patiently, like a nun, or actively toiling for the man she loves. But what is perhaps most astonishing about the contact between separated lovers in Shakespearean comedy is the fact that when it occurs the stereotypical male and female roles established in act 1 are reversed. The happy ending, in fact, ordinarily depends upon the woman's assuming the traditionally male prerogative of action and rescuing, in one way or another, a man who seems quite clearly to have become a stereotypical female, passive and immobile. This startling reversal of sex roles, Shakespeare's insistence upon a relative rather than an absolute view of sexual identity, is more than ironic; it is crucial for the happy ending, and perhaps responsible as well for Shakespeare's characters' seeming, at their best, in the words of Dr. Johnson, "the genuine progeny of common humanity," not simply individuals but "commonly a species."[7]

Though many critics have, of course, pointed to the heroine's adopting a male disguise and self-consciously mimicking male behavior, what has generally been overlooked is the hero's unself-consciously adopting the posture and attitudes of a woman. Nowhere can this shift be seen more clearly than in Bertram's refusing to marry Helena, his letter of rejection, his subsequent flight, the bed-trick, and the recognition scene that lets all end well enough.[8] Richard P. Wheeler has written insightfully on the oedipal tensions at work in this play and in the problem comedies in general, on Bertram's being forced by his guardian, the King, to marry Helena as the King's surrogate, and on the suggestions of incest made explicit in the Countess's insisting, at one early point, on Helena's being like a sister to Bertram.[9] What seems equally clear, as I suggested in Chapter 2, is that the social dynamics at play in II.iii suggest that Helena is the pursuer and Bertram the pursued. "A young man married is a man that's marr'd" (II.iii.298), and a "marr'd" man, at least in the terms this play proposes, is a woman. After all, Bertram's being denied the privilege of traveling to Italy to fight in the Tuscan wars had earlier made him "the forehorse to a smock" (II.i.30); his marriage to a childhood companion— and his being chosen by her—has left him feeling passive, a posture he associates with the feminine, and allowed Helena, to his thinking, to play the active and masculine part.

What this play expects us to believe at the end, however, in spite of its rancor, is that Bertram really does love Helena. What has baffled audiences and critics for generations is not only why Helena would want Bertram, but also why a "detesting lord" (III.v.65), tricked once by an authoritarian King into marrying, would accept that marriage after being tricked a second time by a wife who had seemed to him, at the very least, grasping and devious. The solution to these problems lies in the letter Bertram writes to Helena as he leaves Paris and that she reads to his disappointed mother in III.ii:

> *Hel.* Look on his letter, madam, here's my passport. [Reads.] "When thou canst get the ring upon my finger, which never shall come off, and show me a child begotten of thy body that I am father to, then call me husband; but in such a 'then' I write a 'never.'" This is a dreadful sentence. [56-61]

The letter Bertram has given Helena seems, above all else, an assignment, a set of instructions specifying quite clearly what must be done in order for him to live with her happily ever after. And, in spite of the direness of her tone, Helena herself takes it exactly as one would a challenging assignment: she leaves immediately, fulfills the precise requirements stated in the letter, and when her efforts have been made known to him, Bertram announces, "If she, my liege, can make me know this clearly, / I'll love her dearly, ever, ever dearly" (V.iii.315-16). At the end, Bertram is not begrudging, he does not say that if she has succeeded he will *live* with her as husband and wife; rather, he says he will "love her dearly." In other words, his love will be the product of her having done what he himself asked her to do earlier.

That it is an assignment can hardly be doubted. Helena, in fact, calls the letter her "passport," and although she is being ironical, she does, in fact, use it as a passport.[10] Bertram's syntax makes this abundantly clear, for the letter straightforwardly instructs, " 'When thou canst . . . then call me husband.'" Those critics who do not fault Helena for pursuing so mean-spirited a man as Bertram usually chide her for being underhanded and aggressive, yet they would do well to consider that she does no more than Bertram himself asks her to do. It would seem beside the point for critics to chastise her when Bertram seems entirely pleased with her success.

What happens between Bertram and Helena seems a well-orchestrated play within a play written by Bertram himself, an elaborate rigmarole in which each plays a part without ever breaking character. The script is, of course, the letter assigning Helena her tasks. When critics react to the letter as Bertram's mother, the Countess does, as though its sarcastic tone were its real meaning—as though, in fact, it means the opposite of what it literally says—the rest of the play becomes nonsense. M.C. Bradbrook thinks that "When, with a moral reflection upon his lack of moral sense, she [Helena] strips off her pilgrim's weed to catch her runaway husband by a trick more worthy of him than her, she has become the puppet-figure of an overworked craftsman."[11] However, not even a puppet could act as confusedly as Helena does if we take her subsequent words as literal statements of her intentions. Taking them literally, Anne Barton cannot understand why Helena winds up in Italy after leaving Paris for the shrine of St. Jaques le Grand in Compostela, Spain: "It is never made clear why Helena's route should in III.v bring her to Florence."[12] Like Bradbrook, G.K. Hunter simply assumes that Shakespeare made a "mistake."[13] The warped sense of direction that has sent Helena southeast when she tells us she will travel southwest may be Shakespeare's mistake, but it certainly cannot be Helena's. It is, after all, one thing to take the wrong fork in the road, and another entirely different one to wind up in the same city where one's estranged husband has taken refuge. How can Helena do what Bertram has asked of her without her taking up residence in Florence?

Helena's seemingly impossible task is made a great deal easier when we remember the speed with which Bertram agrees to give Diana his family ring. That puzzling action, giving up a ring "Which were the greatest obloquy i' th' world / In me to lose" (IV.ii.44-45), can make sense on stage or in the study only when interpreted as a deliberate attempt to help Helena succeed, in other words, as his playing the part he himself had written. To agree to go to bed with the very woman to whom he had given the ring is to fulfill, in the most obvious sort of way, the conditions imposed upon Helena in a letter that is anything but a clear-cut statement of rejection. Unless Bertram is as dull-witted as some think Helena, we are left with no choice but to consider that she knows the difference between Spain and Italy and he remembers the terms of the most important letter he has ever written.

In asking Helena to get the ring "That downward hath succeeded in his house / From son to son, some four or five descents, / Since the first father wore it" (III.vii.23-25), Bertram is asking her to separate him even further than he already is from his deceased father and from his family history. In giving up the ring, that symbol that "binds his sexuality to his place in a family tradition," Bertram repudiates "patriarchal loyalties,"[14] bastardizes himself, and thereby creates a sense of himself as independent adult. He cannot be her husband and fulfill the terms of his marriage vows unless he first sees himself as her husband and not as his famous father's son or the King's ward. He asks her to take responsibility for removing his ring, an act he cannot, apparently, do himself. Secondly, and more importantly insofar as it ratifies his giving away his father's ring, Bertram asks Helena to take responsibility for consummating their marriage, for revealing the sexual component in her nature. It is clear that in Bertram "there emerges what appears to be a recoil from sexuality itself,"[15] as though he cannot or will not apprehend Helena's sexuality, though the other young men at the court of France do. When approached by Helena in II.iii each of the young lords is willing to marry her, and enthusiastic at the prospect. When Helena tells the fourth Lord that he is "too young, too happy, and too good, / To make yourself a son out of my blood" (96-97), he answers, "Fair one, I think not so" (98). Earlier, in introducing Helena to the King, Lafew indicates how appealing he and the King find her:

> Nay, come your ways;
> This is his majesty, say your mind to him.
> A traitor you do look like, but such traitors
> His majesty seldom fears. I am Cressid's uncle,
> That dare leave two together; fare you well. [II.i.94-98]

Later, in mistaking the young lords' actions and thinking they reject her, Lafew calls them "boys of ice" (II.iii.93); "Sure they are bastards to the English, the French ne'er got 'em" (94-95). Bertram, like Demetrius in *A Midsummer-Night's Dream*, "will not know what all but he do know" (I.i.229), that his Helena, like Demetrius's, is a sexually attractive woman.

Whether Bertram rejects Helena because "he associates her with the home he is trying to escape," and thus reveals a "covert fear of incest,"[16] or because he simply does not yet know himself well enough to understand his own feelings, being too young and too frustrated to do what he most wants, two points are clear. In the first place, on some level Bertram wants to be happily married to Helena and therefore assigns her tasks, helps her fulfill them, and agrees to love her "dearly" when she has accomplished them; and, second, his handling of their relationship has forced her to become active and stereotypically male, and himself to be passive and stereotypically female: "The sexual roles are almost completely inverted: the woman pursues the man, chastity becomes the aggressor, the gentle female assumes the offensive."[17] If, when these plays begin, the women are to some degree prisoners of family and social tradition, by the second or third act the women transform themselves into models of action and initiative. Helena's gradual assumption of male prerogatives, her decisiveness, is typical. She begins as an orphan living at Rossillion thanks to the goodheartedness of the Countess. Bertram's leaving for Paris activates Helena; she not only follows him but ventures to cure the King on pain of being taxed with impudence, "A strumpet's boldness, a divulged shame, / Traduc'd by odious ballads; my maiden's name / Sear'd otherwise; ne worse of worst—extended / With vildest torture, let my life be ended" (II.i.171-74). She then dares to marry Bertram in spite of his opposition, journeys to Florence, secures the help of Diana and her mother, undergoes the humiliation of the bed-trick, and returns to Paris and accepts Bertram knowing that he had wished her dead. She has traveled geographically and socially, planned, coaxed, and bribed, while Bertram has been the prize, like the lady in a Petrarchan sonnet, impervious to all manner of argument.

Bertram's letter establishes the terms of their relationship by enjoining Helena to become active: "When thou canst get. . . ." Such riddling statements are familiar to us from romantic literature and fairy tales, though they are usually challenges accepted by men in order to win women. Here, and in general throughout Shakespeare, the reverse is true: it is the women who must pursue the men. In *A Midsummer-Night's Dream*, as we have seen, Helena laments that she must chase Demetrius, arguing of women, "We cannot fight for love, as men may do. / We should be woo'd, and were not made to woo" (II.i.241). Helena notwithstanding, in Shakespeare the woman who cannot woo, will not wed and bed the man she loves.

The consummation of their marriage is the play's central action and its deepest mystery. Having finally maneuvered into bed a man who has approximated Marvell's coy mistress, Helena fulfills the second of the two conditions stipulated by Bertram. With the possible exception of Middleton's *The Changeling*, where Beatrice Joanna listens outside the door as Diaphanta substitutes for her on her wedding night, this play takes us as close to the marriage bed as we are likely to come in plays from this period. In IV.iv Helena tells the Widow and Diana what it was like to be with Bertram as they consummated their marriage without his knowing it:

> But O, strange men,
> That can such sweet use make of what they hate,
> When saucy trusting of the cozen'd thoughts
> Defiles the pitchy night; so lust doth play
> With what it loathes for that which is away. . . . [21-25]

Later, when Helena tells Bertram that it was she with whom he slept, and that "when I was like this maid, / I found you wondrous kind" (V.iii.309-10), it is the young Count himself as well as the audience who remembers that he made "sweet use" of her. Arthur Kirsch writes that the bed-trick "releases and incorporates, rather than denies, Bertram's aggressive sexual energies" and that the Count's success "provides the basis for a marriage in which there can be desire as well as affection."[18]

In that awkward encounter in the garden between Bertram and Helena, Shakespeare joined a man who had fled home and all association with father and family to a woman who was at once dead and alive, passive and active, a pilgrim at the shrine of St. Jaques le Grand and a wife in bed with her husband. At the end of the play she is treated as an object of wonder, a wife and a maid, Venus and Diana, the renowned "Dr. She" who ministered to the King no less well than to her husband. Helena has rescued a marriage and a man, for married to Helena Bertram is free to return to Rossillion and claim his birthright by accepting his father's ring from her, thereby reestablishing ties with a family and a tradition he had rejected.

At the same time Shakespeare was writing plays about inconstant men like Proteus, Angelo, and Bertram, he was writing plays, as we have seen, about men who come to suspect their wives and lovers as inconstant. In *The Comedy of Errors*, for example, Shakespeare shows us, in the twin

Antipholus brothers, the two kinds of husbands and lovers in his comedies. Antipholus of Ephesus runs from his wife, Adriana, whom he thinks an impatient scold, to the arms of a courtesan. His flight from wife to whore is in sharp contrast to the ambivalence of his brother, who comes to see in one woman, Luciana, both the modesty of the maid and the sexual allure of the mermaid. Such misapprehension of integrated women is generally the stuff of tragedy, where Othello, for example, sees two Desdemonas, Hamlet orders Ophelia to a "nunnery," and Antony seems unable to settle on one idea of Cleopatra, who complains, "Not know me yet?" (III.xiii.157), though plots centering on men who mistake women are even more typical of the majority of his comedies. In some ways, the problems created for women whose husbands and lovers are inconstant, a Demetrius oscillating between Helena and Hermia, are far less serious than those of women who are thought themselves to embody two contradictory aspects, the beauty of the virgin and the ugliness of the whore. The ambivalent attitude of this sort of male character, and the changing nature of the woman in his eyes, provides perhaps the characteristic dilemma of Shakespearean comedy. The patching up of these more deeply wounded relationships requires more than fairies in the woods. In *As You Like It, The Taming of the Shrew, Much Ado about Nothing, The Merchant of Venice, The Winter's Tale*, and *Cymbeline,* Shakespeare portrays a full range of male characters who misapprehend women and shows us the increasingly complex ways in which the reunions between lovers are brought about.

Though both Orlando and Posthumus Leonatus are poor, exiled, and separated from their fathers, in terms of their attitudes toward those fathers and toward the women whom they love, the two young heroes are polar opposites. Consequently, it is little surprise that what happens to bring about the happy ending in *As You Like It* is radically different from what happens in *Cymbeline.* That is, while both men make contact with a woman from whom they believe themselves separated, and while both are made to address the issue of that woman's sexuality, each experiences his contact with her in a profoundly different way. A sure gradient leads down from Orlando's secure position as the youngest son of Sir Rowland de Boys and his confident attitude toward his Rosalind, to Posthumus's self-conscious posing as a bastard and a murderous cuckold.

When Rosalind encounters Orlando in the Forest of Arden she decides to "speak to him like a saucy lackey, and under that habit play the knave with him" (III.ii.295-97), though she never tells us why she would rather trick him than reveal herself and get on with the business of comedy. In Celia's eyes, Rosalind has "simply misus'd" (IV.i.201) her sex, but it is clear that Rosalind has a method in her "love-prate" (202) that goes well beyond good fun and mischievous eavesdropping. By taking the initiative and playing Ganymede playing "Rosalind," she is able to gauge the depth of Orlando's passion, test his fidelity, and apprise this disenfranchised young man of harsh possibilities in married life.

Orlando passes every test devised for him by Rosalind and proves an apt pupil in the bargain. Even at his most vulnerable, separated from father, country, and woman, in the woods and among the boys (for such Rosalind must now be accounted), Orlando refuses to doubt her fidelity and honesty. Confronted by a "man" with the possibility of Rosalind's being disloyal to him, he simply rejects such a view. It is Rosalind, of course, who insists on his facing the facts about women, who plays the instructor and buzzes about her passive student like a magician around a crystal. Schooled by "an old religious uncle" (III.ii.344) who read lectures against love, and having cured one man of the "lunacy" (403), Rosalind runs down romance in general and Orlando's affection in particular. This "Rosalind" tells Orlando that he does not behave as a lover should nor does he look like one. When he tells her that without Rosalind he will die and that Rosalind loves only him and will always love only him she brands his feelings mere naïveté. His teacher claims that "there was not any man died in his own person, *videlicet*, in a love-cause" (IV.i.96-97). Worse yet, to her, one cannot "desire too much of a good thing" (123-24), and she guesses that Rosalind will probably have twenty men such as Orlando, for with women, "the wiser, the waywarder" (161). But Orlando cannot be talked out of loving her, or into suspecting her, for ""Virtue is no horn-maker; and my Rosalind is virtuous" (64).

As You Like It and *Cymbeline* are dissimilar in tone though similar in structure. In both plays young impoverished men are exiled, separated from women who love them, and tested by hearing damning descriptions of those women from other men. But the tone of these two plays is different and not just because there is real villainy in *Cymbeline* and only a one-dimensional sort of evil in *As You Like It*. The plays differ because these two fully realized and psychologically complex figures, Orlando and Post-humus, react in radically different ways to the cynical remarks about women they hear from others: Posthumus cannot be persuaded that his wife is honest, and Orlando will not be persuaded that Rosalind can be dishonest. After hearing the worst, Posthumus tries to kill Imogen, whereas Orlando marries Rosalind twice, once in a mock ceremony engineered by Rosalind playing "Ganymede" playing "Rosalind," and shortly afterward in earnest. In Orlando, Rosalind has a husband who has been exiled and slandered, and who has heard the worst, and yet remains constant. Orlando reacts, in fact, in a manner much more characteristic of the heroines of Elizabethan comedy, like Margaret in *Friar Bacon and Friar Bungay*, Grissil in *Patient Grissil*, or Luce in *The London Prodigal*, patient and loyal, than of the heroes, and so appears to us from the start a man who thinks and acts like the secure and confident son of a great nobleman.

Because Orlando refuses to believe tales he hears about Rosalind and about women in general, there is a reuniting of the lovers in act 5 but no more need for him to apologize or to change than there is, say, for the doggedly loyal Ralph in *The Shoemaker's Holiday,* and that can be said of very few other Shakespearean heroes. Valentine, Florizel, and Ferdinand are cut from the same cloth as Orlando; none loses faith or interest in the woman he loves, though for all three the conditions of bastardy obtain, and they are separated from fathers and women. Valentine, for example, is exiled from Milan by Silvia's father, the Duke, a man who attacks him primarily on the basis of his lineage: "Wilt thou reach stars, because they shine on thee? / Go, base intruder, overweening slave, / Bestow thy fawning smiles on equal mates" (III.i.156-58). When the Duke later accepts him, he suddenly calls Valentine "a gentleman and well deriv'd" (V.iv.146), and that ought to tell us that occasionally legitimacy is in the eyes of the beholder. Furthermore, Valentine and Florizel are forced to see the women they love in far more sexual terms than they had bargained for, Valentine as a witness to Proteus's attempted rape of Silvia, and Florizel as witness to his father's calling Perdita, "knack" (IV.iv.428), "enchantment" (434), and "fresh piece / Of excellent witchcraft" (422-23). Because all three retain faith in women and are no more seduced into misogyny than Orlando is by Ganymede's lectures (or by Jaques' cynicism), none of these men needs to be reunited with a woman in any sense other than the strictly physical. Each needs access to the woman and her father's permission to marry, but none needs to adjust to life with a woman or to develop a more congenial attitude toward women. Valentine, Florizel, and Ferdinand, like Orlando, are positively motivated toward woman and marriage and cannot be dissuaded or made jealous.

To study Shakespeare's heroes in a sequence that moves from Orlando's assurance to Posthumus's instability is to encounter increasingly insecure and unwilling young men. For example, the males in *The Taming of the Shrew* are like Orlando in their optimism and self-confidence, but even here fear of women and male ambivalence are all too obvious. Although Lucentio and Hortensio seem enthusiastic enough, the play ends with their moralizing and telling us and each other that marriage will not be what they had hoped it would. Their attitudes toward their wives have changed for the worse and have become less sure and more like those of Antipholus of Syracuse or Navarre: ambiguous and muddled. After he loses the wager to Petruchio, Lucentio tells us that it is a "harsh hearing when women are froward" (V.ii.183), and Petruchio adds a coda by telling both men, "We three are married, but you two are sped" (185). Of course, the Elizabethans found few situations more entertaining than a man's marriage to a nag or a shrew, the sort of "woman" Morose thinks he has married in Jonson's *Epicoene*. But the line from impatience to "shrewishness" to disobedience is a sure descent, and a woman who is not a patient Griselda is likely to be charged with "frowardness." If a woman does not react to male insecurity with the patience of Mariana in *Measure for Measure* or the absurd meekness of the abused wife in *A Yorkshire Tragedy*, then she appears "froward, peevish, sullen, sour" (157), "a foul contending rebel, / And graceless traitor to her loving lord" (159-60). Disobedience, of course, could only lead to infidelity, to the scenario Rosalind describes to Orlando when she lectures him on marriage: "maids are May when they are maids, but the sky changes when they are wives" (IV.i.148-49). One might indeed meet his "wive's wit going to [his] neighbor's bed" (168). And after infidelity, was she not capable of murder? What, after all, are Alice, the homicidal wife in *Arden of Feversham*, and Lady Macbeth if not grasping women married to uxorious men? Even Frankford, in *A Woman Killed with Kindness*, is criticized by his wife's own brother for not seeking her life for her infidelity.[19]

Lucentio and Hortensio may be "sped," but Petruchio is not, and he takes Kate's insubordination in deadly earnest. For him, as for all the men in Padua, shrewishness is no laughing matter. Though I think Shakespeare muddies the waters by making Katerina truly ill-tempered rather than merely high-spirited, Petruchio's inability to handle marriage to a free and lively woman is clear in his need to turn Kate into an automaton.[20] All the directorial ingenuity in the world cannot erase the fact that Petruchio has created a woman who will say whatever pleases him, and who has become a watchdog for male supremacy, chastening other women who stray in word or deed from the Elizabethan world picture and its patriarchal viewpoint. Though, like Orlando, Petruchio is well-disposed to marriage—in fact, any woman with money enough will do—he is far less trusting of women. And in Kate, Petruchio finds an exaggeration of all the worst qualities men liked to think women embodied. For him, as for the world of this play in general, it is assumed that women will either toe the line, as Kate is taught to do, or they will simply assume control, as Bianca, the Widow, and the Hostess of the Induction do. In fact, from the males' point of view, *The Taming of the Shrew* reveals a world of opportunistic females; the only obedient women are Kate, a woman playing a part written by her husband, and Christopher Sly's "wife," a man pretending to be a woman. What happens to Sly in a jest, Petruchio engineers in reality: Sly marries a man and Petruchio marries a kind of man in woman's clothing. Of the three newly married women in act 5 only Kate behaves and speaks as the supposedly meek Page in the Induction does:

> *Sly.* Are you my wife and will not call me husband?
> My men should call me "lord"; I am your goodman.
> *Page.* My husband and my lord, my lord and husband,
> I am your wife in all obedience. [Ind. ii. 104-7]

It is just as well that Sly's relationship with the Page never reverses itself and that the story in the Induction does not continue; in this way Sly and his "wife" retain the same sort of relationship that Petruchio and Kate achieve at the end of act 5. The Lord in the Induction creates as a joke an artificial situation in which man is the "lord" and woman the obedient servant; Petruchio makes that his reality.

Petruchio works throughout the play to render Kate passive and himself the master, though the play can be staged, of course, in such a way as to suggest that Petruchio's mastery is as tenuous as Sly's over his "wife." Indeed, Coppélia Kahn thinks that in their interaction we see that "only a woman has the power to authenticate a man, by acknowledging him, *her* master" and that it is "Kate's submission to him that makes Petruchio a man, finally and indisputably."[21] In any case, most recent commentators would, I think, agree that Petruchio trusts women enough to marry, but not enough to marry any woman more independent than a good hunting dog. We have seen evidence of his ambivalent attitude toward women earlier, in Chapter 1, in his describing his journey toward marriage as a thrusting "into this maze," but it blossoms fully in his need to see Kate as "My horse, my ox, my ass, my any thing" (III. ii. 232). To Petruchio, she is indeed an animal, and it is he who uses the taming metaphor and promises to bring her "from a wild Kate to a Kate / Conformable as other household Kates" (II. i. 277-78). To be "conformable" in the sense Shakespeare uses the word here, is to be "of compliant disposition or practice; tractable, submissive, disposed to follow directions," a fairly accurate description of the perfect Elizabethan helpmate.[22] But the "conformableness" Petruchio wants and the "taming" he attempts merely reveal the depth of his own fear. When Baptista and Tranio chide Petruchio for wearing tattered clothing to his wedding, the groom cuts the discussion short and suddenly turns serious: "Could I repair what she will wear in me, / As I can change these poor accoutrements, / 'Twere well for Kate, and better for myself" (III. ii. 118-20). Petruchio's fear of what Kate "will wear in me," that is, will "wear out in me," is so great that he is willing to forgo the pleasures of the wedding night and of several succeeding nights. Instead of consummating the marriage in Kate's "bridal chamber," Petruchio seems entirely satisfied with hectoring her:

> *Gru.* Where is he?
> *Curt.* In her chamber, making a sermon of continency to her,
> And rails, and swears, and rates, that she, poor soul,
> Knows not which way to stand, to look, to speak,
> And sits as one new risen from a dream. [IV.i.182-86]

Though her remarks on Petruchio's "continency" are illuminating, I cannot agree with Irene Dash that his sermon indicates a willingness to forgo "sexually aggressive behavior"; [23] rather, it seems to me, Petruchio reveals all too clearly a fear of Kate's sexuality and of consummating his marriage. Like Hermione in *The Winter's Tale*, who tells Leontes, "You speak a language that I understand not" (III.ii.80), Kate is simply dumbstruck. Petruchio is only one among many males in Shakespeare's comedies who choose "a sermon of continency" over sexual contact, for female impatience and frowardness imply licentiousness, and therefore the possibility of infidelity and rebellion.

Petruchio's fear turns upside down our notions of the stereotypical honeymoon and wedding night, when a sophisticated man must be gentle with his virginal bride. Here it is the bride who is asked to be gentle with the frightened groom. While Kate sits, "as one new risen from a dream," Petruchio lectures her on continency and tears the bed apart: "some undeserved fault / I'll find about the making of the bed, / And here I'll fling the pillow, there the bolster, / This way the coverlet, another way the sheets" (199-202). Othello climbs into bed to kill his wife, and Petruchio climbs into bed to "kill a wife with kindness" (208), as he puts it. The result of his nightly treatment of Kate is a deferral of sexual intercourse until Kate has been "tamed," made patient and docile, made into a man's idea of what a woman ought to be, in other words, transformed into Sly's page or into the "heroine" in *M. Butterfly*, with whom heterosexual intercourse is simply not possible.

Kate represents an exaggeration of the spirit of independence Shakespeare had described in Adriana in *The Comedy of Errors*. Although we feel uncomfortable about Adriana's being stifled by her husband and Aemilia, few would deny that Kate might benefit from change, though even fewer would approve Petruchio's methods or his results. And because Kate is so clearly discourteous and abusive when the play begins, there is no question in this play of her being able to help Petruchio to transform himself from the untrusting and frightened young man into the secure adult. Because Kate is every Elizabethan male's worst dream of what woman can become unless he curb "her mad and headstrong humor" (209), *The Taming of the Shrew* simply reinforces all the male characters' least appealing traits, those that, in later comedies, most often lead to the deepest wounding of the heroine. The difference between Petruchio and Orlando, or between Petruchio and the sort of men we expect the King of Navarre and his courtiers to become, is that Rosalind and the Princess of France are integrated and energetic women, whereas Kate is insecure and childish. It would take a man far less a product of his age than Petruchio to transform Kate rather than to "tame" her, and that mission is clearly an impossibility in Shakespeare, where the men are ordinarily unable to change themselves, let alone another. The men in Shakespearean comedy misapprehend women as a matter of course, perceiving threats where none exist, and perhaps therefore are thoroughly incapacitated when a woman like Kate appears to be a genuine threat. In any event, these plays are almost always about a woman's ministering to a man, and not vice versa. The best a man can do with a needful woman is "tame" her.

In *Much Ado about Nothing* Shakespeare shows us two pairs of lovers and two quite different sorts of men, Benedick, who turns out to be strong enough to accept an independent woman and to relinquish the stereotypically male and authoritarian role, and Claudio, a lover lacking trust and all too willing to see a woman as "Venus" (IV.i.60) or an animal raging "in savage sensuality" (61). This play does not face very squarely the young Count's predisposition to error, and critics and audiences alike do not joy in his contract with the reborn Hero in act 5.

Certainly, the Friar hoped, as I suggested at the start of this chapter, that Hero's supposed death would lead to a good deal more than Claudio's merely admitting that he had been fooled and made a mistake. Friar Francis predicted nothing short of a transformation, that her "death" would make him mourn, "And wish he had not so accused her; / No, though he thought his accusation true" (232-33). Claudio, for whom "beauty is a witch" (II.i.179) under the best of circumstances, is hardly the man to mourn a woman "though he thought his accusation true." Indeed, thinking it true, the most he can say to Hero's grieving father is "Away, I will not have to do with you" (V.i.77). In the presence of Don Pedro and Benedick, Claudio reverts to the old jokes, calls Leonato and Antonio "two old men without teeth" (116), and advises Benedick to cheer up: "What, courage, man! What though care kill'd a cat, thou hast mettle enough in thee to kill care" (132-34).[24] The Friar's prediction, however, though wrong about Claudio, is much closer to the mark as a description of what happens to Benedick. Out of Claudio's terrible attack on Hero in church in IV.i comes

Beatrice's request that Benedick "Kill Claudio" (289), and from that comes the surest sign that he is hers forever.

Claudio proposes marriage to Hero at a time when Benedick and Beatrice are at "war" (I.i.62). "Signior Mountanto" (30) and "Lady Disdain" (118) have been at odds for some time, and as the play begins Benedick pays a visit to Messina where he and Beatrice are later tricked into admitting their love for one another. In order to understand how it is that these two separated and feuding lovers come to a reconciliation in which each accepts the other easily and cheerfully, it is necessary to understand who they are and why they separated in the first place.

About their earlier relationship there is only one piece of information, and it is obviously subjective. Beatrice tells us that at one time Benedick "lent" (II.i.277) his heart to her, "and I gave him use for it, a double heart for his single one. Marry, once before he won it of me with false dice, therefore your Grace may well say I have lost it" (277-82). For Kenneth Muir, "The speech is rather obscure; but it seems to imply that Benedick at one time had made love to Beatrice, and she felt his intentions were not serious."[25] Her conclusion, that he won her love by using "false dice," is never elaborated upon, though it would account for her hostility.

Beatrice makes perhaps one further comment on their separation. After Hero has been slandered and rejected by Claudio, and Benedick tries to console Beatrice, he turns the discussion to their newfound love:

> *Bene.* By my sword, Beatrice, thou lovest me.
> *Beat.* Do not swear and eat it.
> *Bene.* I will swear by it that you love me, and I will make him eat it that says I love not you.
> *Beat.* Will you not eat your word? [IV.i.274-78]

One is reminded here of what the Duke says of Angelo in *Measure for Measure*, that when Mariana's dowry was lost at sea, he "swallow'd his vows whole" (III.i.226). Later in the same scene when Benedick swears again, "By this hand, I love thee" (324-25), Beatrice responds, "Use it for my love some other way than swearing by it" (326-27). Throughout the play Beatrice suggests that Benedick is a man whose actions do not follow his words, in short, that he plays false and is a coward. In act 1, when she hears that he is returning from the wars, she asks, "how many hath he kill'd and eaten in these wars?" (i.42-43). She calls him a "valiant trencherman" (51), and when the Messenger describes Benedick as "a good soldier too, lady" (53), Beatrice comes directly to the point: "And a good soldier to a lady, but what is he to a lord?" (54-55). The question is, will Benedick defend women or, like Bertram and the men in Navarre, hold swords against them. Beatrice's bantering always has a point (in a way that Benedick's does not), and her recurring theme is that men are false and that their words are lies. Her attacks are all the more telling, for this play focuses a great deal of attention on the use and misuse of language in general. And it is for this reason that, when Beatrice asks him to "Kill Claudio" and he finally agrees to challenge his closest friend, Benedick is seen as a man who moves, not only from the world of male comaraderie to that of heterosexual love, but as one who can now trust a woman implicitly and agree to be faithful to her in deed as in language. Furthermore, what Beatrice insists upon is a more honest use of words, a recognition that language divorced from meaning is a kind of faithlessness. Using words less flippantly, this play suggests, is to use them more as women do, rationally, as precise indicators of feelings and intentions. With regard to other of Shakespeare's comedies, Terry Eagleton writes, "for speech to unhinge itself from the world is another name for madness," [26] and it is this sort of male insanity—which makes victims of Kate, Hero, Hermione—that Beatrice has resolved to avoid.

Benedick's transformation is even more remarkable for his having been a professed misogynist, "ever an obstinate heretic in the despite of beauty" (I.i.234-35). His lighthearted gibes always suggest that to marry is to become a cuckold, a more comical way of calling women whores than Claudio's, and, like Claudio, Benedick is obviously "Hippolytan" in his views. It is surprising, then, that Benedick, whose attitudes so much correspond to those of a bastard, and in this play to those of Don John in particular, is not only thought of as Don John's opposite but that he is capable of moving from the views of a Claudio or a Posthumus to those of an Orlando: "I will be horribly in love with her" (II.iii.235). He and Beatrice are popular with audiences partly because of timing: while they are falling in love, Claudio falls "horribly" out of love. The audience, of course, knows from the start that Benedick "is already in love with Beatrice" [27] and that the action of the play will merely reveal to him what we have known all along, that his misogyny is a veil for his love. Nonetheless, his defending Hero against the slanders of his male friends, his acceptance of Beatrice's position, in other words, his willingness to become an advocate for women against the familiar misogyny of the male world of Messina, represents a startling turnabout.

It is difficult to believe that there was ever a time in Benedick's hypothetical past when he was as naive and rigid as Claudio. In Shakespeare, habits of mind are rarely products of one's age, and in his plays there are both wise youngsters and foolish elders. Claudio, Antipholus of Syracuse, Petruchio, Bertram, and others, exhibit minds tyrannized by convention and disabled by insecurity. Separated from parents, alone, wandering in mazes, Shakespeare's young men often lack resilience; though their hearts are in the right place and their intentions generally good, they are incapable of adapting, of seeing themselves from another perspective and as a result seem paralyzed. When their paralysis causes them to stumble and make fools of themselves, they seem Bergson's jolly incompetents, like Sir Andrew Aguecheek, and we call the play a "happy" comedy. When they seize up, however, like an engine without oil, become exaggerations of themselves, give in to their own worst impulses and fears, and victimize others, the play seems uncomfortable to us, there is little happiness, and what is left is an emotional problem for the audience.

Benedick is adaptable, willing to see himself from the outside and to take chances and trust the woman he loves rather than the familiar voice of patriarchal convention. *Much Ado about Nothing* is often compared favorably to *The Taming of the Shrew*, though the focus of such discussions is usually Beatrice and Kate, not Benedick and Petruchio.[28] The differences between the two men, however, though less readily apparent, are of far greater significance than those between the women. Both women are obviously unconventional, Kate abusive physically, Beatrice verbally, as Muir suggests, but theirs is a difference in degree, not kind. Beatrice seems more real, and is skillful at expressing her unconventional attitudes in acceptable ways whereas Kate cannot and perhaps as a consequence is lobotomized as the play ends. But between Benedick and Petruchio the differences are profound and are matters of kind. Petruchio can only become more of himself when challenged by Kate, and he uses unconventional means to achieve supremely conventional ends. Benedick never even attempts to change Beatrice; he simply comes to accept her as she is, unconventional, intelligent, and independent, all that we imagine Kate could have become had Petruchio been less frightened.

From the very start, Benedick combines lightheartedness with cynicism, and if A. P. Riemer is right, that critics have "exaggerated the 'wit'" of Beatrice and Benedick's exchanges,[29] it is nonetheless in his wittiness that Benedick is distinguished from other heroes of Shakespearean comedy. He is the opposite both of the moralist Claudio, whose favorite adjective for Hero is "modest" and for whom women are either virgins or whores, and of the bastard, Don John, for whom women are only whores. Benedick, like Emilia in *Othello*, seems to know that there are more than a dozen women in this world who would cuckold their husbands, and this knowledge, which he playfully shares, makes him less demanding of women and more resilient. He simply thinks all women human, and therefore capable of behaving in a variety of ways. Perhaps because they agree about the nature of women, Beatrice and Benedick seem "the only inhabitants of Messina to demonstrate a capacity for making sure moral discriminations."[30] Such knowledge and discrimination in Shakespeare's women is hardly unusual—what does Beatrice know about love and men that Adriana, Portia, and Rosalind do not? In the men, however, it is far less common.

Benedick's line, of course, is that marriage equals servitude and cuckoldry; it is to wear one's cap "with suspicion" (I.i.198). If ever he loves, Benedick tells Don Pedro and Claudio, then "pick out mine eyes with a ballad-maker's pen, and hang me up at the door of a brothel-house for the sign of blind Cupid" (252-54), or "pluck off the bull's horns, and set them in my forehead" (263-64). But this mocking of love, marriage, and women is not complemented, as it is in Shakespeare's bastards, by the slandering of particular women, including his mother, nor by the noxious tone typical of misogynists like Claudio or Jachimo. Quite the contrary, Benedick explicitly refuses to say one bad word about any woman; he is scrupulous and courteous throughout: "That a woman conceiv'd me, I thank her; that she brought me up, I likewise give her most humble thanks; but that I will have a rechate winded in my forehead, or hang my bugle in an invisible baldrick, all women shall pardon me. Because I will not do them the wrong to mistrust any, I will do myself the right to trust none; and the fine is (for the which I may go the finer), I will live a bachelor" (238-46). This speech may help to explain his past, and it certainly prefigures the future. The man who does not wish to have "a rechate winded in [his] forehead" and who "will live a bachelor" might indeed have "lent" his heart and then broken off the engagement, all of which could have been construed by Beatrice as his having won her heart with "false dice." Such a man might have played falsely, period, for it is clear that Benedick's concern is primarily with himself, not with the woman. What this speech also tells us, however, is that Benedick is as likely to trust a woman as to mistrust her; he cannot say something negative about women without balancing it by saying something positive: he will not "mistrust any," yet he will "trust none." Benedick is not a misogynist, though he sounds like one; he is a cynic, skeptical of pretensions of any kind, especially those to moral superiority, and is the consummate entertainer, an aristocratic Dogberry, a witty corrupter of words rather than a maimer of language.[31] He seems, as Marilyn French claims, "balanced," an adult who "has been a soldier and is respected within the male world," yet who also "shows compassion and sensitivity in his response to Hero's defamation."[32]

In act 2, after being tricked by his friends, Benedick tells us that he loves Beatrice, but he shows us as much only when he agrees to challenge Claudio. When Claudio attacks Hero, Benedick stands dumbfounded, "attir'd in wonder" (IV.i.144), torn between his sure belief that Hero is "wrong'd" (260) and his great friendship with Claudio and Don Pedro.

What Beatrice does is make him choose between his love for her and his love for Claudio, between his new ways and his old:

> *Bene.*   Come, bid me do anything for thee.
> *Beat.*   Kill Claudio.
> *Bene.*   Ha, not for the wide world.
> *Beat.*   You kill me to deny it. Farewell. [288-91]

The man who has been compared by Beatrice to "my lady's eldest son, evermore tattling" (II.i.9-10), is now asked to act, and to act for a woman and on behalf of a woman. Earlier, Beatrice had said Benedick was "a good soldier to a lady, but what is he to a lord?" Now Beatrice wants him to become a good soldier *for* a lady and *against* a lord. The danger had always been that Benedick would become a charming version of Parolles, chatty, vainglorious, and ultimately faithless, the sort of man she describes when Beatrice wishes herself a man so that she might challenge Claudio: "Princes and counties! Surely a princely testimony, a goodly count, Count Comfect, a sweet gallant surely! O that I were a man for his sake! or that I had any friend would be a man for my sake! But manhood is melted into cur'sies, valor into compliment, and men are only turn'd into tongue, and trim ones too. He is now as valiant as Hercules that only tells a lie, and swears it. I cannot be a man with wishing, therefore I will die a woman with grieving" (IV.i.315-23). Of this speech Lisa Jardine writes, "At this moment she [Beatrice] recognises the tongue as the symbol of impotence and inaction, of the threat which will never become a deed";[33] that is, she sees the limits of a woman's power in a man's world, that mere talking is, after all, nothing. Surely, however, the point of this speech, indeed, the point of Beatrice's remarks on the use of language throughout this play, is that it is the men who are "tongue" and render themselves impotent by using words as airy nothings.

In acting for Beatrice, Benedick and she achieve union without resorting to manipulation and disguises; in *Much Ado about Nothing* the woman achieves her ends and still remains a woman, very much alive, partly because Benedick, in a sense, agrees to be Beatrice's male disguise. By becoming an active force for Beatrice, Benedick avoids becoming a liar and a coward, a Parolles, a soldier valiant for lying and swearing to it. More importantly, Benedick dares to be "womanly" in the sense that he agrees to work for women and against men and to use words rationally rather than idiosyncratically, and Beatrice dares to be "manly," in that she finds a man who will act "for her sake," be her surrogate and enable her to develop a stereotypically masculine side without adopting the disguises of Portia and others, or using the subterfuge of "death." In this, in her avoiding both the sequestration of Ariadne and the descent of Alcestis, she is reminiscent of the Princess of France, a woman who defies men, acts according to her own lights, and finally winds up issuing orders to the King of Navarre. With the exception of the ladies in *Love's Labour's Lost*, Beatrice is unique in Shakespearean comedy. Up to this point, women who assert themselves and yet refuse to don disguises, like Kate, or Adriana, are merely put down. Once Benedick does agree to challenge his friend for Beatrice, the two are united as complete human beings. Of Beatrice's action Riemer writes, "we are forced to realize that she is putting Benedick upon his mettle, eliciting from him a guarantee of his moral integrity and concern. This is one of Shakespeare's finest and most subtle touches—the unspoken implications of a relationship are given dramatic substance through the careful portrayal of two fantastical but fundamentally sound people, and through their reaction to a crisis which places their personal morality in the balance."[34]

When Benedick does challenge Claudio, in V.i, it is as though he and Beatrice were speaking with one voice: "Fare you well, boy, you know my mind. I will leave you now to your gossip-like humour. You break jests as braggards do their blades, which, God be thank'd, hurt not" (185-88). Benedick disassociates himself from Claudio, who is now a "boy" and a gossip and braggart, exactly the sort of man Beatrice accused him of being. Unlike Bertram, who had to be tricked into seeing Parolles for what he is, Benedick develops insight into his erstwhile friends and simply loves Beatrice and bonds himself to her.

As the hero's response to love and attraction tends toward Posthumus's misogyny and away from Orlando's self-confidence, we discover increasingly complex female reactions to increasingly complex and serious male problems. For example, the interaction among Bassanio, Portia, and Antonio in *The Merchant of Venice* reveals not only the nature of the threat to romance in Shakespearean comedy, i.e., the impediments offered by the hero himself, but also the startling ways in which the herione effects changes in him that lead to reconciliation. Lawrence W. Hyman argues persuasively that the bond plot helps to indicate "the struggle between Portia and Antonio for Bassanio's love."[35] When Antonio's letter, asking that Bassanio witness his death, arrives at Belmont, Portia asks only that Bassanio marry her before he travel to Venice, for Antonio's "letter creates a direct conflict with Portia's marriage to Bassanio."[36] When Bassanio leaves and the newlyweds are separated, Portia lies to Lorenzo and Jessica, as we have seen in Chapter 5, telling them that she will sequester herself at "a monast'ry two miles off" (III.iv.31) until his return. Privately, she announces to Nerissa her plan that they disguise themselves as men in clothes provided by her cousin, Doctor Bellario, a noted jurist, and "see our husbands / Before they think of us" (58-59). Though she promises to tell Nerissa why she has planned so devious a venture ("I'll tell thee all my whole device / When I am in my coach" [81-82]), we never do find out what has prompted her to leave Belmont, lie to her friends, and argue law in Venice. We do know that in order to be a lawyer in the singularly male world of this play Portia needs to represent herself as a man. What we know in addition, and more importantly, is the result of her actions: Antonio's life is saved, and Bassanio gives away the ring that Portia gave him and that she said would "presage the ruin of your love" (III.ii.173) if lost. Most commentators now follow Hyman and see Portia's saving Antonio as her way of preventing the merchant from sacrificing himself "as a final gesture of his love for Bassanio," as well as of preventing her husband from bonding to the memory of a dead Antonio, and of avoiding a marriage clouded by death.[37] Furthermore, most interpret her asking for the ring as a way of testing his affection for her in relation to his feelings of friendship for Antonio.[38]

What happens between Portia and Bassanio in Venice, however, is not so much a test as it is a lesson, and a lesson characteristically taught by the women in Shakespearean comedy to the men. The point of the lesson is twofold: partly it teaches that marriage is not only a different but also a more sacred relationship than that between two friends; but more particularly its message is sexual, the ring plot being almost exclusively a way of educating Bassanio about the nature of female sexuality.

Marriage releases Portia from her father's grasp and transforms her from "an unlesson'd girl, unschool'd, unpractic'd" (III.ii.159) into "Baltha-zar," a doctor of great learning whose youth belies his wisdom. In Belmont the newlywed Bassanio may be the master and Portia the servant, but in Venice Portia is not only intelligent and resourceful, she is creative, orchestrating Antonio's release and testing Bassanio's faith. Just as she knows how to save Antonio even before she steps into the courtroom, so she knows precisely what and how to teach Bassanio, the husband who had seen her beautiful hair as a "trap." After she wins the law case Portia asks for the ring, and will settle only for the ring. When Bassanio, "upon more advice" (IV.ii.6), succumbs to Antonio's coaxing—for it is his friend who coerces Bassanio into breaking faith with Portia—and hands her the ring, Portia knows that her husband has placed the obligations of friendship above those of marriage. It is as though Bassanio were Valentine and had just offered Silvia to Proteus. That action in The Two Gentlemen of Verona is absurd in part because Silvia seems oblivious to Valentine's gesture. Portia, however, is most acutely aware of what her husband's generosity means, and her point seems to be not that Bassanio should love Antonio less but rather that he needs to be less ambiguous about his love for her. His shallow commitment does not lead him openly to reject a woman, as less healthy men such as Claudio and Posthumus, do, but rather to reject her implicitly by preferring Antonio.

Portia saves her marriage in the same way Helena saves hers, by becoming the active partner, interceding between her husband and another woman—in this play herself, in disguise—and arranging matters so that her husband is, so to speak, faithfully unfaithful. The tactics used by Shakespeare's female characters always seem appropriate to the level of a man's self-awareness. Rosalind need only present a negative picture of herself and suggest that as a woman, she is capable of deception and trickery in order to learn that Orlando is secure enough to trust her. Helena needs to interpose herself physically between Bertram and Diana, to become Diana, in a sense, in order for Bertram to accept her sexuality. Portia's situation is more serious than Rosalind's but not so dire as Helena's. That is, while Bassanio is not nearly as self-aware and confident as Orlando, he is less impulsive and vindictive than Bertram, certainly less doubtful about the nature of women, and less frightened by the reality of marriage.

Complementing the rise of the active woman in this play, of Balthazar, from that version of Portia who deferred to Bassanio as her lord, is our sense that the male world of Venice is an impotent, passive, and static community. The Venetian tableau in front of which Portia works is practically paralyzed by indecision and is symbolized by Antonio, prostrate and willing to die. Her presence in this scene, IV.i, is galvanic: first she works Shylock to a fever of anticipation and then drops him as suddenly and encourages the Christians, led by the cheerleading Gratiano, against Shylock. Her remarks are a combination of incisive questions and terse commands in which she tells various parties what "must" be: "Then must the Jew be merciful" (182); "this strict court of Venice / Must needs give sentence 'gainst the merchant there" (204-5); "It must not be" (218); "And you must cut this flesh from off his breast" (302). Her self-assurance and dynamism are in stark visual and aural contrast to the passivity of the men.

Portia's aggressiveness and her pose as Balthazar do not end with the end of the trial and Shylock's sentencing. If anything, Portia is even more assertive when Bassanio offers to reward her for saving his friend's life (408-12). Of all Shakespeare's disguised women surely Portia comes the closest to representing a stereotype of masculine authority and bravado (Viola is afraid of Aguecheek, Rosalind and Julia swoon), and nowhere more so than in demanding Bassanio's ring. We must remember, however, that her asking for the ring comes after what she has heard from both Bassanio and Antonio about each other and herself earlier, in the courtroom. When Antonio is about to die, he instructs Bassanio,

> Commend me to your honorable wife,
> Tell her the process of Antonio's end,
> Say how I lov'd you, speak me fair in death;
> And when the tale is told, bid her be judge
> Whether Bassanio had not once a love. [273-77]

Bassanio announces to Antonio and the court, in most explicit language, that Antonio's life takes precedence over all else, and especially Portia:

> Antonio, I am married to a wife
> Which is as dear to me as life itself,
> But life itself, my wife, and all the world,
> Are not with me esteem'd above thy life.
> I would lose all, ay, sacrifice them all
> Here to this devil, to deliver you. [282-87]

This is the sort of comment that, in other contexts, critics are quick to defend by pointing to Renaissance treatises on Neo-Platonism and love between men. But there can be no recourse here to platitudes about Bassanio's being a noble spirit or a model of the loyal friend, for Portia takes offense, and does so immediately: "Your wife would give you little thanks for that / If she were by to hear you make the offer" (288-89). Her remarks are seconded by Nerissa after Gratiano wishes his wife "were in heaven, so she could / Entreat some power to change this currish Jew" (291-92): "'Tis well you offer it behind her back, / The wish would make else an unquiet house" (293-94).

Portia's peremptoriness, then, in pressing Bassanio for the ring must be taken in the context of her having heard Bassanio clearly prefer Antonio's life to hers. She demands the ring with the same authority she used in the courtroom to defend Antonio: "I will have nothing else but only this, / And now methinks I have a mind to it" (432-33). Bassanio refuses her, Portia leaves, and Bassanio calls her back after Antonio once again forces him to weigh Portia against his friend: "My Lord Bassanio, let him have the ring. / Let his deservings and my love withal / Be valued 'gainst your wive's commandement" (449-51). Though Norman Rabkin depreciates the importance of "the game she plays with the ring" and sees her behavior here as "trickery and a tendency to domineer, so inconsistent with the moving spontaneity of her emotions both as Bassanio chooses the lead casket and as she speaks of mercy," it is clear that Portia has been carefully and consistently characterized from the start as an authoritative and knowledgeable woman hardly given to playing games.[39] Her seriousness of purpose in asking for the ring suggests the same strength and determination that enable her to play by her father's rules, offer money to save Antonio, follow Bassanio to Venice, and win Antonio's freedom and Bassanio's peace of mind.

The happy ending in *The Merchant of Venice* depends upon Portia's saving Bassanio twice, once in arguing law in the courtroom, which frees his friend from death, and once again in being the woman to whom he gives his wife's ring. In order to succeed at both, she must demonstrate creativity and mental acuity. Our reaction to her dazzling Bassanio later, in Belmont, by showing him the very ring he knows he gave to a lawyer in Venice, is the same as our reaction to her defeating Shylock with his own argument. But however much we may applaud her success, denigrate or praise her methods, we ought not lost sight of the importance of the ring plot and the precise uses to which she puts the token Bassanio has grudgingly given away. Bassanio's being unfaithful to Portia, with Portia, creates the paradox with which *The Merchant of Venice* ends. Her interceding not only prevents Bassanio from being unfaithful in fact, as Helena's bed-trick prevents Bertram, and Mariana's Angelo, but allows her to raise the sexual issue precisely because she knows he has indeed given the ring to a woman. Had she not stepped between Bassanio and his intentions, had he given the ring to a man, the moral of the story would simply be, "Bassanio has listened to Antonio yet again, and has slighted Portia in favor of a male friend." And though, from Bassanio's point of view, he *is* giving the ring to a man, from here on it is Portia who directs events much as Rosalind does in *As You Like It*. What Portia is concerned with now are Bassanio's feelings towards women, not men, and she uses the ring as a way of teaching Bassanio about relations between men and women and about the nature of female sexuality.

Heterosexual love and fidelity are the first of Portia's thoughts when she returns to Belmont in V.i. When Lorenzo tells Jessica that he has heard Portia's voice, Portia raises the issue of cuckoldry by claiming that Lorenzo "knows me as the blind man knows the cuckoo, / By the bad voice!" (112-13). When Bassanio, Antonio, Gratiano and the other men, newly arrived from Venice, salute her and compare her to the sun, Portia's response in greeting Bassanio is again sexual: "Let me give light, but let me not be light, / For a light wife doth make a heavy husband, / And never be Bassanio so for me— / But God sort all! You are welcome home, my lord" (129-32). What Portia insists on Bassanio's recognizing at this time—just before they exit to consummate their marriage as the scene and play end— is that she is a woman and he a man, both capable of infidelity, an option that remains simply a matter of choice. She brings to the fore a picture of their marriage as the union of a cuckold and a whore, an exaggeration of the picture with which Rosalind confronts Orlando, and does so as vigorously and actively as she had argued in court. Once again Portia is dynamic and Bassanio and Antonio static; stereotypical sex roles remain reversed, for it is she who questions, demands, and threatens, though not as the stock harridan of Elizabethan comedy. The point of the scene is not that Portia is a nag but rather that she is a woman. Novy reminds us that "while angry at Bassanio, she is actually uniting the two of them more closely by emphasizing their sexual relationship."[40]

When she pretends to learn that Bassanio has given away her ring, she threatens, "I will ne'er come in your bed / Until I see the ring!" (190-91). Wheeler, I think, undervalues Portia's behavior in this scene, describing it merely as witty and teasing; he reads her approach as "slightly uneasy sexual jesting."[41] But what Portia does goes well beyond a jest. She accuses Bassanio of having given the ring to a woman and settles quickly on the point she will develop for the next forty-two lines, the possibility of her sleeping with another man in response to his infidelity:

> Let not that doctor e'er come near my house.
> Since he hath got the jewel that I loved,
> And that which you did swear to keep for me,
> I will become as liberal as you,
> I'll not deny him any thing I have,
> No, not my body nor my husband's bed. [223-28]

Her speech simply announces what will happen in language as graphic as its meaning is clear, for she will "not deny him any thing I have," "thing" being a popular euphemism for "pudend," as Partridge glosses it,[42] and for "privy member, privy parts," as the *OED* puts it.[43] Significantly, in *Othello* when Emilia tells Iago, "I have a thing for you" (III.iii.301), and he replies, "You have a thing for me? It is a common thing" (302), what she hands him is the most well-known token in Shakespeare, Desdemona's handkerchief. That the token in Shakespeare symbolizes sexual fidelity is not news, but what is important to see is that the "thing" Bassanio rejects in giving away the ring is that bonding in marriage that is exemplified by the sexual union of man and woman. What Portia does not want is to lie with a man, and consummate a marriage to a man, who is ambiguous about women, seeing their sexuality as a "trap," and who, on some level, rejects the intimacy marriage demands. At this point Portia reveals the thing itself, the ring, and baldly tells Bassanio, "I had it of him. Pardon me, Bassanio, / For by this ring, the doctor lay with me" (258-59). Gratiano can only guess, "What, are we cuckolds ere we have deserv'd it?" (265). Bassanio is not the misogynist Claudio is, though his surrendering the ring is as antifemale a gesture in its way as Navarre's is in closing his "gates" against the ladies of France.

Portia's use of the ring certainly shows Bassanio that as wife and woman she has the same sexual options he has, that love "has to be possessed and guarded, even though it is free and belongs exclusively to neither one of those who made the contract,"[44] a notion he must grasp in order to see marriage as a union between equals and to see Portia as an unambiguous and integrated woman. His wife, who can choose to remain chaste and faithful, is precisely the same woman who can choose to be disloyal. It is not that there are two types of women but rather that women have "hands, organs, dimensions, senses, affections, passions" (III.i.59-60) as men do and may use them in two ways. Their sexuality, Portia's parable seems to suggest, like men's, in and of itself is neither good nor bad. In *Othello*, in an obvious redaction of Shylock's speech, Emilia makes the same point: "Let husbands know / Their wives have sense like them; they see, and smell, / And have their palates both for sweet and sour, / As husbands have" (IV.iii.93). And while Emilia, like Portia, makes the comparison between the sexes as a way of restraining husbands and threatening them with "measure for measure," the deeper lesson is simply about the nature of female sexuality, and therefore about female behavior, and the necessity of the man's accepting sexuality as an integral part of womanliness and of marriage. "In the final reconciliation between husband and wife," Novy writes, "the threats of possessiveness and promiscuity are both dispelled, and the vision is one of a sexual relationship in which both partners can maintain their own identity."[45] Surely it is Othello's need to see Desdemona as alternately hypo- and hyper-sexed that obliges him to "sacrifice" (V.ii.65) her, just as it is Petruchio's, Claudio's, Leontes' insecurities and half-formed notions of female sexuality that force them to immure their wives and lovers behind the walls of a narrowly prescribed behavior. Adriana and Kate diminish until they know their places; more typically Shakespeare allows his heroines to teach the men about the sociology of marriage and the nature of female sexuality, and thereby to create a climate more fully comedic. It is the men who are, literally, duplicitous, fearfully apprehending two sorts of women where there is only one, though all the riddles in the play misleadingly ask, "who is Portia, and where is she to be found?"[46]

The movement from separation to reunion in Shakespearean comedy, I have suggested, is clearly a function of the hero's and heroine's willingness to modify, if not switch, stereotyped sex roles. When the woman helps the man, she is usually in disguise and prepared to take the initiative or find a surrogate who will act on her behalf and is quite ready to behave in ways often considered exclusively male. And when the disguised woman meets the man, who is himself not only confused but often bastardized—that is, separated from father, ambivalent about women and marriage, and disenfranchised—he, in turn, has often assumed what appears to be a passive posture that allows him to be taught or changed by example. Though he may have gone to the wars, or "to discover islands far away," or "to the studious universities," his successful reunion with the woman he loves depends on his becoming, in terms of the period's stereotypes, less a "man" and more a "woman," patient and hopeful.

The hero's ability to change depends on his willingness to be taught by the woman herself, as Benedick is, and by experiences she engineers for him, as Bassanio is, and so to transform himself. Here, however, we need to draw a distinction between such transforming and the Renaissance notion that women are the truest teachers. That popular idea, so charmingly espoused by the men of Navarre in the first act of *Love's Labour's Lost*, is antithetical to the sort of teaching Shakespeare's women ultimately wind up doing. Though Navarre and his courtiers agree early on that women's eyes "sparkle still the right Promethean fire; / They are the books, the arts, the academes, / That show, contain, and nourish all the world" (IV.iii.348-50), the men ultimately learn that women must teach them in a far less inspirational and far more active manner, assessing their personalities and accomplishments, assigning them tasks, in short, taking charge rather than silently inspiring. The hero's quoting the Renaissance party line on women as "Promethean" only appears to reinforce the stereotypical notion that women are, or ought to be, passive adjuncts and is hardly the same as a genuine willingness to learn and change, to put oneself under another's influence by trusting. The almost instinctive tendency of some young men in these plays to idealize women, to profess what Carol Thomas Neely calls "the attenuated, formulaic Renaissance version of medieval courtly love," inhibits communication and makes both necessary and unavoidable the women's "debunking" and exposing "the unreliability of male vows of undying love."[47] In large part, Shakespearean comedy enacts the process by which idealization is transformed, through female intervention, into understanding and acceptance of women. When the man does not learn from the woman, when instead it is the man who teaches and the woman who changes, as in *The Taming of the Shrew,* we feel as though a man's bad habits have simply become ingrained.

From Shakespeare's earliest comedies to his latest, role reversal is the path that leads to the reunion of lovers. The women in *Love's Labour's Lost* assign the men tasks, but those tasks, which the men accept, confine them for a year and put them in a position ordinarily associated in comedy with women. The King is asked to

> go with speed
> To some forlorn and naked hermitage,
> Remote from all the pleasures of the world;
> There stay until the twelve celestial signs
> Have brought about the annual reckoning. [V.ii.794-98]

His year will not be so very different from the Princess's, for she vows to shut her "woeful self up in a mourning house" (808). Berowne, who must for a year "Visit the speechless sick, and still converse / With groaning wretches" (851-52), is, in effect, asked to become a male nurse, and he agrees: "Well, befall what will befall, / I'll jest a twelvemonth in a hospital" (870-71). Longaville perhaps speaks for all three men when he says, "I'll stay with patience, but the time is long" (835). Now it is the men who agree to be patient, to live like Silvia in a tower, Jessica in her room, Viola as a statue, Portia at a monastery, or Imogen in prison, segregated from the pleasures of the world and under the direction of the opposite sex. The willingness of the men of Navarre to sequester themselves is all the more important for its being presented to us not as a meaningless rigmarole or as a woman's jealous command, or even as punishment, but explicitly as therapy, a prescribed regimen intended to change them, to exorcise unrealistic images by exposing the men to a real world of pain and death. And because these comedies ordinarily do not end until the men do appear to change, know who the women are, see them more clearly, and treat them as women and not as "signs" (V.ii.469) or objects to be manipulated, *Love's Labour's Lost* cannot end "like an old play" (874). Berowne knows that "These ladies' courtesy / Might well have made our sport a comedy" (875-76), but these ladies do not want to be courteous if that means marrying only to be rejected on their wedding day, or night, or a decade later, as in *The Winter's Tale*.

The Winter's Tale shares with Shakespeare's earlier plays a similar structure. Leontes and Hermione do not reunite until Leontes learns, not merely apologizes; furthermore, his learning is depicted as a consequence of their reversing roles: Leontes must become patient and accept the passive life, while Hermione, through the agency of Paulina, remains omnipresent and active and never leaves Leontes' consciousness. In this play, and to an even fuller extent in *Cymbeline*, the mysterious process predicted by the Friar in *Much Ado about Nothing* truly occurs, for when he hears his wife has died, "Th' idea of her life" does indeed "sweetly creep / Into his study of imagination" (IV.i.224-25). When Leontes denies the truth of the Oracle, learns that Mamillius has died, and sees Hermione swoon, he immediately recovers, comments accurately on his behavior, "I have too much believ'd mine own suspicion" (III.ii.151), and then simply asks forgiveness, vowing to "New woo my queen" (156). But the world of *The Winter's Tale* is not that of *Much Ado about Nothing*, where naive claims of having been mistaken suffice, nor is Leontes as innocent as Claudio, for there has been no "putter-on" (II.i.141), no Don John, misleading him. As if to confirm the difference, no sooner is Leontes' apology spoken than Paulina warns him, "—the Queen, the Queen, / The sweet'st, dear'st creature's dead, and vengeance for 't / Not dropp'd down yet" (III.ii.200-202). It is not, however, "vengeance" that overtakes Leontes as the years pass but rather the "idea" of Hermione's life. If time and the women are more pitying than vengeful in the succeeding sixteen years, it is because Leontes repents his folly, enters fully into his grief, and submits himself to the direction of Hermione, Paulina, and the Oracle of Apollo.

But forgiveness does take sixteen years, not the mere seconds of *The Two Gentlemen of Verona*, or even the year of *Love's Labour's Lost*, though Paulina draws a picture that reminds us of the penance imposed upon the courtiers of Navarre:

> A thousand knees
> Ten thousand years together, naked, fasting,
> Upon a barren mountain, and still winter
> In storm perpetual, could not move the gods
> To look that way thou wert. [210-14]

Paulina can only advise him, "take your patience to you" (231), and he does, for the last we hear from Leontes before the "wide gap" (IV.i.7) of sixteen years is his promise to mourn his dead family: "Once a day I'll visit / The chapel where they lie, and tears shed there / Shall be my recreation" (238-40). Leontes must follow Paulina's lead, here and during the ensuing years. When next we see him, in V.i, we are told that he has "perform'd / A saint-like sorrow" (1-2) and hear him reaffirm his willingness to be led by Paulina: "We shall not marry till thou bid'st us" (82). Earlier, Leontes had charged Paulina with being masculine (he calls her a "mankind witch" [II.iii.68]), and in the last act she exercises prerogatives associated with men. It is Paulina as well who arranges for the statue and orchestrates the reunion between husband and wife, though she and Hermione are hardly to be distinguished from one another and seem instead two aspects of the same female force and presence, one stereotypically "dead," the other confident, responsible, and most active. In other words, Paulina and Hermione seem to embody in two people the same active/passive states Portia, for example, represents as "Balthazar" and "Portia" at the monastery.

At this point in the love story in Shakespearean comedy, the wheel has come half circle. The separated and penitent man appears passive, that is, patient and restricted, and the woman active intellectually and physically. In other words, the woman of act 5 finds herself in the psychosocial position of the man of act 1, and the man of act 5 in that of the woman of act 1. Though the plays, as we shall see, reverse the positions of male and female yet again before they end, it is important to recognize that Shakespeare demands a reversal of sex roles as a prerequisite for the happy ending. Leontes, mourning daily, reminds us of Mariana at the moated grange, Thaisa at the Temple of Diana, the "cloistress" Olivia, the "dead" Hero, the imprisoned Imogen, Ariadne marooned on her island, and, above all, Hermione herself, frozen in time like Viola, "Patience on a monument." One of the ironies of this play is that husband and wife are, in a sense, never closer to one another than during their sixteen years' separation, so fully does Leontes' condition approximate that of his dead wife. Clearly, it is through his penitence, his self-cloistering, his willingness to live in the manner prescribed by Paulina, that he can be reached by "Th' idea" of Hermione's life. Like Benedick, Leontes comes under the tutelage of a woman and accepts the vision and point of view of women before he is transformed into a husband. That change, as critics have noted, is a profound one, and the slow process begins as soon as Leontes owns up to his guilt. For G. Wilson Knight, when Leontes vows to mourn "his speech is calm and lucid; he is now, as never before, kingly."[48]

Leontes' change occurs almost exactly as the Friar in *Much Ado about Nothing* predicts, for as the years pass we sense that Leontes can almost see and hear the "dead" Hermione:

> Good Paulina,
> Who hast the memory of Hermione,
> I know, in honor, O, that ever I
> Had squar'd me to thy counsel! then, even now,
> I might have look'd upon my queen's full eyes,
> Have taken treasure from her lips—
> *Paulina*   And left them
> More rich for what they yielded.
> *Leontes*   Thou speak'st truth:
> No more such wives, therefore no wife. One worse,
> And better us'd, would make her sainted spirit
> Again possess her corpse, and on this stage
> (Where we offenders now) appear soul-vex'd,
> And begin, 'Why to me—?' [V.i.49-60]

Leontes communicates with her in a more real way than he had when she was alive; he reminds us of Othello, who stands over the sleeping Desdemona and promises, "Be thus when thou art dead, and I will kill thee / And love thee after" (V.ii.18-19), and of Admetus who will sleep with Alcestis's likeness after she has died for him: "In dreams shalt thou / Haunt me and gladden me."[49]

Leontes' seeing and hearing Hermione is presented as the result of his patience and suffering. His adoption of characteristics associated with women in literature is emphasized by Shakespeare throughout act 5, and especially in scene 3, when he sees the statue and is reunited with Hermione. Like the trial scene in *The Merchant of Venice*, this scene divides its characters into two groups, Paulina and Hermione, on the one hand, active physically and creative, and Leontes and the others, passive, like spectators at a play but also like witnesses to a miracle, struck dumb with amazement, as the men always seem to be at the end of the comedies. Indeed, Paulina commands all to "stand still" (95), and when Hermione steps down Paulina coaches Leontes, "Start not" (104). Every action that he takes is first ordered by Paulina; in effect what we see are two statues coming to life, Hermione, and the amazed Leontes, who has his own "full awakening" as Derek Traversi puts it.[50] In *Twelfth Night*, when Viola asks to see Olivia's face without the veil, the Countess condescends, saying, "we will draw the curtain, and show you the picture" (I.v.233), and in a sense with that gesture Olivia ceases to be a work of art, or a cloistress, chooses instead to come alive, falling in love with "Cesario" as the first step in her progress to the altar with Sebastian. Twice we hear Paulina offer to "draw the curtain" (68, 83) covering the statue, and, in an action reminiscent of Olivia's but far, far grander, another woman comes alive. Hermione approaches Leontes, and he responds to her, the observations of those watching reflecting his passivity and her activity:

> *Pol.*   She embraces him.
> *Cam.*   She hangs about his neck. [111-12]

When the play ends, Leontes and Hermione seem to have forged a "reciprocal, mutually creative relation between a vigorously rendered manhood, and a comparably complete realization of essential womanly power," as Wheeler puts it.[51]

But if we understand the manner in which Leontes and Hermione reunite after sixteen years, what we find less easy to comprehend is why Leontes has had to wait sixteen years for Hermione to return. The audience is struck by the fullness of his penitence and agrees with his compatriot Cleomines, who counsels him to do "as the heavens have done, forget your evil, / With them, forgive yourself" (V.i.5-6). We feel, too, the sharpness of Paulina's stings in reminding him, apparently often, that "she you kill'd / Would be unparallel'd" (15-16). In short, the connection between Leontes, Hermione, and Perdita is in some ways puzzling. The astonishing dramatic point to bear in mind is that Hermione's only speech in act 5 is addressed not to Leontes but rather to Perdita. After stepping down from the pedestal and embracing Leontes, Hermione greets Perdita:

> You gods, look down,
> And from your sacred vials pour your graces
> Upon my daughter's head! Tell me, mine own,
> Where hast thou been preserv'd? where liv'd? how found
> Thy father's court? for thou shalt hear that I,
> Knowing by Paulina that the oracle
> Gave hope thou wast in being, have preserv'd
> Myself to see the issue. [V.iii.121-28]

And while it is true, of course, that Menandrine New Comedy, as well as the Roman comedy of Plautus and Terence, generally neglects the female characters, who are almost always silent as the play concludes, the problem here is not so much Hermione's silence—the fact that she never does speak to Leontes after awakening or even that the only words she utters after act 3 are addressed to Perdita—as that this speech explicitly tells us and Leontes that she "preserv'd" herself in order to see Perdita, not him. Traversi tells us that it is Hermione's "first act in her new state to beseech the gods to 'look down' and pour their 'graces' upon her daughter's head,"[52] but it is really her *only* act. The play very movingly presents Leontes' repentance, his "painfully working himself from the bondage of sin and remorse into the freedom of nature,"[53] and we feel his contrition and sorrow keenly, yet Hermione seems to ignore his repentence, his transformation, in telling us that she has lived only to see her daughter.

Hermione's focusing on Perdita, and her insistence that she not be reunited with Leontes if, in the words of the oracle, "that which is lost be not found" (III.ii.136), indeed the oracle's insistence on the primacy of Perdita, make great sense given the focus throughout the first three acts on children, childhood, bastardy, and legitimacy. It is Leontes' destruction of his family, his refusal to accept his role in generation, that turns the play from birth to death, from summer to winter, and therefore it seems logical to focus on the child at the end. But Perdita is more than "that which is lost" and more than the final puzzle piece. Perdita may represent spring, or children, or forgiveness, but what she *is*, quite clearly, is a living token, the equivalent of the ring in *The Merchant of Venice*. Her reappearance in Sicilia signals not only the fulfillment of the oracle but also, and more importantly, Leontes' development into a man who can acknowledge his part in the process of generation.

The Winter's Tale is the only one of Shakespeare's comedies in which the supposed infidelity of the woman is discussed in terms of the legitimacy of the children. Leontes' suspicions are aroused in act 1, we are led to believe, while looking at his pregnant wife conversing with his childhood friend and are developed while interrogating his son. For Leontes, proof of Hermione's adultery is, in fact, the infant Perdita herself, and the argument soon comes down to so basic an issue as who the baby looks like, an issue raised earlier by Leontes as he stared at Mamillius. When Paulina brings the infant to Leontes, he repeatedly rejects her as a bastard, even though Paulina, in a sense, offers ocular proof that the child is his:

> It is yours:
> And might we lay th' old proverb to your charge,
> So like you, 'tis the worse. Behold, my lords,
> Although the print be little, the whole matter
> And copy of the father—eye, nose, lip,
> The trick of 's frown, his forehead, nay, the valley,
> The pretty dimples of his chin and cheek, his smiles,
> The very mould and frame of hand, nail, finger.
> And thou, good goddess Nature, which hast made it
> So like to him that got it, if thou hast
> The ordering of the mind too, 'mongst all colors
> No yellow in't, lest she suspect, as he does,
> Her children not her husband's! [II.iii.96-108]

Paulina's concern that Perdita will, in later years, suspect "Her children not her husband's," is, of course, an absurdity. But Paulina's sarcasm does point to the simple fact that heroines in the comedies do not fall victim to the same ideological traps that snare the males; Perdita will not grow into a female version of Leontes or of the bastardized males we have seen in these plays, and reject, in turn, her relation to her children. Although she is rejected by and separated from her parents, set on a deserted shore, and raised in generally impoverished surroundings, Perdita retains her psychological integrity as fully as does, say, Orlando. The possibility of her becoming a female Iago may be hinted at jokingly by Paulina but is virtually unthinkable, such transmutations being strictly the province of the males in Shakespearean comedy.

But Leontes' rejection of a child his subjects and the audience never doubt his raises the same questions about the ideology of illegitimacy we examined in Chapter 4, though we view them here from more than one vantage point. Leontes accuses his wife—indeed, all women—of infidelity and pursues the point against all reasonable objections; he insists on his being a cuckold and develops a murderous attitude. Although Leontes is not treated as an outcast after his rejection of Hermione and never becomes the vagabond we consider Posthumus to be, he does become a sort of eremite, living a "saint-like" existence not at all typical of, nor appropriate for, a king. In addition to these qualities of the bastardized man with which we are familiar, Leontes reveals a dimension we have not seen before in his refusal to acknowledge Perdita his. If the clearest sign of the bastard in Shakespeare is the son's rejection of his father, surely in life it is the father's rejection of the son. Both actions are intimately related and equally indicative of the bastard's frame of mind, for in these plays the man who suspects his mother is the man who accuses his wife.

Thus, Leontes' reversal, his gradual change, his acceptance of Perdita as his own child, is the token for which Hermione must wait. To reestablish his connection with his child is to accept his own legitimacy and the appropriate ideology. If Perdita is his, then Hermione is faithful and perhaps as well the "thousands" of accused women on this "bawdy planet." If Perdita is his, then Leontes stands in as clear a relation to his ancestors as he does to his descendants, to Perdita's children, and her children's children. Hermione's welcoming Perdita and speaking only to her is really to do all that is necessary to cement the family in the healthful bonds associated with legitimacy: "for thou shalt hear that I, / Knowing by Paulina that the oracle / Gave hope thou wast in being, have preserv'd / Myself to see the issue." Perdita is "the issue," that is, not only the answer to the sixteen years' riddle posed by the oracle, or even the outcome, the finish, to the lengthy controversy, but she is "the issue," the child who represents Hermione's marriage to Leontes and Leontes' acceptance of his relation to Hermione as husband to wife, man to woman.[54]

Orlando's security, his refusal to lose faith either in his relationship with his father or in the woman he loves, is paralleled in many plays by Shakespeare's contemporaries but in relatively few comedies by Shakespeare himself. Only Orlando, Pericles, and less central characters, Lorenzo, Sebastian, Florizel, and Ferdinand are loyal in every sense of the word, never bending "with the remover to remove" (Son. 116.4). Orlando's antithesis, as I have suggested, is the more familiar though certainly less congenial Posthumus Leonatus. In our descent from Orlando's joviality to the anger, melancholy, and guilt of Posthumus, we see that as the "mistakes" and misapprehensions of the male become more serious, the reunion between man and woman becomes more dependent on his transforming rather than simply excusing himself with an apology. The more fully the hero approximates the position and attitudes of a bastard, the more complex the interrelationship between him and the woman becomes and the more clearly that reunion depends on the man's changing in the way the Friar in *Much Ado about Nothing* hopes. By the same token, as the man's problems with self and woman become more severe and complex, the more convoluted and, in a sense, mysterious, become the machinations and efforts of the woman. The ways in which the separated Posthumus and Imogen interact in *Cymbeline* provide us with the clearest picture of the reunion between lovers whose relationships remind us of those in tragedy.

When Pisanio confesses to Imogen that Posthumus bade him kill her, Imogen's first thought, ironically, is that "Some jay of Italy / . . . hath betray'd him" (III.iv.49-50). Posthumus, like Claudio, has regressed from lover to misogynist and has become an even more dreadful Hippolytan type than his earlier Shakespearean counterpart. Imogen, guessing herself betrayed, reacts in two ways that distinguish the women from the men in these plays. In the first place, instead of wishing Posthumus dead, Imogen tells Pisanio, "Why, I must die" (74). Secondly, she generalizes about men, but instead of advocating misanthropy, Imogen seems saddened by her notion that Posthumus will "lay the leaven on all proper men; / Goodly and gallant shall be false and perjur'd / From thy great fail" (62-64). Though she is hurt, Imogen is not blinded by her feelings into assuming that there are no "Goodly and gallant" men or that the earth has become a version of Leontes' "bawdy planet." Nor has she lost either her own feeling for her husband or a sense that he has affection for her. She knows that it was "no act of common passage, but / A strain of rareness" (91-92) in herself that allowed her to choose Posthumus over "princely fellows" (90) and to incur her father's displeasure, and she is certain that when Posthumus will "be disedg'd by her" (93) he follows, his "memory / Will then be pang'd by me" (94-95), a thought entirely consonant with Friar Francis's notions about how lost love affects the bereaved.

Imogen is fairly quick to accept the scheme proposed by Pisanio, that she leave the court, pretend she is dead, and disguise herself as a man, all so that she might, Pisanio suggests, "tread a course" "near / The residence of Posthumus" (146-48). One can sense throughout this scene (III.iv) her readiness to do whatever is called for in order to be near her husband. As Pisanio talks, Imogen feels "almost / A man already" (166-67). Like the Duchess of Malfi, who responds to her brother's threats by comparing herself to a man, "as men in some great battles, / By apprehending danger, have achieved / Almost impossible actions . . . / So I,"[55] Imogen feels the change complete even before the disguise is put on: "This attempt / I am soldier to, and will abide it with / A prince's courage. Away, I prithee" (182-84). Her disguising is neither the game that Rosalind seems to play nor the intelligent move Portia makes but rather a more fully developed version of Julia's disguise and flight in *The Two Gentlemen of Verona*, a desperate attempt to be near an estranged man. Her willingness to disguise herself, to be "dead" to and for her husband, necessitates that Alcestian sacrifice that here approaches the literal death of both personas, "Fidele" and Imogen.

To see Imogen as a version of Alcestis, however, is perhaps to read more into the play than is immediately apparent, for we are nowhere invited to see her journeying as a comment on Posthumus's change, and certainly not as a necessary part of his evolution into a healthy man and a fit partner. The obviously puzzling aspect of the separate behaviors of Imogen and Posthumus is their never making physical contact during their long separation, at least not until the recognition scene, V.v. And yet if they never do make contact, how are we to understand in which ways their individual undertakings and trials affect one another, if at all? After all, the relationship between Posthumus and "Fidele" is difficult to understand in a way that those between Orlando and "Ganymede," Orsino and "Cesario," even Bassanio and "Balthazar," simply are not, for these lovers at least speak to one another while they are separated and the woman disguised. What we can see and appreciate is Imogen's attachment to Posthumus, the suffering brought about by his attempt on her life, and the great loss she experiences when she thinks him dead. What we do not see very clearly, and what has left some critics wagging their heads, is how it happens that Posthumus is a changed man at V.i.1, and what, if any, role Imogen has had in his radical transformation from misogynist to contrite husband.

In the interim between his vow at the end of act 2, to write against women, to "Detest them, curse them," and his entrance in act 5, wishing to "die / For thee, O Imogen, even for whom my life / Is, every breath, a death" (i.25-27), he has received a bloody cloth from Pisanio indicating that Imogen is dead. What we are asked to believe is that the knowledge of his having caused Imogen's death has made him remorseful in the extreme and that his repentance flourishes—and this is the crucial point—in spite of his still believing that Imogen has been unfaithful to him: "You married ones, / If each of you should take this course, how many / Must murther wives much better than themselves / For wrying but a little! (2-5). Posthumus, who repents of his crime, seems disposed now to see infidelity as a minor infraction rather than as a sign that his mother and all women are whores. More precisely, Posthumus still believes, with Emilia in *Othello*, that this is a world where some women will be unfaithful, but he now believes them to have "little faults" (12) rather than "All faults that name, nay, that hell knows." This change in Posthumus is not quite the same as his simply coming to believe Imogen innocent, but it is, to quote the Friar yet again, a "greater birth" than any other male transformation in Shake-speare, including Leontes', which comes about only *after* he hears the oracle proclaim Hermione's innocence. Posthumus here starts to sound a little like Imogen, and like the other heroines, especially Portia, who also invokes heavenly mercy as a model for humans to follow.

Critics, however, have not taken easily to Posthumus's change. James Nosworthy writes, "The hero's remorse of conscience is unconvincing. Since he still believes in Imogen's guilt, his attitude towards her should remain unchanged, however much he may repent of the supposed murder. To term her alleged offence 'wrying but a little' seems contrary to the moral code of the play, though, as Professor Ellis-Fermor points out, it is not necessarily inconsistent with the feelings of a human being illuminated by grief and seeing with new eyes."[56] Kenneth Muir, too, raises an eyebrow: "He has forgiven Imogen while he still believes her guilty of what he describes as 'a little fault.' This conversion, extraordinary by Elizabethan standards, should go far to reinstate Posthumus in the eyes of a modern audience"; Muir notes, in addition, "the husband who kills his wife by kindness would never envisage the possibility that he was worse than her."[57]

However much Posthumus's speech may seem anachronistic in terms of Elizabethan attitudes and that stage's stock wounded husbands, most readers, I think, would agree with Ellis-Fermor that his change is certainly logical in terms of human nature, as Muir seems to suggest in speaking of Posthumus's appeal to "a modern audience." In addition to its fidelity to life, Posthumus's "conversion" has been prepared for imaginatively if not literally, in Imogen's obsequies over the headless body of Posthumus's bastardly counterpart, Cloten, as I suggested earlier. In any event, Post-humus's speech at the beginning of act 5 is only partly a description of his feelings about the effects of infidelity on marriage. What he also does is discuss his attitude toward himself, and shape and justify his course for the future. In part to atone for his great sin, he will defend Imogen's kingdom:

> I'll disrobe me
> Of these Italian weeds and suit myself
> As does a Briton peasant; so I'll fight
> Against the part I come with; so I'll die
> For thee, O Imogen, even for whom my life
> Is every breath a death; and thus, unknown,
> Pitied nor hated, to the face of peril
> Myself I'll dedicate. Let me make men know
> More valor in me than my habits show.
> Gods, put the strength o' th' Leonati in me!

To shame the guise o' th' world, I will begin,
The fashion: less without and more within. [22-33]

Posthumus's transformation is an ongoing process rather than a finished business; he has, in fact, only started to change when act 5 begins. Feeling remorse, he can no longer take the Italian side and will fight for the British dressed as a "peasant." In such an outfit, he will be "unknown" to either side and will make his presence known only through his actions, through "the strength o' th' Leonati," rather than through fashion.

Curiously, we see in Posthumus's posing as a peasant signs both of a further descent into bastardy—poverty and anonymity—and yet, at the same time, a newfound healthiness, a regeneration of self-respect, and the development of attitudes that, in Shakespeare as in romance in general, are always to be associated with the heroic. This puzzling contradiction is resolved when we remember the fine but crucial line between the bastard or the "ideologically illegitimate"[58] on the one hand and the suffering hero on the other. Although both types, Don John and Orlando, for example, are separated from women, their fathers, and their patrimony—and thus are outsiders, disenfranchised and unknown—their habits of mind are radically different. The hero does not think all women whores, is certain of his connection to father and family name, and is unknown only to the extent that he feels he has not yet lived up to the high standards established by the patriarchy of which he is the latest member. Thus, while the one thinks the world a corrupt place and its inhabitants diseased, and is often limited by these assumptions, the other thinks life good, full of possibilities from which he is barred solely by circumstances. Therefore, any change of fortune, such as Pericles' finding his father's armor, is apprehended by the healthier man as an opportunity to show the world what he is really made of and what he has felt destined to become all along. And such a change, from ideological bastard to hero, is exactly what Posthumus undergoes; it is a transformation that, in a sense, most of the heroes of Shakespearean comedy must undergo. His mind is no longer tainted with regard to women, and he begins to develop the sort of self-confidence that makes similar characters immune to the misogynistic suggestions and plots of others. With a renewed remembrance of Imogen, and with a renewed understanding of his relationship to the "Leonati," Posthumus is now capable of heroic action and, more importantly, of developing even closer ties to wife and to family.

The point is made graphically seconds later, in scene 2, when Posthumus "vanquisheth and disarmeth Jachimo" (S.D.), who explains his defeat at the hands of "this carl" (4) by telling us that his having "belied a lady" "Takes off my manhood" (2). He then compares Posthumus's clothing to his own in a way that reinforces not only the links between Posthumus and Cloten but especially the point about inner and outer fashion Posthumus made:

> Knighthoods and honors, borne
> As I wear mine, are titles but of scorn.
> If that thy gentry, Britain, go before
> This lout as he exceeds our lords, the odds
> Is that we scarce are men and you are gods. [6-10]

This, from the man who earlier had called him a "beggar" (I.iv.23) and rated him appropriately: "This matter of marrying his king's daughter, wherein he must be weigh'd rather by her value than his own, words him, I doubt not, a great deal from the matter" (14-17).

It is Posthumus's very success on the battlefield that compels him shortly afterward to tell British soldiers that he is a Roman, for he would not advance in anyone's eyes and longs only to end his life "by some means for Imogen" (V.iii.83). For him, incarceration is "Most welcome" (iv.3) bondage, though we see it as the prelude to his subsequent rising. Thus, ironically, without his being aware of it, his jailing is another sign of his having "The fashion: less without and more within." He begs the gods,

> For Imogen's dear life take mine, and though
> 'Tis not so dear, yet 'tis a life; you coin'd it:
> 'Tween man and man they weigh not every stamp;
> Though light, take pieces for the figure's sake;
> You rather, mine being yours; and so, great pow'rs,
> If you will take this audit, take this life,
> And cancel these cold bonds. O Imogen,
> I'll speak to thee in silence. [22-29]

It is not his contrition and humility alone that convince us that Posthumus continues to change and that his change is a true metamorphosis. His soliloquy at V.ii is in many respects a direct response to his earlier soliloquy at II.v.1, when he had declared, "We are all bastards." Then, in his wrath at discovering what he thought was Imogen's great infidelity, he had claimed that his father

>   was I know not where
> When I was stamp'd. Some coiner with his tools
> Made me a counterfeit; yet my mother seem'd

The Dian of that time. So doth my wife
The nonpareil of this. O vengeance, vengeance! [4-8]

Here, the only vengeance he seeks is against himself. But more importantly, the life he offers for Imogen's in act 5 came not from "some coiner"
but is seen as the gods', "you coin'd it." It is their "stamp" he carries and not
that of an unknown father. The counting house imagery remains the same,
but the import is exactly opposite; Posthumus recognizes heavenly antecedents, and this recognition comes just as he falls asleep, dreams of his
parents, and the king of the gods descends to intervene in his affairs. If
"the total effect of *Cymbeline* depends absolutely upon a sympathetic
understanding of Posthumus' contrition and an emotional involvement in
his forgiveness," [59] his turning against himself here in the precise language
he had used earlier to castigate Imogen makes it easier for us to appreciate
that process.

Wilson Knight's fine analysis of the links between "The Vision of Jupiter"
and the established Shakespeare canon has done much to lay to rest the
debate over the authenticity of Posthumus's dream. The dream is thoroughly Shakespearean, not only in the linguistic ways in which Knight's
"study of the harmonies, minute and massive, of Shakespeare's world"
describes it but especially in terms of the development of the hero in
Shakespearean comedy. [60] These plays begin with the separation of a young
man from his father, describe the descent of that boy into a sort of bastardy,
and from *The Comedy of Errors* on, emphasize the incorporation of family
rather than its dissolution. From the start, the power of Shakespeare's
imagination has resided in his ability to see the problems between hero
and heroine in terms of the hero's wider family unit, and to suggest that his
relation to his parents determines his relation to his spouse. Those men
who are surest of their lineage and feel closest to their fathers are least
susceptible to loss of faith in women. It is entirely appropriate—indeed,
necessary—that Posthumus gain a relationship with his family before he
reestablish one with Imogen, and that in this play, which has insisted from
the start on the relation between Posthumus's birth and his marriage to
Imogen, the connection be developed through a "striking transcendental
moment." [61] The dream is not the climax of Posthumus's development, but
it is the one step without which all his other notable achievements would
seem meaningless.

The centrality of the dream is brought home to us, first of all, when we
observe that it has come about as a result of Posthumus's calling on his wife,
"O Imogen, / I'll speak to thee in silence," lying down on the prison floor,
and falling asleep. Though the logic of the sequence—Posthumus's wish-

ing to speak with Imogen, followed by his dreaming of his parents and of Jupiter—is at first clear only intuitively, it soon makes great sense. His separation from Imogen has been understood all along as the product of his wanting to believe the worst of her and of all women, and of his being treated as an illegitimate. It makes perfect sense that in order to "speak" with her, Posthumus first must speak with his parents and establish his own legitimacy and a bond between him and them that the unfortunate facts of his birth denied him. Importantly, from the start of the dream Posthumus's father, Sicilius Leonatus, and his mother stress his ancestry and the conditions of his birth. For them, his lineage and his innate nobility of spirit should have been rewarded, not mocked, and his father brags, "Great nature, like his ancestry, / Moulded the stuff so fair, / That he deserv'd the praise o' th' world, / As great Sicilius' heir" (48-51). Their interpretation of the recent events in their son's life is certainly more charitable than most critics' and simply places blame both on Jupiter for not acting the part of a surrogate father and, more interestingly, on Jachimo, "Slight thing of Italy" (64), whom Jupiter allowed "To taint his nobler heart and brain / With needless jealousy" (65-66). To them—and this is perhaps understandable insofar as they are his parents—Posthumus was the innocent victim of Jachimo's cunning and Jupiter's apathy. That combination caused him to be thrown "From Leonati seat, and cast / From her his dearest one, / Sweet Imogen" (60-62). Their refrain, which suggests in various ways that their son is good, removes all responsibility for his misfortunes from Posthumus and surely is at odds with what we have seen in the preceding four acts. But their insisting on two events, Posthumus's separation from the Leonati and his subsequent separation from Imogen, focuses attention on the central events in his life, and while they do not explicitly suggest that his loss of family has led to his loss of Imogen—after all, they see Posthumus as entirely innocent—what we hear over and again is that the facts of his birth and the loss of his family, physically and psychologically, are of crucial importance in understanding the sort of man, and husband, he has become.

If Imogen's elegiac tone at the funeral of "Posthumus" in act 4 indicates both his similarity to Cloten and, at the same time, the death of the bastard in him, Jupiter's descent to the level of mere mortals at his parents' insistence and on his behalf indicates the birth of that healthier Posthumus only possible as the product of a sure sense of self that—in these plays—comes from a man's identification with father and family. Jupiter's message, "Whom best I love, I cross" (101), seems "rather a simple-minded one"[62] and hardly adequate as an explanation of Posthumus's decline. Then again, Jupiter makes no attempt to explain the precise ways in which he has tried Posthumus and emphasizes instead the young man's rebirth.

This theophany, which ought to have for us all the authority of the oracle in *The Winter's Tale*, is an explicit announcement that "He shall be lord of Lady Imogen" (107) and functions, whether we like it or not—and many have not—as an imprimatur, Jupiter's intercession being yet another sign that Posthumus's repentance is to be taken at full value. "But there is not the slightest reason to take the epiphany as the summation of the play," Robert Grams Hunter argues. "The version of reality given us in *Cymbeline*, as always in Shakespeare, is highly complex. Like Jaques' melancholy, it is compounded of many simples and one of the simplest of these is the truth contained in the theophany. That truth—even though all's not quite right with the world, God *is* in his heaven, and we suffer for our own good—is, in terms of the play, perfectly valid but only partial."63 Posthumus's rebirth is not a *fait accompli* when he enters in act 5 mourning Imogen's death and forgiving her "wrying," but rather an ongoing process, advanced incrementally when he dreams and hears Jupiter.

Though many have remarked on the apparent lack of zip in Jupiter's revelation (Granville-Barker described Posthumus's entire dream as "supererogatory" and "a pointless pageant that he sleeps through"64, few have denied the fullness of Posthumus's transformation and the passionate way in which the dream affects him. The seeds of his rebirth are sown in *The Comedy of Errors*, when Antipholus of Syracuse compares himself, albeit clumsily, to

> a drop of water,
> That in the ocean seeks another drop,
> Who, falling there to find his fellow forth
> (Unseen, inquisitive), confounds himself.
> So I, to find a mother and a brother,
> In quest of them (unhappy), ah, lose myself, [I.ii.35-40]

and in that play's careful relating of Antipholus's love for Luciana to his separation from his own family. Though the characterizations are less full, the structural imperatives are the same. Antipholus's lament, which leads to the joys of act 5 ("After so long grief, such nativity!" [V.i.407]), prefigures the ascent of Posthumus from the depths of despair in the British prison: "Sleep, thou hast been a grandsire and begot / A father to me, and thou hast created / A mother and two brothers" (V.iv.123-25). What tends to become lost in the critical debate over authorship, characterization, or the quality of the poetry in Posthumus's dream is the startling fact that the dream has been written at all. The imagination and understanding that see that associations with father and family are crucial to one's conception of self, hence to one's life with others, are not the less wonderful for their being typically Shakespearean. Nosworthy is surely correct in noting that "it is, perhaps, the necessity of the Vision which, when all else has been said, argues most powerfully for its authenticity," but not, I believe, for the reason he adduces, that "the resolution of discords" can only be brought about as "the result of supernatural intervention."[65] The resolution, the happy ending in this play, is not effected by Jupiter, who simply announces what will happen and approves of what has, any more than the oracle and not a reborn and contrite Leontes is responsible in *The Winter's Tale*. The resolution is affecting precisely because it is psychologically compelling and not because a *deus ex machina* has told us it ought to be.

Thus, the Posthumus who enters in the final scene, though appropriately despairing of his "murder" of Imogen, bitter at Jachimo, and saddened by Imogen's supposed fall, is nonetheless ready for and deserving of a reunion with his wife. From being bastardly, an ideological twin of Cloten, he has become an Orlando or Pericles, destitute only outwardly, not "within," stronger for forgiving Imogen and for speaking with her throughout his ordeal, renewed through his miraculous discovery of father and family, and blessed by Jupiter himself.

The course that leads Posthumus into Imogen's presence in act 5, penitent and sorrowful, in a word, humanized, has been predicated upon his and Imogen's changing places. In act 1 it is Imogen who is locked in her room, and although she is spirited in the defense of Posthumus's reputation, Imogen is associated throughout the first two acts with bondage, as Knight points out, and is patient and passive in a way we can almost feel. Her frustration at being forced to stay at court while Posthumus is away and the pressure applied to her by the Queen and Cloten make us feel her immobility, and that tension is suggested graphically in her chiding Pisanio for not watching Posthumus's ship sail longer than he did:

> I would have broke mine eye-strings, crack'd them, but
> To look upon him, till the diminution
> Of space had pointed him sharp as my needle;
> Nay, followed him till he had melted from
> The smallness of a gnat to air, and then
> Have turn'd mine eye and wept. [I.iii.17-22]

Her description of the breaking of her "eye-strings" lets us see how completely Imogen is anchored and how she will suffer imprisonment and yet retain faith. Her turning Posthumus into a point "sharp as my needle" amplifies the first image, with its insistence on her immobility, by suggesting the stereotypical association among women, art, and domestic occupations. Both images, in turn, are summarized in her telling Pisanio, in a metaphor which, once again, suggests a female stereotype, that her father interrupted her farewell to Posthumus before she could "have charg'd him, / At the sixt hour of morn, at noon, at midnight, / T' encounter me with orisons, for then / I am in heaven for him" (30-33). Nosworthy rejects what he calls the "obvious interpretation" of these lines, that "Imogen sees herself as a goddess whom Posthumus is to worship at certain hours," and suggests instead that Imogen wants Posthumus to join her in prayer at those times "because I shall then be praying for him."[66] It seems to me, however, that both interpretations miss the mark, for she never suggests that she is a goddess, and yet she explicitly says that at certain hours she is "in heaven for him." But Shakespeare has had at least one previous heroine "in heaven" and yet not a goddess, Rosalind, whom Hymen introduces to her father by telling him, "Good Duke, receive thy daughter, / Hymen from heaven brought her, / Yea, brought her hither" (V.iv.111-13). I see no reason not to take Hymen's remarks literally and have no problem understanding Imogen's as metaphorical. Separated from her husband, Imogen feels like a guiding spirit, a heavenly presence. She is, in fact, not only describing herself as the stereotypically patient and prayerful woman (Isabella, in *Measure for Measure,* is thought of as "a thing enskied, and sainted" [I.iv.34]), the forlorn lover whose only activities are needlework and chanting orisons, but is also that quasi-mysterious force with whom Posthumus communes in prison, the inspirational force the Friar in *Much Ado about Nothing* had hoped Claudio would create out of his memory of the "dead" Hero.

But while Imogen remains an icon to Posthumus, she becomes an active figure to the audience. If Carolyn Heilbrun is correct and "the conventional female dream, still preserved in romances," is that "a woman's destiny consists in her rescue by a 'prince'"[67] we must see *Cymbeline,* and other of Shakespeare's comedies, as unconventional, for in them it is the princess who saves the man. Imogen's patience lasts only as long as her relationship seems secure; once she feels Posthumus "at some hard point" (III.iv.16) she becomes "Fidele" and leaves home to be near him in fact as well as in prayer. And it is at this point that Posthumus "seems to have gone completely limp";[68] in an ironic reversal of roles with Imogen, he loses his freedom of movement, prays frequently, and works matters so that it is he who is incarcerated. The Posthumus we see in act 5 is a man as passive as Leontes and as absolute for death as Antonio. He asks the gods, "make me blest to obey" (i.17), engineers a "Most welcome" bondage, and is, in fact, "merrier to die" (iv.171) than his keeper to live, a man on the verge of moving from Leontes' "saint-like sorrow" to a real martyrdom.

7

"The Marriage of True Minds"

Shakespearean comedy ends not with hero and heroine communing with one another during their separation but rather with their face-to-face confrontation in the fifth act. That final meeting is a confirmation and ratification of encounters, physical and spiritual, we witness earlier in the play, and establishes a new relationship between lovers, one that has evolved from their earlier acquaintance into something different and often unexpected. But whether the new relationship merely affirms old stereotypes, demanding that women be silent and consigning them to an inferior social position, or describes a more equal and humane bond between husband and wife has been debated vigorously by commentators with an interest in gender relations in Shakespeare.

Juliet Dusinberre, grounding her argument on what she sees as the liberating effects of Puritanism on Elizabethan attitudes toward women and the family, thinks the period "bred the conditions of a feminist movement" and that Shakespeare, in particular, had a "fascination with women."[1] Lisa Jardine, using similar historical documents, reaches an opposite conclusion in *Still Harping on Daughters*. For Jardine, "the Reformation actually removed some of the traditional possibilities for women's independent thought and action."[2] Queen Elizabeth's brilliant achievements, Jardine argues, indicate little more than an exception to the rule: "I believe that Elizabeth I failed to make other than the impact of a 'token' woman on the patriarchal attitudes of the early modern period."[3] Jardine's readings of individual plays, consequently, are far less sanguine than Dusinberre's. In contrast, Marianne Novy, who reads the comedies as conflicts between mutuality and patriarchy in *Love's Argument*, thinks that "women's gestures of submission are often balanced by similar gestures from the men" and therefore that "none of these arguments [that Shakespeare's comedies end with a return to patriarchally ordered structures] seems "strong enough to overshadow the emphasis on mutuality."[4] Carol Thomas Neely reaches a different conclusion, one closer to Jardine's, though less absolute. For Neely, in spite of the power broken nuptials give women "to resist, control, or alter the movement of courtship," the fact remains that "with the celebration of completed nuptials at the end of the comedies, male control is reestablished, and women take their subordinate places in the dance."5

The debate is not likely to bring about consensus soon, in part because of the difficulty of ascertaining precisely how open an era the late sixteenth century had become with regard to the social position, education, and rights of women. Nonetheless, it seems to me that because Shakespearean comedy depends so entirely on the heroine to teach and transform the male—and therefore to engineer the marriage that signals the happy ending—it is impossible simply to assert that the patriarchy is reaffirmed and women are put back in their place. It is important to recognize that a number of special attitudes and plot elements characterize the meeting between hero and heroine in the last act, and that these militate against our seeing act 5 simply as a reproduction of the domestic and social situations of act 1.

In the first place, there is ordinarily a sense of strangeness that touches the characters who witness the encounter, though it is most often the man who finds himself "amazed" at discovering a woman he had thought lost and who feels their reunion "wonderful." Conversely, it is the woman who is thought to inspire these feelings and who seems, for the most part, an omniscient and surprisingly calm presence at the center of an awe-struck gathering. Second, the lovers' meeting is often considered a second chance, especially for the man, who is usually regarded by himself and others as coming to his senses or achieving adulthood and mental health by agreeing to marry. His final acceptance of the woman not only is seen as a second chance to behave morally and healthfully but is occasionally dramatized quite explicitly as a second marriage, where rings and tokens are exchanged once again and vows reaffirmed. It is this correspondence between a man's errors of judgment or passion and his final reconciliation with a woman that Neely examines so fully. She reminds us that "throughout these plays broken nuptials counterpoint the festive ceremonies, revealing male and female antagonisms and anxieties that impede the movement toward marriage."6 Often the happiness we feel at the end of a comedy has a great deal to do with the knowledge that we have lived for two hours in a world where second chances are indeed possible and where errors are not lasting.

Third, the encounter between man and woman certainly signifies a return to a version of social and political normalcy, that is, to something like the accepted Elizabethan conventions regarding marriage and governance. The reversal of sex roles and attitudes early in the play, when the women dress as men and become active forces and when the men cultivate patience, adopting attitudes more like those traditionally associated with women (the reversal that has, in fact, accounted for the reunion in act 5), is reversed yet again as the play ends. Men become men, and women women, in traditional and easily recognizable ways, most obviously observed in their changes of clothing, the women to sex-appropriate dress, and the men to clothes befitting their social rank. But the new status quo of the fifth act—and it is here that I differ from Neely and tend to agree with Novy—is significantly different from the status quo of the first act, and I am not referring primarily to the changes in governance described by Northrop Frye.[7] Far more important, it seems to me, are the new ways in which hero and heroine apprehend one another as a result of all that they have undergone in the previous four acts. In spite of the hero's becoming the titular "head of the household" and the woman's concomitant reduction in stature, the fact of the matter is that Shakespearean comedy ends with women retaining a sense of the mysterious, and not simply because they seem to have defied the laws of nature by appearing to have been in two places at the same time. More compelling is the fact that when the play ends only the women (and the odd friar) know precisely what has, in fact, gone on; though the women usually promise to explain how they have been lawyers and nuns, boys and girls, virgins and wives, in heaven and on earth, the curtain often drops before their lovers learn what's what, and sometimes before we do. In other words, the intelligence and verve the women have exhibited—which neither we nor the men easily forget— combines with their knowing all the answers (it is the women to whom all the other characters look for explanations in the last act) to produce an Elizabethan status quo of a very special sort. The men often exit in fact holding the purse strings and the women the apron strings, but audiences sense that questions relating to domestic authority are by no means as uncomplicated. The imbalanced relationships of act 1, formed between insecure yet authoritarian males and secure but deferential females, have been transformed into marriages between people who perceive each other as far more equal. Indeed, for the audience more often than not these plays seem to end with women ascendant. The men may control in stereotypical ways—ways that I by no means think of as inconsequential, as we shall see—but it is the values of the women that have been affirmed, and it is the rationality, strength, and loyalty of women that the play glorifies.

These three characteristics of the ending of Shakespearean comedy are as apparent in the early plays as in the later. Though the last act of *The Comedy of Errors* focuses on a family reunion rather than on a reunion between men and women specifically, we still feel how struck all the characters are with the wonder of their finding people they loved and lost. Egeon has found a wife "If I dream not" (V.i.347), and Antipholus of Syracuse will marry Luciana "If this be not a dream I see and hear" (377).

Such good fortune is for the Duke a "morning story" (357) and for the Abbess a "nativity" (407). Part of the new "story" will be old Egeon's assumption of the traditionally masculine role and Aemilia's of the feminine. Although the Abbess is a dominant figure at the end of the play and Egeon, as I have suggested earlier, one of Shakespeare's prototypically passive men (at least when separated from his wife), it is clear that sex roles are about to be reversed a second time. The Abbess is giving up the sisterhood and the authority her career permitted for a revived marriage: "Whoever bound him, I will loose his bonds, / And gain a husband by his liberty" (340-41). I am tempted to make too much of these lines, for they imply rather succinctly how the husband's becoming active as the play closes is directly related to the wife's becoming more passive—it is she who unties him and thereby becomes a wife once again. Aemilia and Egeon's reversal of roles is echoed in Antipholus of Syracuse's marriage offer to Luciana, a woman who had frightened him and whom he had shunned two acts earlier for the security of the abbey. Then she had seemed omniscient and powerful and he frightened and passive. In the last scene, however, he emerges from the abbey to woo Luciana once again, and at the same time that his father is released from his bondage to greet Aemilia as his wife. Thus, in general terms, the social norms have been reachieved: men who have been bound in ways that remind us of the physical, legal, and psychological constraints against women are once again free.

The unions of the fifth act, however, are not mere mirror images of what they once were, and this is clear, for example, in Antipholus's no longer believing the women of Ephesus to be witches, and in Adriana's agreeing to be a patient wife. But there is an equally important sense in which sexual relationships in act 5 are different from those we see and hear about earlier in the play. In the first place, in spite of the fact that in *The Comedy of Errors* the problems are caused by simple mistakes and can easily be explained away, Shakespeare begins here what will be a hallmark of his handling of recognition scenes, and that is the deferral of information vital to the characters' understanding of "miraculous" events until after the play ends:

> *Abb.* Renowned Duke, vouchsafe to take the pains
> To go with us into the abbey here,
> And hear at large discoursed all our fortunes;
> And all that are assembled in this place
> That by this sympathized one day's error
> Have suffer'd wrong, go keep us company,
> And we shall make full satisfaction. [394-400]

Here the explanations are postponed partly because the audience has been in on the joke from the start, and recapitulation would bore. But such withholding of information—a kind of "disclosure without closure," to appropriate one of Catherine Belsey's terms[8]—is a characteristic feature of the ending of Shakespearean comedy, as we shall see, whether the audience has known or not and regardless of the audience's doubts about there being any explanation at all for the wonders we have been asked to accept. What we notice in *The Comedy of Errors* as well, is that the information that can explain the confusion and contradictions of the preceding four acts is in the hands of a woman, and one associated with religion. The woman's having the information and her religious aura become in the later plays strong suggestions that she is at the center of the apparently mysterious events and is more powerful, more in tune with heaven's plan, than is the man. However traditional we suppose the renewed relationship between Egeon and Aemilia, the fact remains that it is the woman who is looked to for explanation and "full satisfaction."

The sense of wonder and of a new beginning that is paralleled by a return to accepted social norms is obvious at the end of *The Two Gentlemen of Verona* as well. Though the play ends with Valentine's offering to explain to the Duke why the page (Julia) has "more grace than boy" (V.iv.166), the mystery of identity has to do only with the woman. When the disguised Julia faints and is revived by Valentine and Proteus, she gives her errant boyfriend two rings, one of which Proteus recognizes as "the ring I gave to Julia" (93). Julia is the first in a long line of Shakespearean heroines to complicate already complicated situations by speaking in oracular tones rather than by explaining in a straightforward manner:

> *Pro.* But how cam'st thou by this ring? At my depart
> I gave this unto Julia.
>   *Jul.* And Julia herself did give it me,
> And Julia herself hath brought it hither. [96-99]

Though she soon identifies herself, her riddling answer helps to create an aura of the supernatural about her, for it suggests that she is two people and capable of being in two places at one time. Perhaps it is this hint of mystery that accounts for the prompt turnabout in Proteus's affections as much as it is his sense of her fidelity and love. In any case, he vows to love her as loyally as she loves him, "Bear witness, heaven, I have my wish for ever" (119), an oath that implies, in "for ever," his acceptance of a second chance to act in his own best interests. Though the play has shown us two transformations, a woman's "shape" and a man's "mind" (109), it is Julia's metamorphosis that prompts Valentine to predict, in the play's last speech, that when the Duke hears the story, he "will wonder what hath fortuned" (169).

The Taming of the Shrew, which ends with a woman's change of attitude and behavior and not a man's, confirms the stereotypes rather than reverses them. Instead of allowing the man to transform himself in response to the woman's efforts to teach him about marriage and female sexuality, *The Taming of the Shrew* begins by caricaturing women in order to confirm male suspicions, to evoke male authoritarianism, and to enjoy with a vengeance a communal reestablishment of the social and sexual status quo. When the play begins, the stage is peopled with passive men and one woman whose actions call into question stereotypical modes of behavior. Kate physically abuses the men and is thought to have a "most impatient devilish spirit" (II.i.151); she is the opposite of the Kate Petruchio sarcastically describes to Baptista in proposing marriage to his daughter, a woman of "affability," "bashful modesty," "and mild behavior" (II.i.49, 50). However, this version of the well-behaved Elizabethan female is precisely the Kate Petruchio finally does create. By the end of the fourth act he has effected a complete reversal of the attitudes we see in acts 1 and 2; Kate is patient and obedient, and Petruchio her sovereign. When Kate obeys Petruchio by coming to him when he calls, Lucentio comments, "Here is a wonder, if you talk of a wonder" (V.ii.106). Their agreement as husband and wife is sealed by their leaving for a second wedding night, "Come, Kate, we'll to bed" (184), and by the play's last line, Lucentio's observation to Hortensio as they are left alone on stage, "'Tis a wonder, by your leave, she will be tam'd so" (189). *The Taming of the Shrew* ends with "wonder," but wonder of a different sort from that which the characters and audience feel at the end of *The Comedy of Errors* and *The Two Gentlemen of Verona*. Here there is a tongue-in-cheek attitude that makes fun of male dominance even as it reasserts it. How wonderful it would be, the four men seem to be saying, if women could be tamed as easily as Petruchio has tamed the notorious Kate. Shakespeare's ending the play with the carefully calculated male victory is not, however, an option he chose to exercise very often in his career. Although the fifth act of a Shakespearean comedy ordinarily reasserts male authority and social norms, it does so only after we have seen the happy ending effected by a general surrender to values represented by women.

In the early plays the Shakespearean denouement is clearest in *A Midsummer-Night's Dream*, where the lovers are baffled by the strange way in which their emotional problems have been sorted out. When asked by Theseus to explain their "gentle concord" (IV.i.143), Lysander can only "reply amazedly" (146), and even old Egeus can only "wonder of their being here together" (131). The odd sensations, as in *The Comedy of Errors*, seem dreamlike, and Hippolyta sums up by concluding that their stories are "strange and admirable" (V.i.27). Though the women in this play do not adopt disguises, the wonder of the ending is still, fundamentally, a matter of the man's settling on the appropriate vision of the woman. In other plays the woman has a more direct hand in manipulating what the man sees of her; Julia decides to disguise herself as a man and, in a sense, Aemilia chooses to become an abbess. While their disguises are direct responses to separation from men, these women, Julia and Aemilia, like Portia, Rosalind, and others, possess two personas they can address, even adjust, at will. In *A Midsummer-Night's Dream* the women are also seen in contradictory ways, but the opposing views are presented solely as the product of the way in which men apprehend and imagine. When the man finally agrees to marry the woman who has loved him all along, the lovers' harmonious story is perceived as "strange" (V.i.1). For the women it is strange that the men have come to their senses, but what amazes the men is the difference in their before and after perceptions of the women.

Like Luciana in *The Comedy of Errors*, Hermia and Helena have done nothing to gain or lose the affection of their boyfriends. Because the audience knows that it is the fairy world that has manipulated emotions, explanations are neither necessary nor, indeed, possible, unless Puck or Oberon were to make himself visible (as Hymen does at the end of *As You Like It*) and reveal flashes of a higher power. But that ignorance does not inhibit the men from feeling amazed at how their images of the women have changed. It is Demetrius's perceptions, in particular, that this play examines:

> my love to Hermia
> (Melted as the snow) seems to me now
> As the remembrance of an idle gaud,
> Which in my childhood I did dote upon;
> And all the faith, the virtue of my heart,
> The object and the pleasure of mine eye,
> Is only Helena. To her, my lord,
> Was I betrothed ere I [saw] Hermia;
> But like a sickness did I loathe this food;
> But, as in health, come to my natural taste,
> Now do I wish it, love it, long for it,
> And will for evermore be true to it. [IV.i.165-76]

Demetrius explains his reborn love for Helena both as the result of his maturing and of his coming into health, notions that reinforce each other, for being unable or refusing to grow up is tantamount to mental illness. This feeling of renewed health reminds us of Puck's description of the love potion as a "remedy" (III.ii.452) that undoes what Oberon calls the "hateful imperfection" (IV.i.63) of one's eyes and is implied in Lysander's abusing Hermia earlier as "loathed med'cine! O hated potion" (III.ii.264).

As a healthy adult, Demetrius pursues Helena rather than she him. On the previous night the opposite was true, and Helena lamented, "Run when you will; the story shall be chang'd: / Apollo flies, and Daphne holds the chase; / The dove pursues the griffin; the mild hind / Makes speed to catch the tiger" (II.i.230-33). Demetrius's flight from Helena, his passivity and her active pursuit, "set a scandal" (240) on her sex: "We cannot fight for love, as men may do. / We should be woo'd, and were not made to woo" (241-42). The mysterious agency through which female characters touch husbands and lovers during their absence is visible here, for we see Puck work things so that "Jack shall have Jill" (III.ii.461) and the old proverb "That every man should take his own" (459) come true. However, because it is the fairy world, and not the women themselves, that intervenes and effects changes in the men, sixteenth-century sexual and social stereotypes are reestablished as the play closes. We do not see women transform men, and in *A Midsummer-Night's Dream* men and women seem equally helpless. Here the credit goes to Oberon and Puck.

The reunions in Shakespeare's later comedies are magnifications, as it were, of those in the earlier plays: essential elements are expanded upon rather than new ones added. Because, however, characterization deepens as Shakespeare develops as a playwright, the reunions are more resonant, and what seems like a sort of psychosocial shorthand in the early plays appears far more realistic in those written later. The encounters between hero and heroine in the fifth act are more convincing and moving not because they are truer to life but because we have seen more fully the steps leading up to the significant changes. In *The Merchant of Venice*, for example, all characters are amazed, and that amazement, as in *The Two Gentlemen of Verona*, has to do essentially with male attitudes toward the nature of the women, Portia and Nerissa, in particular, who delight in confusing the men and in belaboring their explanation of just what sort of creatures women are. And, yet again, this play ends with a woman's agreeing to explain all, as Portia declares,

> It is almost morning,
> And yet I am sure you are not satisfied
> Of these events at full. Let us go in,
> And charge us there upon inter'gatories,
> And we will answer all things faithfully. [V.i.296-300]

The men are "not satisfied" and neither is the audience, for the play ends without Portia's explaining, among other "things," why she changed into "Balthazar" and followed Bassanio to Venice and, perhaps more interestingly, how it came to pass that "an unlesson'd girl, unschool'd, unpractic'd" (III.ii.159) did in fact practice law, and with remarkable success. In other words, Portia remains for us and for the men a mysteriously inexplicable figure. Whereas in *The Two Gentlemen of Verona* there is mystery about Julia's identity but also an explanation, in *The Merchant of Venice* there is mystery and insufficient explanation. In some later comedies, of course, there will be no explanation at all.

The return to a version of the sexual and social status quo in *The Merchant of Venice* is greatly affected by the mystery surrounding Portia, for as heroines like Portia appear more capable and powerful it simply becomes less possible to consign them to their needles as the plays end. Bassanio may be a version of Jason or of Hercules when he wins her, but Portia is the real rescuer in this play. To Bassanio she is now "sweet doctor" (V.i.284); when she announces to Antonio that his ships have come in, he tells her, "you have given me life and living" (286), though he ought to have added, "for a second time." She and Nerissa use the rings to tease Bassanio and Gratiano for 125 lines, adding puzzle upon riddle until the two men are thoroughly baffled by the knowledge and apparent omnipresence of the women, though Portia explains away the complications in only five lines:

> you are all amaz'd.
> Here is a letter, read it at your leisure.
> It comes from Padua, from Bellario.
> There you shall find that Portia was the doctor,
> Nerissa there her clerk. [266-70]

And, as I have suggested, while these lines are a factual summation that both explains how Portia obtained the rings and clears away the sexual ambiguities created by the women's double entendres, they leave entirely unaddressed the question of Portia's intentions and abilities. To her wealth and beauty she has added a natural schooling, all of which make Portia quite a formidable presence in comparison to her prodigal and generally inept husband. From the point at which the men enter (127) to the end of the play (307), she is quite definitely in charge, recreating in her questions, demands, and syntax another courtroom scene and a second triumph of ingenuity, one necessitated both by Bassanio's valuing his friendship with Antonio above his marriage to her and by his fear of female sexuality. Therefore, as she gives herself and her ring to Bassanio for a second time, there are far fewer concessions to the imbalance of power between the two than obtained when he won her; the delicacies of language with which she gave herself to him earlier, when he chose the correct casket, the "royal humility" of which Granville-Barker speaks,[9] are largely eschewed.

It is only in her last speech, however, quoted above ("It is almost morning"), that Portia hints that it is Bassanio who will be "her lord, her governor, her king," as she described him earlier (III.ii.165). In telling the men that she will answer all their questions, Portia describes them as active and she and Nerissa as passive: "charge us there upon inter'gatories, / And we will answer all things faithfully." An "interrogatory" (or, "intergatory") was "a question formally put, or drawn up in writing to be put, to an accused person or a witness."[10] Portia's legalism gives the men the illusion that it is they who are the lawyers, and the women who are commissioned to answer, and is in addition an oblique suggestion that the two women may have overstepped their bounds, perhaps "misus'd" their sex, to borrow Celia's phrase from *As You Like It* (IV.i.201). Finally, in using "faithfully" as her last word in the play, Portia attempts to erase the earlier impression of sexual freedom she had made in swearing that "the doctor lay with me" (V.i.259) and also vows to be obedient in the way that matters most to men in Shakespeare's plays, in precisely the way Bassanio has failed by backing away from a full commitment to his wife. And yet, in spite of these subtle shifts toward the conventional, the impression with which the audience is left is of Portia's grace and mystery. It seems difficult to imagine any production of *The Merchant of Venice* in which the relationship between Portia and Bassanio is not one-sided as the play closes: "To the very end she expands in her fine freedom, growing in authority and dignity, fresh touches of humor enlightening her, new traits of graciousness showing."[11]

From Roman New Comedy and from Italian Renaissance comedy Shakespeare inherited a tradition that prized a happy ending brought about by cunning and trickery and from romance one brought about fantastically. Shakespeare modulates the reunions in his comedies, always (and increasingly) favoring the romantic and improbable but never quite dropping the sort of shenanigans that enable Lucentio and Bianca to outwit their fathers and Lorenzo and Jessica to rob Shylock and elope. For example, although *The Merry Wives of Windsor*, on the one hand, and *Much Ado about Nothing* and *As You Like It*, on the other, achieve happy endings that "amaze" the central characters by magically producing a woman almost from thin air, *The Merry Wives of Windsor* depends for its effects on cunning rather than on mystery, and for all its Englishness the love story's happy ending allies this play to continental comedies of intrigue.

In act 5 Master Page commands his daughter Anne to dress in white so that Slender can identify her in the woods at night, escape with her and marry; her mother orders her to wear green for Doctor Caius's sake. When Fenton learns of their plans, he substitutes boys in white and green, and the would-be suitors and Anne's parents are foiled by a "seemingly obedient" (IV.vi.33) daughter who pleases herself by marrying Fenton, the man she loves. When Slender and Caius discover that they have seized upon boys as wives, the familiar mystery having to do with a woman's whereabouts and identity begins, for Ford asks, "This is strange. Who hath got the right Anne?" (V.v.211). When she appears moments later with Fenton and is asked to explain, her new husband takes over and confesses all to her parents:

> The truth is, she and I (long since contracted)
> Are now so sure that nothing can dissolve us.
> Th' offense is holy that she hath committed,
> And this deceit loses the name of craft,
> Of disobedience, or unduteous title. . . . [223-27]

Though the precise way in which they were deceived is not told her parents, they are as convinced as the audience that her eloping has been the familiar matrimonial sleight of hand her father and mother themselves had planned for her. What amazes the bystanders are not, as it turns out, questions about Anne's nature—"Who hath got the right Anne?"—but rather those having to do with the mechanics of her deception. Ford asks his friends to "Stand not amaz'd" (231), Page consoles himself in thinking that "What cannot be eschew'd must be embrac'd" (237), and Falstaff reduces the event to its most easily understood component: "When night-dogs run, all sorts of deer are chas'd" (238). Anne has taken the masculine initiative by being disobedient and by "committing" an offense, but the fact of its being mere deceit reduces the sense of mystery about her, and makes the transition back to conventional attitudes and behaviors relatively smooth. Fenton explains the night's intrigue while Anne stands by saying only "Pardon, good father! good my mother, pardon!" (216); his controlling the scene seems entirely appropriate, as Anne's activity has been under Fenton's direction all along.

In *Much Ado about Nothing* there is little wonder at the end concerning the marriage of Beatrice and Benedick, not so much because they have been more realistically handled as because Beatrice has all along been an integrated personality, a woman unique in Shakespeare for not having had to disguise herself, to create a fictitious persona in order to help a man and revive a relationship. The wonder at the end of this play has, instead, to do with the reappearance of the "dead" Hero. It is in her emergence that we can see a radically different treatment of women from that in *The Merry Wives of Windsor*, and this in a play where there is in fact no behavior that cannot be easily explained.

When Claudio stands before the masked Hero, thinking he is about to marry her cousin as penance for having slandered her, he seems eager though perhaps a little too slick, and yet that mood contrasts nicely with the only verbal reaction he is allowed when he discovers that Hero lives, "Another Hero!" (V.iv.62). Only thirteen lines are devoted to this discovery, but the sense of wonder generated, and the knowledge that this is Claudio's second and last marriage, are very strong, partly because, as in *The Two Gentlemen of Verona*, the woman uses repetition and alliteration to reinforce the mystery of her appearance:

> *Claud.*   Give me your hand before this holy friar—
> I am your husband if you like of me.
> *Hero.*   [*Unmasking.*] And when I liv'd, I was your other
>   wife,
> And when you lov'd, you were my other husband.
> *Claud.*   Another Hero!
> *Hero.*   Nothing certainer:
> One Hero died defil'd, but I do live,
> And surely as I live, I am a maid.
> *D. Pedro.*   The former Hero! Hero that is dead!
> *Leon.*   She died, my lord, but whiles her slander liv'd.
> *Friar.*   All this amazement can I qualify,
> When after that the holy rites are ended,
> I'll tell you largely of fair Hero's death.
> Mean time let wonder seem familiar,
> And to the chapel let us presently. [60-71]

Here we have a literal second marriage, reinforced by their language, "your other wife," "my other husband," the "former Hero," "One Hero died," and so on. However, the wonder is not a product of the characters' sense that this is a world where second chances are given but rather of the mystery that enshrouds Hero from the moment she unmasks, bestowing upon her an ethereal quality (unmerited in her case not so much because she never really died as because she seemed so slight a character when alive). Nonetheless, the amazement is kept deliberately high, for the Friar, a fine surrogate and advocate for female values (as most clerics are in Shakespeare's comedies), never does tell the men how it comes that Hero lives again, though he implies that he will do so but not in the "Mean time."

His promise to explain stifles all discussion, and the play ends with fifty lines centering on Beatrice and Benedick.

What happens at the end of *As You Like It* is uniquely "wonderful" in Shakespearean comedy, though, as in *The Merry Wives of Windsor* and *Much Ado about Nothing,* the central action involves a woman's mysterious appearance. The uniqueness depends not simply on the fact that a god appears and mingles with mortals in a way we have not seen before but that Hymen seems so obviously Rosalind's factotum, presenting her to father and future husband, and endorsing her and her cryptic ways. What had seemed to be Rosalind's joking little love game with Orlando suddenly expands, revealing behind it a higher truth to which she has, apparently, had access and the others have not. It is as though Shakespeare's previous suggestions that women were more adequately "schooled" or tutored have set us up to think Rosalind merely another trickster, when suddenly the heroine appears with a god, and one who then refuses to answer any questions. In previous plays the audience knew the answers if the men did not or knew that the women could give rational answers if they had a mind to. But here there are no answers we can conjure up short of believing that Rosalind truly has supernatural connections. What Shakespeare tells us, furthermore, is that Rosalind is perhaps literally capable of being in two places at the same time, on earth and in heaven. The significance of the theophany in this play cannot be overestimated, especially because *As You Like It,* for all its pastoralism, seems to be so firmly grounded, through the first four and a half acts, in what we sense to be a realistically portrayed world. The shift from the physical to the metaphysical is abrupt and because of its suddenness seems a revelation on Shakespeare's part not so much of a heavenly dimension as of how women function in the imaginative worlds of these plays and of how men apprehend them.

In the play's last act, Hymen interrupts the casual banter among Touchstone, Jaques, and Duke Senior to announce, "Good Duke, receive thy daughter, / Hymen from heaven brought her" (V.iv.111-12). Critics often treat Hymen like a poor relation, some ignoring the character, others transforming him into a mortal, and one who is part of an elaborate deception engineered by Rosalind.[12] Not only is there no justification in the First Folio for reducing Hymen from god to man or for assuming Rosalind has gotten up a charade, but such a diminishing of the "wonderful" is clearly at odds with the tone of the last scene and with the reactions of the characters. Mere trickery (such as we see in *The Merry Wives of Windsor*) simply is not consonant with the air of the mysterious and magical Rosalind herself induces earlier when she promises Orlando, Silvius, and Phebe that they will wed the following day: "[*To Phebe.*] I will marry you, if ever I marry woman, and I'll be married to-morrow. [*To Orlando.*] I will satisfy you, if ever I satisfied man, and you shall be married to-morrow. [*To Silvius.*] I will content you, if what pleases you contents you, and you shall be married to-morrow" (V.ii.113-118). When she enters with Celia and Hymen in the last scene she sustains the tone of ritual: "[*To Duke Senior.*] To you I give myself for I am yours. [*To Orlando.*] To you I give myself, for I am yours" (V.iv.116-17). Her father and Orlando are astounded, the Duke because his daughter has suddenly materialized, and Orlando because the promises made by an enigmatic young boy have come true. And while Orlando is allowed only one line to respond to his good fortune, "If there be truth in sight, you are my Rosalind" (119), and then says no more, Rosalind continues to astound the gathering: "I'll have no father, if you be not he; / I'll have no husband, if you be not he; / Nor ne'er wed woman, if you be not she" (122-24). Indeed, it takes an injunction by Hymen to put an end to Rosalind's delphic and repetitive utterances and to silence the befuddled crowd. In other comedies when Shakespeare's women use trickery to amaze the men, there is always a suggestion that answers will be forthcoming and that what seemed magical can be explained, as when Portia tells Bassanio, "Portia was the doctor" and "we will answer all things faithfully," or when the Friar in *Much Ado about Nothing* informs the men, "All this amazement can I qualify." Here, however, Shakespeare takes the tone of *Much Ado about Nothing*, for example, one step further, by producing a god in fact and by having that god simply "bar confusion" (125) and promise no easy answers—indeed, no answers at all. It is as though the fairies of *A Midsummer-Night's Dream* have made themselves visible: "Whiles a wedlock-hymn we sing, / Feed yourselves with questioning; / That reason wonder may diminish / How thus we met, and these things finish" (137-40). Celebrants and onlookers will have to settle for questions rather than for answers, and reason will be diminished, not by explanation—what explanation will we accept for the news that Rosalind has been with Hymen in heaven?—but rather by an immersion in the wondrous.[13]

The hymn is sung and the play devotes its final fifty lines not to exposing Rosalind as the master of ceremonies but rather to news of Duke Frederick's conversion and of Jaques's removal to the abandoned cave. The Friar in *Much Ado about Nothing* suggests that for the "Mean time let wonder seem familiar," in effect putting a limit on the "wonderful," as though the answers to Hero's apparent rebirth, although inevitable, are in some ways unwelcome, and the interim ("Mean time") between mystery and knowledge ought to be savored to the fullest. In *As You Like It*, however, Hymen wants wonder to diminish reason and puts no limit at all on mystery's reign. In this way Shakespeare prepares us for the even greater mysteries of his later plays, in which the dead are reborn and reason *must* be dissolved by faith and wonder.

As *You Like It* reveals Rosalind's power, her prodigious abilities and her otherworldly connections, but at the same time reverses previous reversals of sexual stereotype by granting to Orlando the social position and material advantages we feel ought to have been his all along, and which were jealously denied him by Oliver. At the moment he marries Rosalind, who, of course, finally enters dressed as a woman, Orlando becomes heir to the dukedom; when Jaques de Boys announces that Duke Frederick has retired to a hermitage, Orlando's position becomes clear:

> *Duke S.*   Welcome, young man;
> Thou offer'st fairly to thy brothers' wedding:
> To one his lands withheld, and to the other
> A land itself at large, a potent dukedom. [166-69]

The language Duke Senior uses may not be subtle, but it is an effective indication that the power that has always been in the hands of men will remain with men; ultimately, such power is Orlando's, not Rosalind's. Whatever ties bind her to the heavenly, they do not extend so far as to rewrite the social structures which existed when the play began: material wealth, "real" estate, is controlled by men; what awaits Rosalind is a husband, and what awaits Orlando is "a potent dukedom." Although Northrop Frye is right in seeing a change in the political scene when a comedy ends, the change is merely one man for another, hardly a radical or structural change at all, especially when we consider how extraordinary the women are and how they strike us as far more capable and efficient than the men. But what Shakespeare has done is to balance real estate with a sort of heavenly estate, male power with female mystery. The appearances and disappearances of the women left unexplained, for audience as for male characters, Rosalind's abilities and connections must, of necessity, appear as "potent" as Orlando's new kingdom. Her teaching Orlando, her imaginative use of language, her apparently intuitive understanding of the relations between men and women and of the stresses they experience in marriage, are part of the dowery she brings to her wedding. It is little wonder that Orlando is mute as the play ends.

In the problem plays, *All's Well That Ends Well* and *Measure for Measure*, though Shakespeare's formula for bringing comedies to closure remains generally the same, the effects are different, and what we sense ought to be wonderful—the apparent rebirth of those thought dead, the restoration of lost lovers—is merely nice, at best. The flatness of the fifth act revelations is easier to account for in *Measure for Measure* than in *All's Well That Ends Well*, for in the former play Shakespeare toys with the romantic formula in a way he never had before. A woman's apparent ability to be everywhere at once, so effectively used to astound the men in *The Merchant of Venice* or *The Two Gentlemen of Verona*, for example, is vitiated here by Shakespeare's focusing instead on men—by the Friar's turning into the Duke, and especially by Claudio's "rebirth" later in the last act. The muted effect, a product of Isabella's not saying one word to Claudio as the play ends and of Angelo's never responding to the astonishing news that it is Mariana with whom he has slept, is amplified by the emphasis on the magical appearance of men rather than of women. The Duke and Claudio have been in two places at the same time, as have Mariana and Isabella, and neither the men nor the women seem particularly impressed with the wonder of it all.

Though Shakespeare occasionally uses the rebirth of male characters as part of the happy ending in comedies, as in Egeon's being rescued and finding wife and family in *The Comedy of Errors*, and in Alonso's and Ferdinand's discovery that each other lives in *The Tempest*, such miraculous appearances are clearly only addenda tacked on to more glorious discoveries in those plays. Shakespearean comedy relies for its central effects on the male reaction to the wonders apparently performed by the women, and not vice versa. The formula had been outlined in *The Two Gentlemen of Verona*, as I suggested earlier, in Julia's reaction to Proteus's betrayal: "It is the lesser blot, modesty finds, / Women to change their shapes than men their minds" (V.iv.108-9). It is the women who are the rescuers in these plays, and not the men; it is the women's loyalty and their willingness to descend, their ability to be here and there, that saves the men from their own worst intentions. In Shakespearean comedy, changes women make are external and are in reaction to internal changes men make. To toy with this formula, as Shakespeare does in *Measure for Measure* (and, in a slightly different way, in *The Taming of the Shrew*), by having a man, the Duke, save both Isabella and Mariana, and by having men and women change their shapes while only Angelo changes his mind, is to spread the wonder far too thin and consequently to blur the focus. Shaw gets away with such a reversal in *Pygmalion* partly by relying on witty conversation, but in general the idea of a man's stooping to help a woman smacks of redemptive literature and its assumption of male intellectual and moral superiority, and of patriarchal attitudes in the occasional nineteenth-century novel, but not of Shakespearean drama where the woman is almost always presented as the more competent and impressive partner.

It is not surprising, then, that some critics read *Measure for Measure* as a Christian allegory; this play and the Bible share an emphasis on the wonderfulness of males, not females. The conjunction of political, economic, and spiritual power in the hands of a man, here the Duke, is reinforced by the ending that, like those in other comedies, tends in general terms to reestablish the social and sexual status quo and to confirm male dominance. The wonder of Isabella's and Mariana's omnipresence, an ability that surrounds other female characters with an aura that often seems far more potent than the real power commanded by the men, is here dissipated by the more compelling dramatic device of the Duke's machinations. At the end of the play, the accomplishments of the women, having been suggested by a man all along (as Anne Page's are by Fenton), seem less wonderful than merely successful. Tillyard points out that the Isabella of the second half of the play is but a pale shadow of the Isabella of the first half, the essence of whose disposition "is decision and the acute sense of her own independent and inviolate personality."[14] Later in the play, however, "the Duke takes charge and she proceeds to exchange her native ferocity for the hushed and submissive tones of a well-trained confidential secretary."[15] What we are given in exchange for that earlier Isabella is a more powerful Duke, though strong males are not what conduce to happy endings in Shakespearean comedy: "That the Duke is in his way impressive, that he creates a certain moral atmosphere, serious and yet tolerant, in the second half of the play need not be denied; yet that atmosphere can ill bear comparison with that of the early part of the play."[16] And, to add insult to injury, to his omniscience and omnipresence the Duke adds omnipotence in announcing to Isabella that he has "a motion much imports your good" (V.i.535), that, in fact, he intends to marry her. Shakespeare has centralized all forms of power in the masculine figure of the Duke, much against his traditional manner of delineating character and effecting reunions.

The ending of *All's Well That Ends Well* is far more typical of Shakespearean comedy than that of *Measure for Measure*, much more like those of *The Merchant of Venice*, *Much Ado about Nothing* or *As You Like It*, and for that reason somewhat more successful. What has left critics unsatisfied, however, are what seem to be both Bertram's ingrained character flaws and Helena's deviousness. Of these two complaints, the more serious in terms of the denouement is the charge against Helena, for Shakespearean comedy right along assumes problematic males whether the audience likes it or not.

Helena suffers to a certain extent from her association with the King, indeed, her identification with him, and seems a part of his political power, almost its agent, rather than a separate entity struggling to survive in spite of that power. As such, she reminds us, though to a lesser degree, of Isabella, who also becomes, or is made to become, an extension of the will of the Duke and thereby a symbol of male authority rather than an independent woman. It is no accident that in all the comedies in which women seem most potent, the males, especially the governors, seem weak or ineffectual. The Duke in *The Comedy of Errors* is at best a bureaucrat; Silvia's father surrenders to Valentine; Duke Senior is manipulated by Rosalind; Duke Orsino merely languishes in office; Portia saves lives and the financial reputation of Venice in a way the Duke of Venice cannot; Pericles is resuscitated by Marina, Leontes by a combination of Paulina and Hermione. In the problem plays, however, it is the women who are dominated by the men, and though Helena manipulates Bertram into doing what he has wanted to do all along, it is difficult for Bertram and for the audience to separate Helena from the King. Does she use the King to help her win Bertram, or does the King use her to assert his reborn power over a younger generation of males?

All's Well That Ends Well ends well enough, at least more satisfactorily than does *Measure for Measure,* and that is directly attributable, I think, to Helena's being perceived—in spite of her association with the King—as more fully autonomous than either Isabella or Mariana. Although her interests and those of the King of France are seen as identical, Shakespeare contrives events in such a way as to keep the King in the dark both about Helena's devices and, in fact, about her very existence. Thus, when Bertram learns that Helena is alive, the King and all his court learn it at the same time, and while the wonder of it all is fully explainable and the audience knows all the answers, the male characters, including the King, do not. It is once again the women—Helena, the Widow, and her daughter Diana—who speak in the mysterious tones, riddling and teasing the men who are exasperated and, finally, astonished in those familiar ways we have seen in earlier comedies. *All's Well That Ends Well,* therefore, retains for the women a far greater sense of mystery than does *Measure for Measure* and is capable of reaching, if not a joyous conclusion, at least a satisfactory one. Perhaps this is the point Tillyard is getting at when he suggests that "for all the realism of the characters, the moral earnestness of *All's Well* never approaches that of *Measure for Measure.*"[17]

Thus, although Helena is perceived as a confederate of the King, his ignorance about her whereabouts—identical to Bertram's and Lafew's— makes Helena seem more capable and perceptive than the King or Bertram, indeed, more capable than the court of France as a whole. The King's ignorance and Helena's knowledge meet head-on in the play's last scene, V.iii, when Diana, Helena's surrogate at the court of France, confuses him to the point of anger with riddles about how she came into possession of Bertram's ring. As Diana pulverizes her audience with innuendo and paradox, the King is stupefied by Helena's sudden appearance:

> He knows himself my bed he hath defil'd,
> And at that time he got his wife with child.
> Dead though she be, she feels her young one kick.
> So there's my riddle: one that's dead is quick—
> And now behold the meaning.
>   *Enter* Widow *and* Helen. [300-4]

The King can only ask, "Is't real that I see?" (306), and Helena prolongs the confusion by answering, "No, my good lord, / 'Tis but the shadow of a wife you see, / The name, and not the thing" (306-8). Once again, as in *The Merchant of Venice*, the man's acceptance of "the thing" as well as "the name" is a crucial step in the play's evolution into a full-fledged comedy. What is immediately apparent to Bertram, who interjects, "Both, both" (308), is that he is now a husband in deed as in name.

Having fulfilled the terms of Bertram's assignment, Helena is now ready for her second chance at married life with him, a union, she reminds him, reflecting his acceptance of her sexuality:

> O my good lord, when I was like this maid,
> I found you wondrous kind. There is your ring,
> And look you, here's your letter. This it says:
> "When from my finger you can get this ring,
> And [are] by me with child, etc." This is done.
> Will you be mine now you are doubly won? [309-14]

"Doubly won" not only emphasizes that second beginning that the last act ordinarily implies but emphasizes as well to how great an extent sex roles have been reversed: it is the woman who has rescued or "won" the man, and not vice versa, as our everyday notions of romance suggest. With regard to his relationship with Helena, Bertram has been the object of desire, passively awaiting his wife's intervention. And we ought not overlook, either, Helena's explicit reference to her sexual relations with Bertram. She had found him "wondrous kind," and in her reminding him of the pleasures of their brief encounter we find not only the clearest reason why Bertram would be willing now to be hers, now that he is "doubly won," in word and in body, but also precisely what it is that Helena has "done" for him. Without her having doggedly followed him to Florence and manipulated him into bed with her, Bertram would never have learned the "wonder" of sex within the bounds of marriage and the odd way in which his wife really is both Helena and Diana, a sexual creature and the goddess of chastity at one and the same time.[18]

The ingenuity (or cunning), the loyalty and courage Helena shows in her single-minded pursuit of full marriage to Bertram make it well-nigh impossible to reduce her to "wife" in yet another reversal of sex roles once she and Bertram reunite. Unlike the final arrangement in *As You Like It*, in which Rosalind's power and mystery are balanced by Orlando's receiving "a potent dukedom," the fifth act here offers no prize to the young count, partly because he has all along been enfranchised, but especially because Helena simply cannot be summarily demoted from "Dr. She" to a version of Anne Page. In fact, not only does *All's Well That Ends Well* conclude without a second reversal of sex roles, without a movement back toward Elizabethan social norms, it reaffirms the axis that aligns the King and governance with women rather than with the male nobility, for he offers to Diana, in the play's last speech, the power to choose a husband as he had done earlier with Helena: "If thou beest yet a fresh uncropped flower, / Choose thou thy husband, and I'll pay thy dower" (327-28). It is as though the King were establishing a new set of rules governing courting, one which empowers the women and encourages them to become more active, and which simultaneously renders the men passive and powerless young lords.

The startling fifth act reappearance of the lost woman is ordinarily treated by Shakespeare as a response to the various ways in which hero and heroine relate to one another, not only when together as the play begins but especially when separated. In *All's Well That Ends Well*, for example, Helena's rebirth, her Alcestian journey back from her supposed death to life, is seen as a consequence, like it or not, of her having slept with Bertram earlier and of her having fulfilled the terms of his challenge; we understand that had she not done so, she would have been consigned to what in comedy's terms can only be called a living death, the sort we see in Aemilia, the Abbess of *The Comedy of Errors*, and in Thaisa before each is found by her husband. Likewise, Portia's avowed willingness to live the life of a faithful wife at the end of *The Merchant of Venice* is clearly predicated upon her having taught Bassanio something about marriage and female sexuality, just as Julia, Hermia, and Helena find in marriage a culmination of all that they and Proteus, Lysander, and Demetrius have gone through. In the same way, it is clear to us why the Princess of France and her ladies are not willing to marry the men of Navarre and why Isabella says nothing when Duke Vincentio proposes marriage. Whether Shakespeare's comedies end with separated lovers, forced marriages, or warm-hearted nuptials, the conclusion is ordinarily more than simply a requisite happy ending: it is psychologically relevant and seems inevitable in terms of what has gone before.

The coherence of Shakespearean comedy makes the fifth act of *Pericles* all the more anomalous, for the hero's reunion with Thaisa seems no more understandable in psychosocial terms than does Egeon's fortuitous discovery of Aemilia in Shakespeare's earliest play, *The Comedy of Errors.* Instead of a rapprochement that evolves from the specific nature of their separation and travail, Pericles' discovery of Thaisa at the Temple of Diana seems merely the final incident in a turbulent career. It is as though Shakespeare suddenly allows the love story to be drained of all meaning until events in succession are their own reward, a comedic equivalent of revenge drama, where vengeful acts justify their own slender motivation. We seem to witness "the disappearance of character into design," to transplant one critic's description of the ending in *Measure for Measure.*[19]

The problems that have, historically, plagued critics of *Pericles* stem not so much from its doubtful origins—its being excluded from the First Folio and its attendant questions of authorship—as from the sense that the play is, finally, meaningless. Hazlitt objected to "the far-fetched and complicated absurdity of the story" and quoted Schlegel, who felt that "Shakespear here handled a childish and extravagant romance of the old poet Gower, and was unwilling to drag the subject out of its proper sphere."[20] Modern criticism occasionally reads the story as a myth of death and rebirth, as a dream, as an allegory on patience in suffering, or looks to *Pericles'* affinities with *King Lear* and with his earlier comedies and later romances, or with the tragicomedies of Beaumont and Fletcher. The typical refrain, however, has to do with the play's apparent incoherence. For Larry S. Champion, *Pericles* "lacks the conflict built on character which by this point has come to be the hallmark of Shakespearean comedy. The spectator remains outside, as it were, observing the amazing events which entertain for their own sake, not because they arouse interest in what happens to a certain character or how he is affected."[21] James G. McManaway writes *Pericles* off as "an experimental play in its content and in its form. It consists of striking incidents selected from a long romance with small regard for causality";[22] and Derek Traversi sees the play simply as "an experiment in poetic symbolism."[23] For F. D. Hoeniger, *Pericles* must have "extreme interest" for students of the later plays, for here "Shakespeare can be seen groping for much that was to be given consummate expression in his final work."[24] Hallett Smith claims that "from any realistic point of view, the spectacular scenes of *Pericles* are of course utter nonsense."[25]

Pericles, who seems an innocent victim of irrational forces, is one of very few Shakespearean heroes who never loses faith in the woman he loves; he is a good man whose attitudes remain antithetical to those of Claudio or Posthumus, for example, and yet he suffers at least as deeply. Therefore, in order for the play to end happily, it is not the hero who must change, but circumstances, and such an ending, as I have suggested, is not typical of Shakespearean comedy, where it is the hero who is transformed, not his external world.

The structure of the narrative in *Pericles,* however, is typical of that in the comedies and that structure suggests that the hero *is* responsible for his lot. Consequently, what we find in this play is a hero—whom we feel to be an innocent victim—undergoing the trials associated with the typical flawed hero. The salient features of the play—Pericles' separation from his father, his loss of Thaisa, his living the life of a vagabond, his passivity and immobility, his rescue by his daughter, his eventual reunion with a wife presumed dead who has become a religious votaress, and his final assumption of power and the prerogatives of the ruling class—all describe a narrative that in the context of Shakespeare's approach to comedy as a whole implies at the least a hero laboring in error about women, and at the most a hero who has become a self-righteous misogynist. The problem is not that "Pericles and Marina are totally flat; they do not develop as characters"[26] but rather that, flat or round, Pericles is not seen as responsible for the peculiarly Shakespearean story in which he is caught. Proteus is a "flat" character, but *The Two Gentlemen of Verona* seems a coherent play, for we understand that Proteus's actions bear a direct correspondence to his evolving relationship with Julia. The same simply cannot be said of Pericles' relationship with his wife.

If the events that make up the Shakespearean love story are the same in *Pericles* as they are in earlier plays, the shape of the play as a whole is different. The fourteen-year gap in time between acts 3 and 4, the "fast-growing scene" (IV.ch.6) to which Gower refers, and the consequent shift in focus from Pericles to the grown Marina, necessarily reduce the importance of Thaisa, just as the gap in time in *The Winter's Tale* reduces, or at least defers, the impact Hermione makes in favor of that of Perdita. One of the far-reaching results of this discontinuity is that in *Pericles* husband and wife are not shown interacting in any meaningful way during their separation. In fact, as Hallett Smith points out, Shakespeare tosses logic to the wind by insisting on Thaisa's complete isolation: "Thaisa, the lost wife, who is resurrected through the remarkable medical skill of Cerimon, is less prominent, since once she is saved she does not seek Pericles but retires to a nunnery. Why? The plot of romantic fiction will have it so. Probability and plausibility must give way to the demands of the marvelous and the spectacular."[27] "Why?" indeed. The answer cannot be that "the plot of romantic fiction will have it so," for Shakespeare had written romantic fiction for twenty years without jettisoning coherent characterization, at least in the major characters. Aemilia is separated from Egeon in *The Comedy of Errors*, but her taking orders seems logical because we know that she assumes her family drowned. What Shakespeare does in *Pericles* is violate precisely the sort of "plot of romantic fiction" he had always written. It is clear that Shakespeare wants to substitute daughter for wife, perhaps because, as some critics suggest, his interest had been piqued by *King Lear*, but handles the substitution poorly here, much less skillfully than in *The Winter's Tale*, where Hermione's absence and Perdita's appearance are directly related to Leontes' character rather than presented as apparently random events.

Thaisa is reduced in importance not only because she is out of sight and out of mind but also because in *Pericles* it is Marina, rather than her mother, who is the misapprehended woman, the female about whom men hold contradictory views. Her marriage to Lysimachus, in itself an abbreviated version of Shakespeare's typical love story, implies that Lysimachus must choose between two contrary visions of a woman, just as, say, Antipholus of Syracuse, Benedick, or Claudio do. That he sees Marina as a virgin in spite of her setting—a feat Claudio consistently fails to achieve with regard to Hero—is all to the good, though her position is one usually reserved for the wife of the hero himself and not for his daughter. Thus, her subsequent saving of Pericles does not make sense in the way that earlier interactions between male and female characters do. Pericles has not misunderstood Marina and accused her of infidelities; there is no reason why she, and not her mother, should be the inspirational force in her father's life. Then, too, she has taken on at least one other important attribute ordinarily reserved for the hero's lover or wife: Marina is the active counterpart to her passive mother. In earlier plays, active and passive personas are either two aspects of the same woman or two women of roughly the same age who, in some ways, are seen as surrogates for one another. Part of the reason one is tempted to see incest as a major theme in *Pericles* is that Marina functions as a surrogate for her mother but cannot be considered sexually interchangeable in the way that Hermia and Helena, Viola and Oliva, Helena and Diana, or Isabella and Mariana can. In *The Winter's Tale*, although Leontes' interest is piqued by Perdita's arrival and he temporarily confuses her with his memories of her mother, Shakespeare does not reunite father and daughter on stage but rather reports that meeting to us, reserving for the play's climactic scene Leontes' reunion with Hermione. Here it is Pericles' reunion with Thaisa that seems an addendum, and one that simply does not convey the same emotional impact as the scene in which the ailing Pericles is revived by and recognizes Marina.

Marina is active not only in comparison to her mother—that is, as the woman who recovers her husband for Thaisa—but in comparison to Pericles as well. It is Marina, the rescuer, who plays the traditionally male role, saving a father, a "kingly patient" (V.i.71), who plays that of the woman, and the two are quite self-consciously aware of this role reversal, a reversal, we will remember, usually reserved for lovers. In the fifth act she cajoles her father from his catatonia, at which time he recognizes his passivity and the blurring of sexual stereotypes:

> Tell thy story;
> If thine, considered, prove the thousand part
> Of my endurance, thou art a man, and I
> Have suffered like a girl. Yet thou dost look
> Like Patience gazing on kings' graves, and smiling
> Extremity out of act. [134-39]

Marina's combination of stereotypically masculine and feminine traits—her assertiveness and her patience—lasts, however, only as long as Pericles suffers "like a girl." That is, as he emerges from his life of silence and grief and slowly regains the ability to think and question clearly, Marina becomes less active and retreats into silence. The role reversal, in other words, reverses itself again, as we have seen elsewere, and Pericles becomes a masculine figure of authority. When Marina sings and speaks to him, Pericles awakens more suddenly than we might expect for a man so deep in grief. He is disoriented, and pushes her back, grunting "Hum, ha!" (83), Shakespearean shorthand for confusion. Pericles' next speech, however, does make sense, and we know that he has been listening to her and following her story: "My fortunes—parentage—good parentage— / To equal mine—was it not thus? What say you?" (97-98). By his third speech it is clear that he has recovered fully enough to use language grammatically, and his fourth, in which he compares Marina to Thaisa, is a complete and coherent statement. When he is certain that Marina is his daughter, he seems to have regained not only his equilibrium but his sense of command as well. After he sees Diana in a vision, there is no question of his being both King and father:

> My purpose was for Tharsus, there to strike
> The inhospitable Cleon, but I am
> For other service first. Toward Ephesus
> Turn our blown sails; eftsoons I'll tell thee why.
> [*To Lysimachus.*] Shall we refresh us, sir, upon your shore?
> And give you gold for such provision

As our intents will need?
> *Lys.*   Sir,
> With all my heart, and, when you come ashore,
> I have another [suit].
> *Per.*   You shall prevail,
> Were it to woo my daughter, for it seems
> You have been noble towards her.
> *Lys.*   Sir, lend me your arm.
> *Per.*   Come, my Marina. [252-65]

Pericles has become a governor, sounding the appropriately martial tone with regard to Cleon and assuming the prerogatives of a father in directing his daughter. Marina, on the other hand, has collapsed into the pose of the demure girl, standing quietly by as her father offers her to Lysimachus (about whom she ought to have some questions, having first met him in a brothel).

When Pericles falls asleep and in a vision sees the goddess Diana who orders him to Ephesus and effectively reorders the play's priorities, our attention is turned from Pericles and Marina to Pericles and Thaisa. Act 5, scene 3, however, at the Temple of Diana, seems simply a reiteration of scene 1, and a rather less full version, and that ought to indicate the consequences of Shakespeare's substituting daughter for mother and of allowing Marina to revive her father. In the earlier scene, which Kenneth Muir calls "the great Marina-Pericles scene,"[28] Pericles is saved by Marina, while in the later scene it is Pericles who does the saving, traveling to Ephesus and recovering Thaisa, once when she faints upon seeing and hearing him, and once again when he learns who she is and greets her as his wife. Marina is identified as "Thou that beget'st him that did thee beget" (V.i.195), but Thaisa is asked by Pericles, "come, be buried / A second time within these arms" (43-44). The images of birth and death, used to describe daughter and mother, respectively, complement one another nicely, but it is the first we associate with lovers and the happy ending in Shakespearean comedy, where the heroines are so often apprehended as tutors and doctors, bringing health and life to benighted men. Even the joy that is felt at Pericles' discovering Thaisa has been anticipated by the "great sea of joys" (V.i.192) that rush upon Pericles when he finds Marina.

What Shakespeare does retain for Thaisa, however, is the sense of mystery, for although Cerimon promises to explain "How she came plac'd here in the temple; / No needful thing omitted" (67-68), neither the audience nor Pericles hears details concerning Cerimon's magic or learns why Thaisa chose to serve Diana rather than search for her husband and daughter. However, the wonder of Thaisa's rebirth and the interest taken in her by Diana, who leads Pericles to her temple, have been adumbrated by all that we have seen and heard in acts 4 and 5 of Marina, "all happy as the fairest of all" (V.i.49). Though Thaisa's return from the dead cannot be explained to us, and Marina's escape from murderers and panderers can, it is the daughter's preservation that strikes us as the more joyous and wonderful.

Understanding the precise nature of his love story helps us to evaluate the consequences of Shakespeare's substituting daughter for mother in *Pericles*. Judging by critical reaction, the swap has served neither to bring into relief issues related to incest nor to clarify the relationship between character and action in general. What is clear is that at this late point in his career Shakespeare was increasingly drawn to father/daughter relationships which, after all, comprise one of the richer veins in literary romance. However, in *King Lear* and *The Tempest* the mother is dead at the start, and in *Cymbeline* and *The Winter's Tale* the relationship between husband and wife—rather than that between parent and child—remains the focus. But if *Pericles* is a failure on stage (its history is undistinguished), in the study the play points to the extraordinary pull that the psychosocial configuration of his typical love story had on Shakespeare. What we learn is that although the daughter is substituted for the mother in *Pericles*, the storyline itself will not adjust in the least to so drastic a shift. Those elements in his story that usually point to significant events in the hero's development as an independent adult and to his evolving relationship with a woman here are cut loose, rendered less meaningful by their being linked to his relationship with his daughter. The love story to which Shakespeare had devoted his career is a rich vehicle for exploring lovers' attitudes, but it is by no means a flexible instrument; it makes sense not as a general formula for illuminating a variety of relationships but only as a powerful series of behaviors for couples who are, were, or will be sexual partners.

The problems of focus and emphasis at the end of *Pericles* are absent from the last act of *The Winter's Tale*, which, for all its theatricality, concludes in a far more typically Shakespearean manner. There is a relationship between character and event in this play that is missing from the earlier romance, where what happens—the comedic storyline—seems to have a life of its own, unrelated to the attitudes of the central characters. But then narrative always takes precedence in Shakespearean comedy, and it is the characters who must accommodate themselves to the story, so to speak, and not vice versa. Perhaps the disjunction we feel between character and story in *Pericles* is the result of that play's having been begun by someone other than Shakespeare, a hand unfamiliar with the idiosyncratic ways in which Shakespeare develops plot.

At the end of *The Winter's Tale* Leontes, we feel, is reunited with daughter and wife not simply because an appropriate number of years has elapsed but because he is profoundly different from the man who had accused his wife and attempted to murder his daughter. In the fifth act he is no longer the manic husband and father we saw earlier; he speaks in quite different tones and is patient, even deferential. His transformation is so complete that, as with Lear, it is impossible for us to imagine his regressing into the tyrant of the first two acts. In fact, Leontes never quite recovers from his mourning or from the passive stance Paulina instructs him to maintain as the statue of Hermione comes to life. When Hermione steps down from her pedestal and offers her hand to Leontes, he is stupefied and remains immobile. Paulina chastises him, "Nay, present your hand. / When she was young, you woo'd her; now, in age, / Is she become the suitor?" (V.iii.107-9). We have seen that in Shakespearean comedy the woman (or her surrogate) must "become the suitor," must reverse sex roles with the male in order for the play to end happily. Here, the reversal is so complete that it is the man who seems made of marble and the women who seem active and independent. As we watch the scene, Hermione is the cynosure not only because she is the active party, stepping down, walking to Leontes, embracing her husband, but also because she is the mysterious figure as well, and one whose praises "are on a level even higher than Perdita's."²⁹ It is here that *The Winter's Tale* succeeds where *Pericles* fails, for Perdita's story in no way eclipses her mother's. When she sees the statue, Perdita kneels before it and asks, "Lady, / Dear queen, that ended when I but began, / Give me that hand of yours to kiss" (44-46). In a sense, when Hermione comes to life, when she "begins" a second time, it is Perdita who "ends." The daughter's only other line in the final scene, "So long could I / Stand by, a looker-on" (84-85), indicates how fully Hermione occupies center stage and especially with regard to Leontes' resurrection from a despair perhaps as deep as Pericles'. In this play, it is unquestionably the mother, not the daughter, who saves husband and father. And while the wonder of Thaisa's preservation is muted by that of Marina, here the *coup de théâtre* of Hermione's apparent resuscitation cannot help but make Perdita and the others simply "lookers-on."

The Winter's Tale ends as the other comedies do, with a mystery surrounding a woman, and with that mystery's being understood only by the women. When Polixenes asks Paulina to "make it manifest where she has liv'd, / Or how stol'n from the dead" (114-15), Paulina likens the story to "an old tale" (117) and coyly suggests that he "Mark a little while" (118). And though Hermione tells Perdita that she has "preserv'd" (127) herself to see her daughter, Paulina refuses to allow Perdita to answer her mother's questions, telling Hermione: "There's time enough for that; / Least they desire (upon this push) to trouble / Your joys with like relation" (128-30). The Friar in *Much Ado about Nothing* asks Claudio and Don Pedro to "let wonder seem familiar," Hymen enjoins the crowd in *As You Like It*, "Feed yourselves with questioning," and Paulina too encourages joy at the expense of reason. Whether Shakespeare refused to explain mysteries because he thought the audience, knowing the story, would only yawn, or because he could not explain Hymen's presence, Thaisa's rebirth, and Hermione's preservation, one thing is clear: these plays end with male characters (and, in *The Winter's Tale*, audience as well) mystified about the central female characters, questioning their existence and their very natures as human beings. In this regard, Shakespeare's comedies end as *Alcestis* does, with men dumbfounded and women aligned with the supernatural. "What shall I say? Gods! Marvel this unhoped for!"[30] says the awestruck Admetus when Hercules reunites him with Alcestis; "My wife do I behold in very sooth, / Or doth some god-sent mockery-joy distract me?" (1124-25). *Alcestis* ends with the chorus drawing attention to "the works of the Gods" (1159) rather than to Alcestis, who is mute (Hermione speaks only once after awakening) and may not speak "Ere to the Powers beneath the earth she be / Unconsecrated, and the third day come" (1145-46).[31]

In respect to their happy endings, *Alcestis*, *Pericles*, and *The Winter's Tale* are similar, a "new reality," as Northrop Frye puts it, having been created "out of something impossible but desirable."[32] That is, in comedy, Frye suggests, "we see a victory of the pleasure principle that Freud warns us not to look for in ordinary life."[33] Shakespeare's heroes wind up with the women they love rather than with statues, their own prayers or their misogynistic fantasies, and Admetus with his wife instead of her effigy. But what most Shakespearean comedies do—with the salient exception of *Pericles*—that Euripides' play does not, is relate the "victory of the pleasure principle," the happy ending, to the newly developed actions and attitudes of the male characters rather than to the whims of fate or "the works of the Gods." Again with the exception of *Pericles*, the theophanies of Shakespearean comedy point to changes in humans, such as Posthumus and Leontes, rather than to the divinity itself. While we can conceive of *Pericles*' ending with a paean to the gods, as *Alcestis* in fact does, we cannot conceive of such a conclusion to *The Winter's Tale*, for the gods seem to function in this play merely as forces that ratify and recommend the transformations of the human males.

Although Alcestis is a mysterious figure as the play closes, she is seen (as are Aemilia, Isabella, Thaisa, and even Helena) as something of a pawn in the hands of a male universe. Alcestis saves Admetus by dying in his stead, but Hercules (hardly an apt surrogate for female values) saves her as a way of repaying Admetus for his kindnesses. Her silence at the end, and the chorus's interpretation, which calls attention to the power of the gods, reduce her almost to the level of a character in a morality. *The Winter's Tale*, however, closes with the women, and not the oracle, signifying the deepest mysteries of human behavior. The social, if not political, status quo, we sense, has been changed forever, and not in the way Frye suggests. The contest has not been primarily between generations, but rather between two opposite world views, one represented by women and the other by men. Leontes' questions about Hermione's resurrection (he wonders aloud in the play's last speech) are not answered, and although he anticipates hearing more from the women, the sense is that "There's time enough for that":

> Good Paulina,
> Lead us from hence, where we may leisurely
> Each one demand, and answer to his part
> Perform'd in this wide gap of time, since first
> We were dissever'd. Hastily lead away. [151-55]

Perhaps because "no play of Shakespeare's boasts three such women as Hermione, Perdita, Paulina,"[34] no other play gives itself over at the end quite as fully to values which Shakespeare seems to have associated with women and to have esteemed from the first. Paulina, leading at the end as, in a way, she has throughout, promises to permit questions and to provide answers, Shakespeare teasing us "once more with the promise that everything will be explained to everyone—off-stage."[35]

Cymbeline may not be the most affecting of the comedies, but it seems to me to afford a particularly full view of the attitudes and behaviors of lovers in Shakespearean comedy, and seems, therefore, an appropriate play with which to conclude this study of the love story. Act 5, scene 5, in which "the business of the plot evidently thickens,"[36] has been ridiculed for its "exaggerated discoveries,"[37] but is helpful here for it recapitulates plot elements and devices that characterize these plays. As Mark van Doren puts it, V.v "might seem to have been designed as a recognition scene to end all recognition scenes, since it has everything in it and more."[38]

What the last scene has in it, however, is less important than what it all adds up to, a pageant whose theme is the central issue in these plays: male perceptions of the nature of women. The issue is raised almost as soon as the scene begins, with the news, at line 27, that "The queen is dead."

When Cymbeline learns that his wife "Abhorr'd" (40) and "never lov'd" (37) him, and that Imogen "Was as a scorpion to her sight" (45), the King moves, as Posthumus had earlier, from reviling a particular woman to slandering her sex: "O most delicate fiend! / Who is't can read a woman?" (47-48). In *Macbeth* when Duncan reacts to Cawdor's execution for treason, he generalizes, "There's no art / To find the mind's construction in the face" (I.iv.11-12). Cymbeline's reaction to learning of his wife's perfidy is gender-specific in a way that Duncan's is not, and he meticulously separates what Posthumus earlier called "the woman's part" from the man's. Cymbeline's analysis of his blindness to his wife's evil,

> Mine eyes
> Were not in fault, for she was beautiful;
> Mine ears, that [heard] her flattery, nor my heart,
> That thought her like her seeming. It had been vicious
> To have mistrusted her [62-66],

is couched in terms reminiscent of those in Posthumus's misogynistic diatribe in act 2, "Some coiner with his tools / Made me a counterfeit; yet my mother seem'd / The Dian of that time. So doth my wife / The nonpareil of this" (II.v.5-8), and is reminiscent of similar moments and statements in other comedies, of Claudio's "Out on thee seeming!" and of all such angry responses to the supposed difference between what a woman appears to be and what a man thinks she is. Reconciling the testimony of his senses, that is, what the hero apprehends of a woman through his eyes and ears, to what he thinks he knows of her is a central question in *Cymbeline* as in Shakespearean comedy in general. A good deal of this book has described and analyzed the ways in which Shakespeare's heroes descend into a psychological state in which information seems to contradict and over-power "th' attest of eyes and ears," as Troilus puts it, or in which a woman's very beauty becomes the surest sign of her guilt, "for beauty is a witch" and golden hair merely a subtle means to drown, or simply a "mesh t' entrap the hearts of men."

Heroes such as Valentine, Orlando, and Florizel always trust that a woman's beauty indicates honesty. Troilus trusts too, as does Pericles when he dares all for the Princess of Antioch, and these two, like Cymbeline, pay dearly for what is, after all, the rarer action, Othello's tendency to think "men honest that but seem to be so" (I.iii.400). But the majority of men in the comedies simply cannot trust, at least not for very long. For most men, like Leontes, beauty ultimately indicates evil and smiles are deceptive; to maintain faith in Hermione, as Camillo does, is reasonable only if one confesses "To have nor eyes nor ears nor thought" (I.ii.275).

Throughout these plays men suspect, as Antipholus does, that "error drives our eyes and ears amiss"; their wits war with their senses and the results portend no good for women. They fall, and rather precipitously, into ambivalence, depression, and anger, and come to sound like the world-weary speaker in the sonnets. Cymbeline's language, the way in which he chides himself for relying on "eyes" and "heart," is found, for example, in Sonnet 137, where the speaker laments the fact that "In things right true my heart and eyes have erred" (13), and where he regrets that his eyes are "anchor'd in the bay where all men ride" (6). Sonnet 140 describes the speaker's "tongue-tied patience" (2) in the face of the woman's "proud heart" (14), and in Sonnet 141, he upbraids himself for the pain he bears for separating his heart from his "five wits" and "five senses" (9). With a sort of *fin de siècle* resignation Sonnet 138 touts "seeming trust" as "love's best habit" (11) concluding, "Therefore I lie with her, and she with me, / And in our faults by lies we flattered be" (13-14).

Cymbeline, however, seems less angry or resigned than simply befuddled: what are men to do in a world where beautiful women are sometimes false, even malevolent? "Who is't can read a woman?" To assume the worst and mistrust the testimony of appearances, as we see Posthumus do, would be "vicious," though Cymbeline's trusting his eyes, ears, heart, has caused his daughter, among others, needless suffering. It is as though his were a world in which both the gold and the lead caskets contain death's-heads. But what we need to remember is that *Cymbeline* is not a play about a trusting king and an evil wife but rather about Posthumus and Imogen, a mistrusting husband and a faithful wife. And what this comedy and others like it explore is the variety of ways in which a young man falls quickly into the suspicious attitudes of the tragedies and sonnets, but in a world where women *are* faithful. Given a choice between the misogyny of what Jachimo calls his "Italian brain" (196) and the naïveté of Cymbeline's "duller Britain" (197), over and again these plays demand that one trust "eyes," "ears," and "heart" in the faith that beauty and virtue reside in the same house. The comedies leave for Hamlet the assumption that "the power of beauty will sooner transform honesty from what it is to a bawd than the force of honesty can translate beauty into his likeness" (III.i.110-13).

This long final scene, having dealt with the queen, now focuses, as it must, on the ways in which men have apprehended and misapprehended Imogen. I can think of no other scene in Shakespeare in which one woman stands in such distinct relation to so many other people, all male. Imogen is at once lost daughter to the King, dead and living wife to Posthumus, faithful page to Lucius, courageous mistress to Pisanio, sister to Guiderius and Arviragus, beloved page to her brothers and Belarius, and slandered woman to Jachimo. She is female and male, dead and alive, faithful and faithless. Thus, the scene needs nearly five hundred lines principally to reveal to a succession of men who Imogen is and what relation she bears to each of them. Her adopted name, Fidele, has been criticized in comparison with the names Marina, Perdita, and Miranda, though it quite appropriately directs our attention to moral issues, to Imogen's relation to others (most of whom stand near her) rather than merely to the conditions of her birth or her appearance.[39]

The resuscitation of the play's central relationship, between Posthumus and Imogen as husband and wife, depends upon Imogen's reviving her lost reputation. Her first order of business, therefore, is to demand of Jachimo, with Cymbeline's backing, of whom he had the ring which she, of course, recognizes as the token she gave Posthumus when he left her. Jachimo's confession, in turn, propels Posthumus forward, and his lamentation leads to the discovery that the young page is Imogen. The issue developed through each of the successive steps, however, has primarily to do with the nature of women and the various ways in which men "read" women mistakenly. For example, Jachimo confesses to Cymbeline that he was taught "Of your chaste daughter the wide difference / 'Twixt amorous and villainous" (194-95), and he invites us to compare, as we have seen, his "Italian brain," with its assumption that all women are whores, to the King's "duller" British thinking, which made it seem "vicious / To have mistrusted" the testimony of his eyes. Hearing Jachimo confess that he lied about sleeping with Imogen, Posthumus learns instantly that he had been a "most credulous fool" (210) and Imogen "The temple / Of virtue" (220-21). Posthumus thus becomes the third man in this scene to confess an inability to "read a woman," and to admit a consequent error in judgment. His mistaking his wife's character, her essential nature, like Othello's mistaking Desdemona's, is echoed now in his mistaking her physically, for when she rushes forward to comfort him he strikes her.

The hero's striking the heroine is a plot element that seems to have derived from Greek romance, where that apparently gratuitous bit of violence is typical. Although neither in *Cymbeline* nor in the romances "does the blow advance the plot,"[40] it is a graphic recapitulation of Posthumus's earlier spurning of Imogen, and also a very effective way of turning the boy "Fidele" into the woman Imogen, and of reversing husband's and wife's reversed sex roles. Posthumus hits a young man whom he thinks interfering; the man falls to the ground, undergoing what Pisanio sees as a kind of death ("You ne'er kill'd Imogen till now!" [231]) or, at the least, a second sleep ("Wake, my mistress!" [233]), only to rise as a woman and embrace her husband. The falling and rising is not only a far more effective, and dramatic, way of transforming boy to woman than, say, Viola's merely promising Orsino to change her clothes, or even Rosalind's exiting as a boy and entering as a woman, but also, and more importantly, graphically describes the arc of female sufferance in the comedies, where women fall into degradation, into sleep, death, and the frozen condition of stone or works of art. We see a page, not Imogen, fall from Posthumus, but we see Imogen rise up to him, and while it is she who does the moving, it is he who has done the changing, her physical ascent being simply a confirmation of his worth.

The recognitions of this final scene have as their central characters a woman who has undergone incredible suffering because of and for her husband, and a man who has moved from the ideology of the illegitimate to that of the true-born. Just as this scene affirms from the start that the play has largely been about the various ways in which men interpret women (rather than about varieties of women), so it insists from the start on a new reading of Posthumus. We have heard him call Imogen's supposed infidelity "wrying but a little," have seen him fight courageously, not so much for Britain as for Imogen and then for death itself, and have felt his penitence in welcoming the "bondage" of incarceration. In this scene, Posthumus's true worth is confirmed for us in the praise of the King and Belarius:

> Woe is my heart
> That the poor soldier that so richly fought,
> Whose rags sham'd gilded arms, whose naked breast
> Stepp'd before targes of proof, cannot be found.
> He shall be happy that can find him, if
> Our grace can make him so.
>   *Bel.*   I never saw
> Such noble fury in so poor a thing;
> Such precious deeds in one that promis'd nought
> But beggary and poor looks.
>   *Cym.*   No tidings of him?
>   *Pis.*   He hath been search'd among the dead and living;
> But no trace of him.
>   *Cym.*   To my grief, I am
> The heir of his reward, [*To Belarius, Guiderius,
>   and Arviragus*] which I will add
> To you, the liver, heart, and brain of Britain,
> By whom, I grant, she lives. [2-15]

It is significant that the two fathers in this play, Cymbeline and Belarius, express their regard for Posthumus in pecuniary imagery. Three times Posthumus is called "poor"; he wears rags and looks like a beggar. His actions, however, "sham'd gilded arms," for he "richly fought" and did "precious deeds," making Cymbeline "The heir of his reward." He has now lived up to the estimate of him made by the First Gentleman in I.i, "I do not think / So fair an outward and such stuff within / Endows a man but he" (22-24), to Philario's description of him as a man made "both without and within" (iv.9-10), and to his own conception of himself forged when he first proposed to fight as a British peasant, adopting the fashion "less without and more within" (V.i.33). At this point Posthumus's new identity is, in a sense, ratified by the especial regard in which he is held by the King and others. Most importantly, the terms in which that esteem is conveyed, through images from finance, implies that Posthumus is, like Edgar in *King Lear*, not simply the downtrodden and anonymous hero of romance but finally an anti-bastard, the ideological opposite of Cloten or of Edmund. It is the bastard, after all, who craves material wealth and fine clothing in order to mask moral and spiritual poverty, while it is the legitimate son whose innate nobility shines through his rags. It is significant, of course, that one of the many affinities between *Cymbeline* and *King Lear* is the use both plays make of commercial and sartorial imagery, and the ways both explore the relation between such imagery and questions of legitimacy. Posthumus and Edgar are legitimate sons who come to adopt, consciously or not, the philosophy of the illegitimate, but while Posthumus truly becomes the Hippolytan misogynist, Edgar remains the loyal hero of romance, like Orlando or Pericles, a man whose external circumstances cannot taint the true temper of his mind.

The fullness of Posthumus's transformation is brought home to us in his treatment of Imogen after he strikes the "page" and his "dead" wife rises to him. In lines that have been universally praised, Posthumus is revealed to us as a new man, all the more secure for his having suffered earlier, patiently and prayerfully, like a woman:

> *Imo.*   Why did you throw your wedded lady [from] you?
> Think that you are upon a rock, and now
> Throw me again.   [*Embracing him.*]
>   *Post.*   Hang there like fruit, my soul,
> Till the tree die! [V.v.261-64]

The image that Posthumus uses, of himself as a tree and Imogen as the fruit of that tree, his soul, suggests that he sees them as connected in the deepest and most natural way and that to have rejected Imogen was to have committed, in essence, an insanely irrational act, which reminds us of Albany's horrible insight into Goneril, "She that herself will sliver and disbranch / From her material sap, perforce must wither, / And come to deadly use" (IV.ii.34-36). Posthumus's images here are revealing as well in terms of the changes in sex roles husband and wife have undergone. We have seen Imogen move from the chamber in which her father had locked her, to the relative freedom conferred by her disguise as a man, to the limbo of her death-like state after drinking the Queen's potion. We have seen, as well, a graphic recreation of her descent in her falling to the ground when Posthumus strikes her. Posthumus has moved from the physical freedom of the male world to the sterility and loneliness typical of the life of the ideologically illegitimate, and then to the immobility and patience of incarceration, so characteristic of the female stereotype. Re-united with Imogen, Posthumus plays the part of the male in his being the "tree" and in supporting Imogen, whom he wants to "hang there," depending on him in a stereotypically female way (Hamlet complains of Gertrude's behavior with his father, "Why, she would hang on him / As if increase of appetite had grown / By what it fed on" [I.ii.143-45]). And yet Posthumus's image is uncharacteristic of male views of males in the tree's being, by definition, incapable of movement. It is no coincidence, in fact, that trees play an important part in the iconography of Patience, suggesting exactly that blend of constancy and hope that has informed Posthumus's new conception of himself.

Those depictions of Patience, which we discussed in Chapter 5, help, I think, explain as well Imogen's puzzling reference to "rock" ("Think that you are upon a rock"). Glosses of the line invariably include a question mark, and most editors settle for reminding the reader of Dowden's emendation of "rock" to "lock," a wrestling term, like "throw." Although this change makes sense of the line, "it lacks the ring of truth"[41] and is utterly un-Shakespearean in its lack of relation to Posthumus's response, "Hang there like fruit." But if Dowden's emendation is of little help, Imogen's speech does make perfect sense in terms of the iconography of Patience. As we have seen, Patience is almost always shown sitting on a stone or a "monument," occasionally in front of or near a tree. In Bruegel's engraving, for example, which I discussed earlier, a large, dead tree dominates the landscape immediately behind Patience, and in the distance dead trees are prominent. In *Patientia and Fortitudo*, a sixteenth-century engraving by Hendrik Goltzius, Fortitude is seated next to a column while Patience sits in front of trees in leaf.[42] The clearest association of trees and Patience can be seen in *Victrix Patientia Duri*, in George Wither's *A Collection of Emblemes, Ancient and Moderne*. The emblem simply depicts a leafy tree bearing a large stone in its branches, and the motto reads, "*No Inward* Griefe, *nor outward* Smart, / *Can overcome a* Patient-Heart."[43] It is important to remember that the message Jupiter leaves with Posthumus when he sleeps is, in part, a prediction that

Posthumus and Britain will not stop suffering until "from a stately cedar shall be lopp'd branches, which, being dead many years, shall after revive, be jointed to the old stock, and freshly grow" (V.iv.140-43) (interestingly, the device Pericles gives Thaisa at the tournament at Pentapolis shows "A withered branch, that's only green at top; / The motto: *'In hac spe vivo'*" [II.ii.43-44]).

Scholars who accept "rock" as genuine, as Nosworthy notes, frequently read Imogen's speech as an invitation to Posthumus to "think of himself as a shipwrecked sailor who has at last run upon the rock of security."[44] Cymbeline's remarks later in the scene, "See, / Posthumus anchors upon Imogen" (392-93), are then seen as confirmation of this reading, which, it seems to me, is certainly valid. But the anchor, like the tree, was conventionally associated with Hope, the virtue most closely allied in the sixteenth century with Patience. For example, the stone, anchor, and tree are all depicted in *Patientiae Triumphus*, where Patience sits on a block of stone in a wagon pulled by Hope, who carries a large anchor and near whom the leaves of a tree can be seen.[45] The reunion scene between Posthumus and Imogen thus uses symbols conventionally associated with Patience, and these reinforce our sense that the new relationship between husband and wife is a blend of stereotypically male and female virtues. The active patience Imogen evinces in following Posthumus and in retaining faith in him, is echoed in Posthumus's renewal of faith in Imogen even when he believes her guilty of "wrying but a little" and in his patient endurance on the battlefield and in prison. Posthumus's new sense of himself has arisen from the ashes of his old; anger is transformed into patience, and belief in mere externals into an abiding trust in women and in that "within."

There is, however, a somewhat different way of reading the beautiful exchange between Posthumus and Imogen at V.v.261. Most editors follow Malone in adding the stage direction *"Embracing him"* when Imogen asks Posthumus, "Why did you throw your wedded lady [from] you?" The direction helps to elucidate a murky passage but inevitably leads to our seeing Posthumus as the tree and Imogen as the fruit. What is, in a sense, an ever better reading—better in the consistent way it interprets all the images—is to see Imogen as the tree and Posthumus's soul as the fruit. Their embracing one another, of course, leaves open to directors the choice of making one or the other appear more or less dependent. Imogen, after all, compares herself to a "rock," and Cymbeline observes that "Posthumus anchors upon Imogen." It is entirely fitting, then, that Posthumus see himself as dependent, as fruit, and Imogen, especially after her ordeal, see herself as loyal, patient, and solid as rock or tree. Interpreting Posthumus's line, "Hang there like fruit, my soul," as a reference to himself, his soul, rather than to Imogen, makes even more emphatic his transformation from active misogynist to integrated and healthy husband, a man now as trusting and loyal as a woman, a man, like Benedick, who can rely on a woman's judgment and depend on her in the fullest sense of the word. Imogen, in turn, combines the patience and loyalty of the stereo-typical woman with the strength and activity so commonly associated with men. Here more clearly than elsewhere, Murray Schwartz's argument that Shakespeare, as person and playwright, "accepted these differences" ("masculine and feminine . . . self and other") and "merged them into identities," seems both insightful and correct.[46]

Though V.v has gone far toward explaining the various ways in which Imogen relates to all the men on stage, she has much to explain before Cymbeline, for one, can see her as she is. But this play will conclude, as others have, retaining for Imogen some of the aura of mystery that surrounds her as she revives after Posthumus strikes her. Though the audience knows all the answers, her father does not, and he yearns for a longer story than the "abridged" version he must settle for at this time:

> When shall I hear all through? This fierce abridgement
> Hath to it circumstantial branches, which
> Distinction should be rich in. Where? how liv'd you?
> And when came you to serve our Roman captive?
> How parted with your [brothers]? How first met them?
> Why fled you from the court? and whither? These,
> And your three motives to the battle, with
> I know not how much more, should be demanded,
> And all the other by-dependances,
> From chance to chance; but nor the time nor place
> Will serve our long interrogatories. [382-92]

As always in Shakespearean comedy, it is the man with the questions and the woman who can provide the answers; as in *The Merchant of Venice*, the "interrogatories" must wait, for the play will end with a woman at the center of the mysteries that confuse the men.

The reversals of sex role that turn the boy "Fidele" into the woman Imogen and Posthumus into her husband and Patience itself are complemented by Cymbeline's appropriating for himself the role of mother as well as of father. Just as Leontes is courted by his "suitor" Hermione and Pericles suffers "like a girl," so Cymbeline becomes a self-conscious blend of the masculine and the feminine when he discovers his lost sons: "O, what, am I / A mother to the birth of three? Ne'er mother / Rejoic'd deliverance more" (368-70). His arrogating to himself the roles of mother and father, of woman as well as man, characterizes male behavior in the romances. But what Cymbeline does in rejoicing as a "mother" differs only in degree from the behavior of other males in earlier plays. Shakespearean comedy demands that male characters learn to appreciate values associated with women and to experience losses that encourage patience and develop loyalty and trust.

The rejoicing here is a product not only of the miraculous appearance of a woman thought dead, as it is in other comedies, but especially of the restoration of a family whose reunion implies the restoration of Britain's national spirit. The sense of incorporation is stronger here than in any play since *The Comedy of Errors*. Cymbeline's family is reunited; Posthumus and Imogen are given a second start; Imogen will consider old Belarius a "father too" (400), and Cymbeline simply tells his old friend, "Thou art my brother" (399). Most importantly, Posthumus is now husband to Imogen, son-in-law to Cymbeline, and brother to those who will rule Britain in days to come:

> *Arv.*   You holp us, sir,
> As you did mean indeed to be our brother;
> Joy'd are we that you are. [422-24]

This play's botanical imagery, which has as its central metaphor Posthumus's lines, "Hang there like fruit, my soul, / Till the tree die," begins with the 1st Gentleman in act 1 complaining, "I cannot delve him to the root" (i.28). Posthumus has grown and flourished, and Cymbeline, with his sons returned, regains those "lopp'd branches" (438) "now reviv'd, / To the majestic cedar join'd, whose issue / Promises Britain peace and plenty" (456-58). The patience of the individual is reflected nationally in Cymbeline's submitting "to Caesar, / And to the Roman empire" (460-61), adopting as state policy the sort of patience and charitable attitude Imogen shows to Posthumus and Posthumus to Jachimo, whom he forgives. Britain, in effect, takes on the stereotypical female virtues and, as in a marriage ceremony, submits herself to "imperial Caesar" (474), who "should again unite / His favor with the radiant Cymbeline, / Which shines here in the west" (474-76). The peace will be ratified in the temple of Jupiter and sealed with feasts, as though it were, indeed, a marriage. In *Cymbeline*, the regeneration of the individual implies that of the nation, for the roots and branches that revive and grow become the lofty cedar that is the state. Nosworthy captures fully the emotions with which this play closes:

> It is not extravagant to claim that *Cymbeline*, in its end, acquires a significance that extends beyond any last curtain or final *Exeunt*.

There is, quite simply, something in this play which goes "beyond beyond," and that which ultimately counts for more than the traffic of the stage is the Shakespearean vision—of unity certainly, perhaps of the Earthly Paradise, perhaps of the Elysian Fields, perhaps, even, the vision of the saints. But whatever else, it is assuredly a vision of perfect tranquillity, a partial comprehension of that Peace which passeth all understanding, and a contemplation of the indestructible essence in which Imogen, Iachimo, atonement, the national ideal have all ceased to have separate identity or individual meaning. [47]

Conclusion

The great heroines of Elizabethan/Jacobean drama, Beatrice-Joanna, Anne Frankford, the Duchess of Malfi, for example, all play out their sad stories virtually alone, dying for, or because of, men whom audiences think shallow and unworthy of their passionate, misguided assaults on the restrictions of patriarchy. Much the same can be said about the tragic heroines of the nineteenth-century novel, Emma Bovary or Anna Karenina, women who spiral downward while weak or mean-spirited husbands relax in their armchairs or respond only as ignorant spokesmen for repressive cultures. In those stories, husbands and lovers are often presented as part of the problem, witting or unwitting instruments of larger, socioeconomic forces, and the tragedy's effects depend, more or less, on the extent to which we appreciate a woman's lonely struggle against an unavoidable fate.

In contrast, the tragic possibilities that confront Shakespeare's protagonists are eliminated or at least blunted, not because social forces are any the less daunting or because their appetite for adventure or desire for revenge is less strong but rather because Shakespeare conceives of man and woman as the most basic sort of allies. The hero in Shakespearean comedy is truly partnered, and his choices, no less tragic or self-defeating than Emma Bovary's, necessarily involve the woman who loves him. Her sensitivity and acuity, her heroic response, render the comedies stunning *pas de deux*; we watch lovers construct a relationship together, woman responding to man, man responding to woman. Social and psychological pressures are thus alleviated in fundamentally social ways.

Shakespeare sees two lovers as a single entity; for him romance implies sympathetic reactions of the sort we witness when even separated couples affect one another for the better. Indeed, what the hero recognizes in the last act's recognition scene is the fact that he has never really been alone at all. The complementary roles man and woman play, however, tend to focus the audience's attention on the hero, and it is his struggle to forge healthful attitudes toward women and marriage that comedy celebrates. For the most part, the heroine is conceived of as the play's moral center, and she is apprehended as such by the audience and by the major characters themselves. Our orientation derives from her position, ideological, emotional, even geographical; we assess the hero's behavior only in relation to the heroine's well-being. It is her patience for human failing and her almost intuitive understanding of sexual relationships men approximate as the plays end. Finally, it is her level of happiness as she leaves the stage that determines ours as we leave the theater. To say as much is to indicate her role and importance, certainly, but also the ways in which her options as a character are limited. To serve as the play's "ever-fixèd mark" is to assert values associated with the female but also to be denied not sexual feelings but rather the freedom to act upon those feelings. The fun audiences derive from hearing Rosalind describe women as "the wiser, the waywarder" (IV.i.161) or Portia threaten, "I'll have that doctor for [my] bedfellow" (V.i.233), has to do with our being in on the joke, of course, but also with our sure knowledge that the ladies' games are only verbal.

Elizabethan cultural imperatives, which banished women from the stage and defined their representations along lines most reassuring to patriarchy, are responsible in the first place for that narrowed range of female sexual behavior enacted in comedy. Shakespeare, however, uses the twin ideals of female virginity and chastity imposed on comedy by literary tradition and cultural history to accentuate male eccentricity, i.e., as foils for the hero's aberrant behavior. In other words, because there is no suspense with regard to, say, Posthumus's brutal accusations, the question the plot poses, rather obviously, becomes, what has led a man, in love with such a woman, to toss her aside? "Why did you throw your wedded lady [from] you?" Imogen asks in act 5, as the audience turns to the hero for an explanation of his strangely, dangerously, contradictory behavior. Hence, the audience's interest in Shakespeare's love story derives in large part from dramatic irony: the hero is blind to the very qualities of character in a woman that we see most clearly.

Our sense that Shakespearean comedy is primarily about men in no way implies that the woman's part in these stories is less important, or that the female characters are less complex. Indeed, few students of these plays fail to be impressed with the way Shakespeare seems to create genderbalanced communities out of casts composed of three or four times as many males. Nonetheless, the story he tells is clearly precipitated by men, and for that reason centers on men. In *Measure for Measure*, for example, Isabella's being a novice (in Shakespeare's sources the heroine is unaffiliated) serves to draw our attention to Angelo, as he himself is quick to realize. Aroused by the novice, who all along has only asked for "a more strict restraint" (I.iv.4), the deputy asks, "Is this her fault, or mine? / The tempter, or the tempted, who sins most, ha? / Not she; nor doth she tempt;

but it is I" (II.ii.162-64). Isabella's being a virtual fidelity machine, the play's immovable object, has admittedly cost her dearly on stage, for comedy, as Frye and Bergson point out, abhors rigidity. However, her steadfastness functions as a kind of touchstone against which we see all the more clearly the human and all too flexible attitudes of at least four men, Angelo, the Duke, Claudio, and Lucio.

If the heroes in *Measure for Measure,* as in other comedies, can seem more human for their failings and the heroines less so for their constancy, Shakespeare nonetheless allows us to *feel* the effects of male attacks on women, and even a character as tightly circumscribed as Isabella demonstrates an interior life that can be quite effectively presented on stage. In a 1975 production at Stratford, Ontario, set in Victorian England and featuring Martha Henry as Isabella, audiences were stunned in the final moments by the novice's pain. After proposing, or rather announcing his marriage plans, the Duke ushered all but Isabella from his office. Of that final scene a reviewer wrote, "The prospect of marriage to the Duke filled her with revulsion, and the theatre darkened around her face twisted in agony."[1] Productions such as this, which try to shift the focus to the woman and show that her loyalty to principle (or to a man) need not render her a flat character, are in part the result of the growing feminist reappraisal of Shakespeare and can make for fascinating theater. Although they make the important point that the heroine, no less than the hero, is a fully realized, psychologically complex character, they will remain in the minority. When all is said and done, Isabella has not one line after the Duke's, "Dear Isabel, / I have a motion much imports your good" (V.i.534-35). Though her silence speaks volumes, what it tells us has to do with men, that is, with the effect on women of male behavior.

Far more often, of course, productions focus on the hero, though they occasionally reduce that convoluted figure of Shakespeare's imagination to the sort of chap who would seem more at home on a television "drama." For example, again at Stratford, again in the mid-1970s, I saw a *Much Ado about Nothing* that, centering on Claudio, never indicated for a moment that he was anything other than a callous poseur. Because the audience had been largely composed of high school students, when the play ended the actor who performed Claudio came on stage to take questions, the very first of which was, "How do you like being such a bad man?" That evening, Claudio had been the heavy, and his rejection of Hero a dastardly and unforgivable act. Unfortunately, such a boo-hiss approach to male behavior—with consummate irony—turns these comedies right back into the simple-minded affairs Shakespeare was clearly moving from in his insistence that the impediment to romance lie in the psyche and social circumstances of the hero. To direct *Much Ado* so that night after night

Claudio is seen as the Elizabethan equivalent of an evil landlord tying the heroine to the railroad tracks is to shortchange Shakespeare, the audience, and the poor actor. Any performance that leads to the audience's calling that poor fellow on the carpet seems to me to miss the point of these plays entirely. What sense does it make from a psychological, sociological, even dramaturgical point of view to replace the *senex* of Plautus with a one-dimensional version of the angry, destructive, self-destructive hero of Shakespeare? There is, after all, a qualitative difference between the interfering father—Prospero, or Polixenes, or Egeus—and the interfering lover, who slanders as he woos. By turning the hero into his own worst enemy, Shakespeare challenges us to confront the complex nature of love itself and to fathom the ways in which male and female responses to beauty and attraction are contingent upon family history and cultural bias. Claudio's insecurities, his fear of women and dependency on men, merit productions sensitive to the coherent picture Shakespeare has drawn.

From Antipholus through Bassanio to Posthumus, Shakespeare takes pains to create males whose behavior is rooted in attitudes fostered by a host of social circumstances. Though his poetry is far richer in *Cymbeline* than in *The Comedy of Errors,* and though characters are, in general, increasingly substantial as his career progresses, there is from the very first a psychological profile available to the actor playing the male lead. Between the hero as simpering swain, for whom an impossibly sweet love is destroyed by meddling others, and the hero as moody villain, victimizing women almost by nature, there are left a wide range of portrayals that can help us get to the heart of these compelling stories of slander and self-denigration. In the comedies no less than in the tragedies, Shakespeare begins with stock types, embeds them in recognizable social settings, and the result is an interaction between the sexes that is affecting precisely because it is comprehensible intellectually and viscerally. I think it is fair to say that while tragedy's simplistic world of black and white morality ended with the fifth act of *Richard III*, comedy's died in the first act of *The Comedy of Errors.*

Notes

Journal Abbreviations

BuR	*Bucknell Review*
CJ	*Classical Journal*
CompD	*Comparative Drama*
CritQ	*Critical Quarterly*
ELH	[Formerly, *Journal of English Literary History*]
ELR	*English Literary Renaissance*
MLQ	*Modern Language Quarterly*
MLR	*Modern Language Review*
N&Q	*Notes and Queries*
PR	*Partisan Review*
PMLA	*Publications of the Modern Language Association of America*
RenQ	*Renaissance Quarterly*
RES	*Review of English Studies*
SEL	*Studies in English Literature, 1500-1900*
ShakS	*Shakespeare Studies*
ShS	*Shakespeare Survey*
SQ	*Shakespeare Quarterly*
TSLL	*Texas Studies in Literature and Language*

Introduction

1. *The Maine Woods*, ed. Joseph J. Moldenhauer (Princeton: Princeton Univ. Press, 1972), 71.

2. *Pilgrim at Tinker Creek* (New York: Harper's Magazine Press, 1974), 8.

3. *Desert Solitaire* (Salt Lake City: Peregrine Smith, 1981), 194.

4. *The Snow Leopard* (New York: Viking, 1978), 30.

5. *Pilgrim*, 137.

6. *The Panda's Thumb* (New York: Norton, 1980), 182.

7. Richard P. Wheeler takes exception to Frye's schema and thinks the *senex* in Shakespeare "rarely a competing suitor." He discusses the generally helpful attitudes of parents in Shakespearean comedy in *Shakespeare's Development and the Problem Comedies* (Berkeley: Univ. of California Press, 1981), 45-46. Carol Thomas Neely notes that in Shakespearean comedy "the most important impediments to comic fulfillment lie within the couples themselves and not, as Northrop Frye has influentially argued, within the blocking figures, repressive laws, and humor characters of an anticomic society in need of transformation" (*Broken Nuptials in Shakespeare's Plays* [New Haven: Yale Univ. Press, 1985], 26). And, earlier, Sherman Hawkins arrived at a very similar conclusion in "The Two Worlds of Shakespearean Comedy," *ShakS* 3 (1967): 62-80. Noting that Frye's green world theory does not explain *The Comedy of Errors*,

Love's Labour's Lost, Much Ado about Nothing, and *Twelfth Night*, Hawkins described two sorts of comedies, those that begin with "expulsion" (comedies in which the action moves to Frye's green world), and those that begin with "intrusion." In the latter, Hawkins suggested, resistance to love "comes from the lovers themselves": "Love is denied by lovers; husband turns upon wife; youth is divided against itself." Hawkins's pattern seems to me a particularly valuable way to see the plays; what I argue throughout this book—and especially in Ch. 3—is that the real obstacles to true love are always internal and almost always male (the angry fathers and so on being merely conventional hindrances, perfunctorily dismissed when the hero rejects the heroine in earnest).

8. Cited by John F. Danby, *Shakespeare's Doctrine of Nature* (London: Faber and Faber, 1948), 228.

9. *Shakespeare's Festive Comedy* (Princeton: Princeton Univ. Press, 1959), 4.

10. *Illegitimacy* (Ithaca: Cornell Univ. Press, 1982), 132. Teichman uses the term in her discussion of illegitimacy in literature.

11. *Broken Nuptials*, 38.

12. *Friends and Lovers: The Phenomenology of Desire in Shakespearean Comedy* (New York: Columbia Univ. Press, 1985), 4-5.

13. In *Shakespeare and the Nature of Women* (London: MacMillan, 1975), Juliet Dusinberre argues that the Reformation and the Puritan emphasis on marriage and the family led to a drama "feminist in sympathy" (5). For her, "Shakespeare's feminism consists of more than a handful of high-born emancipated heroines: it lies rather in his skepticism about the nature of women" (305). Marianne Novy, in *Love's Argument: Gender Relations in Shakespeare* (Chapel Hill: Univ. of North Carolina Press, 1984), argues that in Shakespeare's plays "women's gestures of submission are often balanced by similar gestures from the men" (43), while Neely sees such equality only fitfully, in *The Winter's Tale, The Merchant of Venice*, and in the mediating influence of Helena's child in *All's Well That Ends Well*. Others, notably Lisa Jardine (*Still Harping on Daughters* [Brighton: Harvester, 1983]), take very different positions, arguing that the patriarchy only appears to concede power to women, retaining, in the final analysis, its full vigor. Catherine Belsey, who has written extensively on gender relations in Elizabethan/Jacobean drama in general (see "Disrupting Sexual Difference: Meaning and Gender in the Comedies," in *Alternative Shakespeares*, ed. John Drakakis [London: Methuen, 1985], 166-90, and *The Subject of Tragedy* [London: Methuen, 1985]), argues that in terms of gender relations, "the period was one of enforced silence, and of intense and violent conflict, producing an order which still bears the marks of the conflict and the violence, and perhaps of the silence too. This reading foregrounds the resistance . . ." (*Subject of Tragedy*, 222).

14. *Man's Estate: Masculine Identity in Shakespeare* (Berkeley: Univ. of California Press, 1981), 217.

1. *"The Spirit of My Father"*

1. Only Proteus, in *The Two Gentlemen of Verona*, and Troilus, in *Troilus and Cressida*, develop a relationship with a woman before their fathers die or before they leave home or assume, even temporarily, a new identity (as, for example, Lucentio does when he becomes "Cambio" in *The Taming of the Shrew*).

2. *Endeavors of Art* (Madison: Univ. of Wisconsin Press, 1964), 157. See also Northrop Frye, *Anatomy of Criticism* (Princeton: Princeton Univ. Press, 1957), 163-86.

3. Marvin T. Herrick, *Comic Theory in the Sixteenth Century* (Urbana: Univ. of Illinois Press, 1964), writes that "It is well known that Renaissance comedy was modeled principally upon the plays of Terence" (1), and Doran remarks that Terence was studied in the classroom "as a source of elegant Latinity for boys to emulate"

(*Endeavors of Art*, 151). In his translation of *The Comedies of Terence* (New York: Bobbs-Merrill, 1967), Frank O. Copley notes that "In every one of the six plays this relationship [between fathers and sons] is subjected to some degree of study" (xviii).

4. See Francis MacDonald Cornford, *The Origin of Attic Comedy* (Gloucester, Mass: Peter Smith, 1968).

5. For the history of the *Menaechmi* in the Renaissance, see *Narrative and Dramatic Sources of Shakespeare*, ed. Geoffrey Bullough (London: Routledge and Kegan Paul, 1957), 1:4-5.

6. For a discussion of the origins of the Shakespearean New Comedy plot see Doran, *Endeavors of Art*, and Leo Salingar, *Shakespeare and the Traditions of Comedy* (Cambridge: Cambridge Univ. Press, 1974).

7. Antipholus of Syracuse, Antipholus of Ephesus, Valentine, Proteus, Lucentio, Troilus, Florizel, and Ferdinand.

8. Lawrence Stone and Jeanne C. Fawtier Stone, *An Open Elite?* (Oxford: Oxford Univ. Press, 1984), 85; see also Ch. IV, "Transitions: Intra-Familial Inheritance," 105-47.

9. *Plautus*, trans. Paul Nixon (London: William Heinemann, 1959), II, 10.

10. *The Family, Sex and Marriage in England 1500-1800* (New York: Harper and Row, 1977), 191.

11. Ibid., 88.

12. See Marilyn Williamson, *The Patriarchy of Shakespeare's Comedies* (Detroit: Wayne State Univ. Press, 1986), for a discussion of prodigality "as a life-script for the Elizabethans," 65ff.

13. *Love's Argument*, 56.

14. Thomas Kelly, "Shakespeare's Romantic Heroes: Orlando Reconsidered," *SQ* 24 (1973): 15, points out that Orlando "is an anagram for Rowland." Orlando's identification with his father is thoroughgoing. In *The Myth of the Eternal Return*, trans. Willard R. Trask, Bollingen Series 46 (New York: Pantheon, 1954), 42, Mircea Eliade describes "mythicization," or "the metamorphosis of a historical figure into a mythical hero," as part of his analysis of the subjects of epic poetry. However, his conclusions would seem to account for the way in which the older generation is remembered in Shakespearean comedy, where fathers almost always seem to their sons to have been exemplary. It would seem that "mythicization" has worked upon the world's memory not only of Orlando's father, but of the fathers of most young heroes in these plays. Men such as Sir Rowland de Boys are remembered by friends and relations as having been superb warriors and statesmen, models for a less noble age. Such idealization perhaps illustrates the thesis that "historicity does not long resist the corrosive action of mythicization" (42). On the relation of myth to character and action, see Northrop Frye, *A Natural Perspective* (New York: Columbia Univ. Press, 1965), 61-71; "Characterization in Shakespearean Comedy," *SQ* 4 (1953): 271-77; and *The Secular Scripture* (Cambridge, Mass: Harvard Univ. Press, 1976).

15. In "The King and the Physician's Daughter: *All's Well That Ends Well* and the Late Romances," *CompD* 8 (1973): 311-27, and in "Marriage and Manhood in *All's Well That Ends Well*," *BuR* 21 (1973): 103-24, Richard P. Wheeler explores Bertram's rejection of Helena as a rejection, in part, of a second childhood forced on him by a King who seems a surrogate father. For a discussion of Bertram's relationship with both parents see W. Speed Hill, "Marriage as Destiny: An Essay on *All's Well That Ends Well*," *ELR* 5 (1975): 344-59.

16. James Trombetta, "Versions of Dying in *Measure for Measure*," *ELR* 6 (1976): 64.

17. *Philaster*, ed. Robert K. Turner, in *The Dramatic Works in the Beaumont and Fletcher Canon*, ed. Fredson Bowers (Cambridge: Cambridge Univ. Press, 1966), 1:I.i.195-204.

18. For a discussion of generational problems see Alexander Welsh, "The Loss of Men and Getting of Children: 'All's Well That Ends Well' and 'Measure for Measure'," *MLR* 73 (1978): 17-28. Welsh discusses, with some cogency, the "biological reasoning" of the problem plays. See also David Sundelson's psychoanalytic study, *Shakespeare's Restorations of the Father* (New Brunswick, N.J.: Rutgers Univ. Press, 1983), 13-18.

19. *A Yorkshire Tragedy*, in *Shakespeare and His Fellow Dramatists*, ed. E.H.C. Oliphant (New York: Prentice-Hall, 1929), 2:ii.219-21, 254-55.

20. *A Woman Killed with Kindness*, ed. Brian W.M. Scobie (London: A.C. Black, 1985), x.7, vii.15-24.

21. *The Shoemaker's Holiday*, ed. D.J. Palmer (London: Ernest Benn, 1975), II.iv.52-3.

22. *The Knight, the Lady and the Priest* (New York: Pantheon, 1983), 37.

23. *Life in the English Country House* (New Haven: Yale Univ. Press, 1978), Chapter 1, *passim.*

24. Stone, *An Open Elite?*, 69-70.

25. Stone, *Family, Sex and Marriage in England*, 87.

26. I am discussing here the kinds of strategies for discovering self and for perceiving and relating to others that are the focus of Coppélia Kahn's *Man's Estate* and W. Thomas MacCary's *Friends and Lovers*. See also Leo Salingar, *Shakespeare and Traditions of Comedy*, 222: "For Shakespeare's characters are not merely capable of being surprised by what happens to them, dismayed or delighted, like the people in Italian comedies; they can be carried out of their normal selves, 'transformed', observe themselves passing into a new phase of experience, so strange that it seems like illusion."

27. Bullough, *Narrative and Dramatic Sources*, 1:vii.29-32.

28. Ibid., 1:112.

29. Welsh, "Loss of Men," 17.

30. See the excellent discussion of the language of Adriana's speech in Vincent F. Petronella, "Structure and Theme through Separation and Union in Shakespeare's 'The Comedy of Errors'," *MLR* 69 (1974): 31-8.

31. *A Traveller in Italy* (New York: Dodd, Mead, 1964), 108ff.

32. Bullough, *Narrative and Dramatic Sources*, 2:316.

2. *"We Cannot Fight for Love"*

1. *Reinventing Womanhood* (New York: Norton, 1979), 139.

2. *Becoming a Heroine* (New York: Viking, 1982), 35.

3. Thomas Middleton and William Rowley, *The Changeling*, ed. George W. Williams (Lincoln: Univ. of Nebraska Press, 1966), II.ii.109.

4. Gustave Flaubert, *Madam Bovary*, trans. Francis Steegmuller (New York: Random, 1957), 101.

5. Henry James, *The Portrait of a Lady*, ed. Leon Edel (Boston: Houghton Mifflin, 1963), 133.

6. It is not clear whether Shylock is more protective of his daughter or his money, though the two, as his dearest possessions, are certainly identified with one another, as MacCary, following Kahn, points out: "his keeping her bound in his house, out of circulation, is an example of his oft expressed attitude toward money generally: he wants it to increase and reproduce itself, but does not want to run risks with it" (*Friends and Lovers*, 36).

7. It is difficult to ascertain with any degree of accuracy just how fully women were emancipated in Renaissance Europe. Lisa Jardine, who uses historical documents more fully than do most commentators on Shakespearean comedy, finds that "social historians are generally significantly less optimistic than literary critics" on the

issue of how free women were in the sixteenth century" (*Still Harping on Daughters*, 63). Although some women "achieved standards of proficiency in the specialist skills of humanism," according to Jardine, from "their male intellectual colleagues these women earned the tribute of being 'beyond their sex', 'like men', honorary members of the male community" (56). An opposite conclusion with regard to the position of women and to their representation in the drama of the period is reached by Dusinberre in *Shakespeare and Nature of Women*. Some women did, of course, achieve notable success in the business world as well as in "the specialist skills of humanism." For example, Beatrice Beech, in "Charlotte Guillard: A Sixteenth-Century Business Woman," *RenQ* 36 (1983): 345-67, describes in great detail the ways in which the Parisian guild system of the sixteenth century enabled women to take over their husbands' businesses when the men died. "One result of this was that many Parisian women led active and varied economic lives" (345). And in a review essay entitled "The Family as History" in *PR* (1986), Edmund Leites discusses recent books that attack standard interpretations of patriarchy in early modern Europe, such as those by Lawrence Stone, Steven Marcus, and Philippe Aries, works ascribing the development of caring relations between husbands and wives and parents and children to the Enlightenment. Although Leites can find no unanimity of opinion in works by Steven Ozment, Linda Pollock, and others, what he does see at work is "a distinctly conservative trend," "an unwillingness to see modernity as morally advanced" (124) over earlier periods, an insistence that family life in the Renaissance was as caring and humane as it is today. For background information see Frances and Joseph Gies, *Women in the Middle Ages* (New York: Crowell, 1978), and Eileen Power's classic study, *Medieval People* (London: Methuen, 1924). For a fascinating analysis of the relationship between political and religious views of women as represented in the visual arts, see John N. King, "The Godly Woman in Elizabethan Iconography," *RenQ* 38 (1985): 41-84.

8. Thomas Kyd, *The Spanish Tragedy*, ed. J.R. Mulryne (London: Ernest Benn, 1970), III.ix.2, 12-14.

9. *Changeling*, III.iii.2-3.

10. John Ford, *The Broken Heart*, ed., Donald K. Anderson, Jr. (Lincoln: Univ. of Nebraska Press, 1968), II.i.i.

11. *Othello*, ed. H.H. Furness (Philadelphia: Lippincott, 1886).

12. The *OED* indicates that the term "husband" originally signified a person owning both house and land, a freeholder. To a military man such as Othello, owning land would imply the exact opposite of the freedom conferred by the seas. Othello's stereotypical attitudes toward the worlds of men and women are reinforced by the not-so-subtle sexual pun in the speech at I.ii.24, which can be read as a fairly straightforward description of sexual intercourse. That he would not put his "unhoused free condition" into "circumscription" for "the sea's worth," is to say he would not have sex at all, save for his loving Desdemona. This reading becomes clearer when we remember that an Elizabethan playwright might well rely on the audience's hearing "cee" ("sea") and recognizing a reference to female genitalia (as in *Twelfth Night* when Malvolio says, "These be her very c's, her u's, and her t's, and thus makes she her great P's" [II.v.86-88]). See John H. Astington, "'Fault' in Shakespeare," *SQ* 36 (1985): 330-34.

13. *Medieval English Nunneries c. 1275 to 1535* (1922; rpt., New York: Biblo and Tannen, 1964), 38.

14. *Medieval English Nunneries*, 506.

15. *The Merry Devil of Edmonton*, in *Shakespeare and His Fellow Dramatists*, ed. E.H.C. Oliphant (New York: Prentice-Hall, 1929, 1:V.i.136.

16. Power: "Unfortunately a large number of girls who became nuns had no vocation at all. They were given over to the life by their families, sometimes from childhood, because it was a reputable career for daughters who could not be dowered for marriage in a manner befitting their estate. They were often totally unsuited for it,

by the weakness of their religious as well as of their sexual impulses. The lighthearted *Chansons de Nonnes*, whose theme is the nun unwillingly professed, had a real basis in fact" (*Medieval English Nunneries*, 437). According to Power, excluding houses that contained both brothers and nuns, there were well over one hundred nunneries in England c. 1270-1536 (1).

17. *Medieval English Nunneries*, 443.

18. This argument, that the woman's male disguise restricts her by eliminating the possibility of sexual encounter with a man, and thereby ironically reinforces conventional restrictions on her, runs counter to some recent interpretations. See, for example, Carolyn Heilbrun, *Toward a Recognition of Androgyny* (New York: Knopf, 1973), 29: "disguise for Shakespeare is not always falsification, or not evilly so. Disguise may be another indication of the wide spectrum of roles possible to individuals if they can but find the convenient trappings of another persona."

19. For Jardine, the transvestized young boys of the Elizabethan stage had a distinctly homoerotic appeal for the audiences. See *Still Harping on Daughters*, Ch. I.

20. Robert Greene, *Friar Bacon and Friar Bungay*, ed. Daniel Seltzer (Lincoln: Univ. of Nebraska Press, 1963), x.160-62.

21. Hardin Craig, ed., *The Complete Works of Shakespeare* (Glenview, Ill.: Scott, Foresman, 1961), note to III.ii.63.

22. *Shakespeare and the Experience of Love* (Cambridge: Cambridge Univ. Press, 1981), 115. Richard P. Wheeler, whose work on the problem comedies highlights the unconscious, incestuous component in Helena's relationship with Bertram, describes the sexual appeal and attraction she has for the court of France in *Shakespeare's Development and the Problem Comedies*, 75-81.

23. "The Argument of Comedy," in *Shakespeare, Modern Essays in Criticism*, ed. Leonard F. Dean, rev. ed. (Oxford: Oxford Univ. Press, 1967), 80.

24. On issues of social class in the play see John M. Love, "'Though many of the rich are damn'd': Dark Comedy and Social Class in *All's Well That Ends Well*," *TSLL* 18 (1977): 517-27. Also see A. P. Rossiter, *Angel with Horns* (New York: Theatre Art Books, 1961), 106.

25. See, for example, Lawrence W. Hyman, "The Rival Lovers in *The Merchant of Venice*, *SQ* 21 (1970): 109-116, and Keith Geary, "The Nature of Portia's Victory: Turning to Men in 'The Merchant of Venice'," *ShS* 37 (1984): 55-68. Leonard Tennenhouse, "The Counterfeit Order of *The Merchant of Venice*," in *Representing Shakespeare*, ed. Murray M. Schwartz and Coppélia Kahn (Baltimore: Johns Hopkins Univ. Press, 1980), 54-69, discusses in part "the betrothal of self to friend" (60).

26. *Shakespeare and Traditions of Comedy*, 221.

27. Ibid., 222.

28. *The Merchant of Venice*, ed. George Lyman Kittredge (New York: Ginn, 1945), note to III.ii.41.

29. See Anthony Lewis, "An Allusion to Orpheus in 'The Merchant of Venice', III.ii.43-7," *N&Q* 25 (1978): 126-27.

30. In Sonnet 68 Shakespeare refers to similar themes, once again relating hairpiece to "fleece":

> Thus is his cheek the map of days outworn,
> When beauty liv'd and died as flowers do now,
> Before these bastard signs of fair were born,
> Or durst inhabit on a living brow;
> Before the golden tresses of the dead,
> The right of sepulchres, were shorn away,
> To live a second life on second head;
> Ere beauty's dead fleece made another gay. . . . [1-8]

31. Ben Jonson, *Epicoene*, ed. L.A. Beaurline (Lincoln: Univ. of Nebraska Press, 1966), I.i.88-90.

32. John Webster, *The Duchess of Malfi*, ed. John Russell Brown (Cambridge: Harvard Univ. Press, 1964), II.i.23, 35.

33. Raymond B. Waddington, "Blind Gods: Fortune, Justice, and Cupid in *The Merchant of Venice*," *ELH* 44 (1977): 469, sees Bassanio's reference to "snaky locks" as "a demonic version of his own description of Portia's 'sunny locks'." In *Shakespeare's Restorations*, 88, David Sundelson writes, "The spider Bassanio links with Portia symbolizes not only an engulfing mother but also androgyny, the fusion of the sexes perceived as horrifying, not charming."

34. Richard Horwich, "Riddle and Dilemma in *The Merchant of Venice*," *SEL* 17 (1977): 195.

35. Sundelson, *Shakespeare's Restorations*, 80-81.

3. *"Any Bar, Any Cross, Any Impediment"*

1. R.S. White, "Metamorphosis by Love in Elizabethan Romance, Romantic Comedy, and Shakespeare's Early Comedies," *RES* 35 (1984): 31. Carol Thomas Neely (*Broken Nuptials in Shakespeare's Plays*) and Sherman Hawkins ("The Two Worlds of Shakespearean Comedy") to varying degrees both see the lovers themselves as the true obstacles to marriage in the comedies. But whereas Neely and Hawkins see the problem in the couple, I see it rooted in the hero's thoughts and actions.

2. Howard Felperin, *Shakespearean Romance* (Princeton: Princeton Univ. Press, 1972), 60.

3. *Anatomy of Criticism*, 44.

4. Ibid., 164-65.

5. Ibid., 167, 173.

6. Doran, *Endeavors of Art*, 225.

7. Herrick, *Comic Theory*, 159.

8. Doran, *Endeavors of Art*, 216.

9. See Doran's chapter in *Endeavors of Art* on "Character," Leo Salingar's section on "Character and Plot" in *Shakespeare and Traditions of Comedy*, and especially the chapter entitled "Comic Characterization" in Robert Y. Turner's *Shakespeare's Apprenticeship* (Chicago: Univ. of Chicago Press, 1974).

10. Larry S. Champion, *The Evolution of Shakespeare's Comedy* (Cambridge, Mass.: Harvard Univ. Press, 1970), 9, 13.

11. White, "Metamorphosis by Love," 14. White summarizes the problem well: "The hinge of romance and comedy in the Elizabethan age is the transformation of the personality effected by love between the sexes. In the hands of mediocre artists there is little more than a formula 'X was metamorphosed upon falling in love with Y'. The greatest writers, however, use the formula to explore the creative potential for change that exists in all individuals, if they are prepared to submit themselves to the destructive and creative power of love" (15). Similarly, in "Identity and Representation in Shakespeare," *ELH* 49 (1982): 339-62, Barry Weller remarks, "It is evident that inadequate characterization is not the only charge which critics have levelled against the early comedies, but in nearly every case the characters' status as 'human puppets' is seen, if not as the cause, at least as the symptom of the play's other shortcomings. The paradox of this judgment is that all of these plays are concerned, in one way or another, with the search for identity, and although 'character' might be seen as a condition which is prior to identity, both terms designate the distinctive attributes of an individual and clearly overlap in their significance. If the characters of the play seek to individuate themselves and the spectators judge that they have failed, either the playwright has

failed in some rather fundamental way or he is commenting on the very enterprise of self-individuation" (345).

12. See Salingar, *Shakespeare and Traditions of Comedy,* 208-11.

13. According to the *OED,* in the sixteenth and seventeenth centuries "mermaid" and "siren" were synonyms, and "mermaid" suggested "prostitute." Antipholus's epithets for women recall similar descriptions in the *Menaechmi.*

14. Margaret Loftus Ranald, "'As Marriage Binds, and Blood Breaks': English Marriage and Shakespeare," *SQ* 30 (1979): 74.

15. Barbara Everett, "Much Ado About Nothing," *CritQ* 3 (1961): 319.

16. See Joyce H. Sexton's remarks on unmotivated villainy in *The Slandered Woman in Shakespeare, English Literary Series,* No. 12 (Victoria, B.C.: Univ. of Victoria, 1978), 41. See also J. Dennis Huston, *Shakespeare's Comedies of Play* (New York: Columbia Univ. Press, 1981), 122-25.

17. In "Those 'soft and delicate desires': *Much Ado* and the Distrust of Women," in *The Woman's Part,* ed. Carolyn Ruth Swift Lenz, Gayle Greene, and Carol Thomas Neely (Urbana: Univ. of Illinois Press, 1980), 79-99, Janice Hays suggests "that Claudio's allegiance is still invested in the sphere of male bonding and male achievement, perhaps as a defense against the anxieties occasioned by heterosexuality, and that he is not yet ready to take his place in the measured dance that signifies marriage and adult responsibility" (85).

18. The quotation is taken from Annie Dillard's discussion of the fascinating conclusions concerning the newly sighted drawn by Marius von Senden in *Space and Sight (Pilgrim,* 26).

19. *OED,* s.v. "impediment."

20. *The Arden Shakespeare: Cymbeline* (1955; rpt., London: Methuen, 1966), note to I.v.77-78.

21. The *OED* cites this line from *Cymbeline* as an example of one meaning of "reflect," "to bestow attention or regard *upon* a person or thing; to set a value on."

22. Ben Jonson, *Volpone,* ed. Alvin B. Kernan (New Haven: Yale Univ. Press, 1962), II.v.67-8, 6-7.

23. *Shakespeare and Experience of Love,* 147.

24. Ford, *Broken Heart,* II.i.39-40.

25. Middleton and Rowley, *Changeling,* II.ii.60-63.

26. Heywood, *Woman Killed with Kindness,* xiii.135-37.

27. Theodore Spencer, *Shakespeare and the Nature of Man* (New York: Macmillan, 1958), 192.

28. Louis Auchincloss, *Motiveless Malignity* (Boston: Houghton Mifflin, 1969), 133.

29. Harley Granville-Barker, *More Prefaces to Shakespeare* (Princeton: Princeton Univ. Press, 1974), 20.

30. Marilyn French, *Shakespeare's Division of Experience* (New York: Summit, 1981), 314.

31. *The Arden Shakespeare: The Winter's Tale* (1963; rpt., London: Methuen, 1972), lxxxii.

32. *Shakespeare* (New York: Holt, 1939), 316. The passage is quoted by Pafford.

33. For Pafford, "thy intention" in line 138 refers to "Affection," and he paraphrases the first few key lines as "Lustful passions: your intensity penetrates to the very heart and soul of man." Pafford's reading not only strains the syntax but creates more problems than it solves. In the first place, "intensity" is not, I think, an acceptable definition of "intention"; the *OED* lists "strain" and "tension," but not "intensity." Secondly, it simply makes more sense to assume that it is Hermione's "intention," which Leontes feels "stabs the centre," and therefore that it is Hermione who "dost make possible things not so held." Indeed, the syntax demands that "Hermione" be the

antecedent of "thou" later in the speech, and the subject of the series of verbs culminating in, "then 'tis very credent / Thou may'st co-join with something; and thou dost." In *Friends and Lovers*, MacCary, who devotes his entire final chapter to these lines, reads the speech, in general, as I do: Leontes' "own peculiar fears and desires have taken control of him, and like sexual creatures communicate with dreams" (207).

34. Clifford Leech, *Twelfth Night and Shakespearian Comedy* (Toronto: Univ. of Toronto Press, 1965), 78, sees Leontes' yearning for youth less as a reflection of a problem with Hermione than as a desire to be with Polixenes, his friend from child-hood, once more: "There may well be a hint in it all that Leontes is more jealous of Polixenes than of his wife Hermione, that it is the loss of a boyhood friend that is the unacknowledged root of his anguish. Certainly Polixenes' elaborate description earlier in the scene of his shared boyhood with Leontes, and the indication of their joint sense of loss when they grew up, separated, and married, give support to this."

35. Champion, *Evolution of Shakespeare's Comedy*, 156.

36. *Wooing, Wedding, and Power: Women in Shakespeare's Plays* (New York: Columbia Univ. Press, 1981), 145.

37. See Patricia Southard Gourlay, "'O my most sacred lady': Female Metaphor in *The Winter's Tale*," *ELR* 5 (1975): 375-95: "It is a sign of the schism between their worlds that even the best disposed of the men think of women generically rather than individually. Antigonus' offer to geld his daughters if Hermione is guilty, so that they will not 'bring false generations,' points ironically to the conclusion Leontes has already made: there is no woman who is not corrupt" (382).

38. Van Doren, *Shakespeare*, 314.

39. Joseph Campbell, *The Hero with a Thousand Faces*, 2nd ed., Bollingen Series 17 (Princeton: Princeton Univ. Press, 1968), 7.

40. *The Riverside Shakespeare* (Boston: Houghton Mifflin, 1974), 445.

41. *Troilus and Criseide*, in *Chaucer's Poetry*, ed. E.T. Donaldson (New York: Ronald Press, 1958), Bk. 5, lines 1772-75.

42. *Shakespeare's Problem Plays* (Toronto: Univ. of Toronto Press, 1949), 81. Tillyard's attempt to justify the poetry is almost as tortured as Troilus's thinking itself: "He does in fact for a brief time inhabit two incompatible worlds. But the self-control he maintained while the evidence for one of these incompatible worlds was accumulating enables him to subject the incompatibility to his will and to transform one incompatible into something that can fit the rest of his experience" (81-82).

43. *An Approach to Shakespeare*, 3rd ed., rev. (Garden City, N.Y.: Doubleday, 1956), 339.

44. "Characters of Shakespear's Plays," *The Complete Works of William Hazlitt*, ed. P.P. Howe (London: J.M. Dent, 1930), 4:221.

45. *Johnson on Shakespeare*, ed. Arthur Sherbo (New Haven: Yale Univ. Press, 1968), 8:938.

46. Ibid., 7:69.

4. *"We Are All Bastards"*

1. *Mucedorus*, in *Three Elizabethan Plays*, ed. James Winny (London: Chatto and Windus, 1959), IV.ii.14.

2. George Wilkins, *The Miseries of Enforced Marriage*, ed. Glenn H. Blayney (1607; facsimile rpt., Oxford: Malone Society, 1964), 2:494-95.

3. *Arden Shakespeare: Cymbeline*, 71.

4. The *OED* glosses the transitive form of the verb "colt" as "to befool, cheat," and quotes Posthumus here. However, it is clear from the *OED's* definition of the noun "colt" and of the intransitive forms (usually implying "wantonness"), that Shakespeare is thinking primarily of its sexual implication.

5. Posthumus's attitude is, of course, related to the popular Renaissance notion that women simply equal sin. The husband in *A Yorkshire Tragedy*, for example, complains, "That heaven should say we must not sin, and yet made women!" (in Oliphant, *Shakespeare and His Fellow Dramatists*, 2:iv.83-85).

6. "Interpreting Posthumus' Dream from Above and Below," in Schwartz and Kahn, *Representing Shakespeare*, 208.

7. "Fond of issue" is a phrase that has puzzled critics. Nosworthy sums up the difficulties by noting that the expression is "usually taken to mean doting on or desirous of offspring, but the sense is surely that Sicilius had abandoned hope of having further children" (note at I.i.37).

8. "Posthumus," or "Postumus," was a common Latin given name, and Horace addressed Ode XIV, Book II, a poem lamenting the inevitability of death, to his friend Postumus. The name is used infrequently in Elizabethan and Jacobean literature: the phrase, "Posthumius' son," appears in *Locrine*, and Julius Posthumus is a minor character in Jonson's *Sejanus*. Neither Kyd nor Marlowe uses the name and, more importantly, in no other play does Shakespeare use the word either as a name or as an adjective. The problem of sources for *Cymbeline* is "baffling," as Nosworthy puts it (*Arden Shakespeare: Cymbeline*, xvii), though it seems Shakespeare decided on the name "Posthumus" for its Latin ring, inasmuch as his probable sources, the prose tale *Frederyke of Jennen* and Boccaccio's *Decameron*, use Ambrosius of Jennen and Bernabo of Genoa, respectively, for the comparable character. The effect of his choice, however, is to emphasize both Posthumus's loneliness and his separation from his father. Posthumus, and the female form, "Posthuma," continued well into the nineteenth century.

9. On Edmund as bastard see Danby, *Shakespeare's Doctrine of Nature*, and William R. Elton *King Lear and the Gods* (San Marino, Calif.: Huntington Library, 1966), especially 131-35.

10. E.R.C. Brinkworth, *Shakespeare and the Bawdy Court of Stratford* (Chichester, England: Phillimore, 1972), 166.

11. *Patriarchy*, 81.

12. Ibid., 83.

13. See Teichman, *Illegitimacy*; Crane Brinton, *French Revolutionary Legislation on Illegitimacy, 1789-1804*, Harvard Historical Monographs, 9 (Cambridge, Mass.: Harvard Univ. Press, 1936); Maurice Baudin, *Les batards au theatre en France de la Renaissance à la Fin du XVIIIe siècle*, Johns Hopkins Studies in Romance Literatures and Languages, 21 (Baltimore: Johns Hopkins Univ. Press, 1932); Oscar Helmuth Werner, *The Unmarried Mother in German Literature* (1917; rpt., New York: AMS Press, 1966); and Howard B. White, *Antiquity Forgot* (The Hague: Martinus Nijhoff, 1978), Ch. Four, "Bastards and Usurpers," 44-73.

14. (London: 1594), 1.

15. Williamson quotes Philip Stubbes and contemporary records on the treatment of bastards and pregnant women, *Patriarchy*, 82-84.

16. *Endeavors of Art*, 15. There was a French edition of *Hippolytus* in 1507, but English editions of Euripides in general are few. In *Euripides and His Influence* (New York: Longmans, Green, 1928), F.L. Lucas argues that the English preference for the atrocities of Seneca obscured Euripides' achievement, though his plays "were doubtless extensively performed at both Universities" (104).

17. *Shakespeare's Ovid, Being Arthur Golding's Translation of the Metamorphoses*, ed. W.H.D. Rouse (Carbondale: Southern Illinois Univ. Press, 1961), Bk. 15, lines 562-64.

18. *Hippolytus*, trans. Arthur S. Way (London: William Heinemann, 1964), 4:616-24.

19. *Hippolytus*, trans. John Studley, in *Seneca, His Tenne Tragedies*, ed. Thomas

Newton (Bloomington: Indiana Univ. Press, 1964), 144. All references to Seneca's play are to this edition.

20. Laurence Sterne, *Tristram Shandy*, ed. James Aiken Work (New York: Odyssey, 1960), 456.

21. *Illegitimacy*, 132.

22. Hays, "Those 'soft and delicate desires'," 84.

23. Robert Grams Hunter, *Shakespeare and the Comedy of Forgiveness* (New York: Columbia Univ. Press, 1965), 158.

24. Joan Hartwig, *Shakespeare's Tragicomic Vision* (Baton Rouge: Louisiana State Univ. Press, 1972), 62. See also Skura, "Interpreting Posthumus' Dream," 209; and Kirsch, *Shakespeare and Experience of Love:* "the stuff within Posthumus does indeed so belie his outward appearance that Cloten begins to seem like his double" (154).

25. Clothing was an especially important element in plays of the sixteenth and seventeenth centuries. As the rhetoricians made abundantly clear, ornament could either enhance and amplify, making the noble nobler, or could disguise and mislead. For example, in a letter to her husband and Shakespeare's colleague, Edward Alleyn, Joan Alleyn writes of a neighbor who was "gulled" by a young man who borrowed a horse and did not return. "I feare me he gulled hym thoughe he gulled not vs the youthe was a prety youthe & hansom in appayrell we know not what became of hym" (*Henslowe's Diary*, ed. R.A. Foakes and R.T. Rickert [Cambridge: Cambridge Univ. Press, 1961], 298). For Elizabethans it was axiomatic that the villain uses clothing to assert his position and to disguise his intentions.

26. *OED*, s.v. "bastard," definition five.

27. *The Growth and Structure of Elizabethan Comedy* (1955; rpt., London: Chatto & Windus, 1979), 87.

28. *Shakespeare's Doctrine of Nature*, 48.

29. Cyril Tourneur, *The Revenger's Tragedy*, ed. R.A. Foakes (Cambridge, Mass.: Harvard Univ. Press, 1966), IV.iii.12.

30. Michael Taylor, "The Pastoral Reckoning in 'Cymbeline'," *ShS* 36 (1983): 102.

31. Hartwig, *Shakespeare's Tragicomic Vision*, 81: "The identification of Cloten and Posthumus has been very carefully and pointedly prepared for by Cloten's insistence that there was little physical difference between them. And though the audience tends to disregard the validity of Cloten's insistence upon this point, when the identification occurs [by Imogen of Cloten's headless body], we immediately recognize its truth and proceed to evaluate its implications."

32. See Nosworthy's note on "Richard du Champ," and his reference to the useful article by Robert J. Kane, "'Richard Du Champ' in *Cymbeline*," *SQ* 4 (1953): 206, at IV.ii.377 (*Arden Shakespeare: Cymbeline*).

33. "Pastoral Reckoning," 98.

34. *Approach to Shakespeare*, 597.

35. On Pericles' goodness see Peggy Ann Knapp, "The Orphic Vision of *Pericles*," *TSLL* 15 (1973): 615-26.

36. *Mucedorus*, III.i.22, 39, 41.

37. *The Merry Devil of Edmonton*, in Oliphant, *Shakespeare and His Fellow Dramatists*, vol. 1, V.i.136.

38. On the relationship between father and son and its effect on social position and power see Herbert Marcuse, *Eros and Civilization* (Boston: Beacon Press, 1966), especially Chapter 3, "The Origin of Repressive Civilization (Phylogenesis)," 55-77. The following quotation indicates the direction of Marcuse's inquiry:

The monogamic family, with its enforceable obligations for the father, restricts his monopoly of pleasure; the institution of inheritable private property, and the universalization of labor, give the son a justified expectancy of his own sanctioned pleasure in accordance with his own socially useful performances. Within this framework of objective laws and institutions, the processes of puberty lead to the liberation from the father as a necessary and legitimate event. It is nothing short of a mental catastrophe—but it is nothing more. Then the son leaves the patriarchal family and sets out to become a father and boss himself." [75]

39. *Shakespeare's Doctrine of Nature*, 20, 191.

40. Perhaps Bertram is doing—albeit unconsciously—no more than young men have done for centuries. Georges Duby describes marriage in medieval France as "a way of striking out on one's own: some knights, by taking or stealing a wife or receiving one at the hands of their lord, managed to escape from another man's house and found one of their own" (*Knight, Lady and Priest*, 94). In *Seize the Day* (New York: Viking Press, 1956), Saul Bellow writes of Tommy Adler, "Yes, it had been a stupid thing to do, but it was his imperfect judgment at the age of twenty which should be blamed. He had cast off his father's name, and with it his father's opinion of him. It was, he knew it was, his bid for liberty" (25).

41. Gourlay, "'O my most sacred lady'," 387. See also James Edward Siemon, "'But It Appears She Lives': Interation in *The Winter's Tale*," *PMLA* 89 (1974): 10-16: "It cannot be chance that twice in this play a princess of Sicilia is accused of sexual irregularity with a prince of Bohemia" (13).

42. William E. Slights, "Nature's Originals: Value in Shakespearian Pastoral," *ShS* 37 (1984): 74.

43. Erich Segal, *Roman Laughter* (Cambridge, Mass.: Harvard Univ. Press, 1968), 57. See also *Plautus: The Darker Comedies*, trans. James Tatum (Baltimore: Johns Hopkins Univ. Press, 1983). Tatum describes Strabax, a young man infatuated with the courtesan in *Truculentus*, as "gleefully . . . throwing his mother and father's wealth to the 'wolves' ('lupae,') which is also slang for 'whores')" (150). *Truculentus*, Tatum contends, "reduces paternity and maternity to matters of finance" (150).

44. Segal, *Roman Laughter*, 60, 17. Salingar, *Shakespeare and Traditions of Comedy*, thinks that "the typical motive for intrigue [in Shakespeare] has become the securing of love, not the finding of monetary means to enjoy it" (172).

45. Segal, *Roman Laughter*, 27.

46. Plautus, *Mercator*, trans. Paul Nixon (London: William Heinemann, 1924), 3:9.

5. *"Patience on a Monument"*

1. Gerald J. Schiffhorst, "Some Prolegomena for the Study of Patience," in *The Triumph of Patience*, ed. Gerald J. Schiffhorst (Orlando: Univ. Presses of Florida, 1978), 3.

2. *Broken Nuptials*, 75.

3. See Carole McKewin, "Counsels of Gall and Grace: Intimate Conversations between Women in Shakespeare's Plays," in *Woman's Part*, 117-32: "Private conversations between women in Shakespeare's plays provide opportunities for self-expression, adjustment to social codes, release, relief, rebellion, and transformation. . . . In the sororal atmosphere of feminism, when the dialogue of women has been emphasized as a vital part of our collective and individual self-realization, we should especially appreciate Shakespeare's art of overhearing the voices of women in an oppresive context, or the voices of women who are free, or discovering how to be free" (129).

4. *Friends and Lovers*, 76, 64.

5. Granville-Barker reminds us in his essay on *Twelfth Night* that with boys

playing women's roles, for the Elizabethans "the strain of make-believe in the matter ended just where for us it most begins"—with the entrance of a boy disguised as a boy (*More Prefaces to Shakespeare*, 28).

6. Adrienne Rich writes in "Women and Honor: Some Notes on Lying," in her collection of prose, *On Lies, Secrets, and Silence* (New York: Norton, 1979), that "women have been forced to lie for survival, to men" (189), and that "truthfulness has not been considered important for women, as long as we have remained physically faithful to a man, or chaste" (188).

7. Flaubert, *Madam Bovary*, 101.

8. Schiffhorst, "Some Prologomena," 2. See Ralph Hanna III, "Some Commonplaces of Late Medieval Patience Discussions: An Introduction," in Schiffhorst, *Triumph of Patience*, 65-87.

9. Schiffhorst, "Some Prolegomena," 20. J.J. Anderson tells us that "feminine personifications of moral qualities are particularly common in English allegory of the later Middle Ages" (*Patience*, ed. J.J. Anderson [1969; rpt., Manchester, England: Manchester Univ. Press, 1977], 51).

10. The translation is by H. Arthur Klein, *Graphic Worlds of Peter Bruegel the Elder* (New York: Dover, 1963), 216.

11. "Some Prolegomena," 14.

12. George Wither, *A Collection of Emblemes*, South Carolina Press, 1975), 81.

13. Leonard Barkan has written insightfully on the problems of verisimilitude inherent in Hermione's appearing as a statue, in "'Living Sculptures': Ovid, Michaelangelo, and *The Winter's Tale*," *ELH* 48 (1981): 639-67.

14. Heywood, *Woman Killed with Kindness*, i.59-60, 64.

15. Thomas Dekker, *Patient Grissil*, in *The Dramatic Works of Thomas Dekker*, ed. Fredson Bowers (Cambridge: Cambridge Univ. Press, 1962), 1:IV.ii.123-24.

16. George Farquhar, *The Beaux' Stratagem*, in *The Works of George Farquhar*, ed. Shirley Strum Kenny (Oxford: Oxford Univ. Press, 1988), 2:III.iii.415-22.

17. *Still Harping on Daughters*, 113.

18. *Broken Nuptials*, 75.

19. Rouse, *Shakespeare's Ovid*, Bk. 8, lines 237-45.

20. *Man and the Natural World* (New York: Pantheon, 1983), 43.

21. *Man and Natural World*, 43.

22. *Miseries of Enforced Marriage*, lines 914-15.

23. Ford, *Broken Heart*, IV.ii.158-59.

24. *Subject of Tragedy*, 178.

25. *Greek Tragedy* (New York: Hill and Wang, 1960), 188.

26. Euripides' tragedies are frequently compared to later comedies and to the romance tradition in general. In his *Introduction to Classical Drama* (New York: Bantam, 1966), 75, Moses Hadas writes, "The happy ending, the importance of the love element, the concern for verisimilitude, the criticism of contemporary mores, are all indices of the descent of tragedy from the heroic to what I have called the bourgeois." Norwood, *Greek Tragedy*, 311, suggests that "Menander is the successor of Euripides, not of Aristophanes; and in *Secular Scripture*, Northrop Frye speaks of a "modulation," "the change from Greek tragedy through Euripides to New Comedy and thence to prose romance" (90). Leo Salingar, too, in *Shakespeare and Traditions of Comedy*, 147, finds the world of Euripidean tragedy akin to that of comedy: "it can be said that Euripides' influence . . . shaped romantic fiction and drama down to the Renaissance."

27. *Alcestis*, trans. Arthur S. Way (London: William Heinemann, 1964), 4:141. All references to *Alcestis* are to this edition.

28. *Secular Scripture*, 88.

6. *"Th' Idea of Her Life"*

1. *Shakespeare and Traditions of Comedy*, 20.

2. "On Shakespeare and Ben Jonson," *English Comic Writers* (1910; rpt., London: J.M. Dent, 1930), 30.

3. David Lloyd Stevenson, *The Love-Game Comedy* (New York: AMS Press, 1966), 194.

4. *Wooing, Wedding, and Power*, 12.

5. *Secular Scripture*, 88.

6. *Subject of Tragedy*, 170

7. Sherbo, *Johnson on Shakespeare*, 7:62.

8. Ruth Nevo, *Comic Transformations in Shakespeare* (London: Methuen, 1980), 17-18, briefly discusses role reversals in Shakespearean comedy; Arthur Kirsch, *Shakespeare and Experience of Love*, 110-11, discusses role reversal in *All's Well That Ends Well*. Marianne Novy, *Love's Argument*, discusses in Ch. Nine the passivity of men in the romances and their willingness "to apply to themselves imagery of women's close biological relationship with children" (171). On Pericles' passivity see John Arthos, "*Pericles, Prince of Tyre*: A Study in the Dramatic Use of Romantic Narrative," *SQ* 4 (1953): 269; also, Knapp, "Orphic Vision," 624-25.

9. See Wheeler, *Shakespeare's Development*, and his earlier article, "Marriage and Manhood," 103-24. For a brief discussion of the incest theme in the play see Robert Rogers, "Endopsychic Drama in *Othello*," *SQ* 20 (1969): 205-15.

10. The *OED* uses Helena's line as one of its quotations illustrating the definition, "a certificate intended to introduce, or secure admission, a voucher." G.K. Hunter, in *The Arden Shakespeare: All's Well That Ends Well* (London: Methuen, 1967), reads "passport" as a "license to wander abroad as a beggar." Hardin Craig, Arthur Case, and others seem to take the best course by not glossing the word at all.

11. *Growth and Structure of Elizabethan Comedy*, 80.

12. *Riverside Shakespeare*, 524.

13. *Arden Shakespeare: All's Well That Ends Well*, note to III.iv.4.

14. Wheeler, *Shakespeare's Development*, 44-45.

15. R.B. Parker, "War and Sex in 'All's Well That Ends Well'" *ShS* 37 (1984): 102.

16. Ibid., 106.

17. Kirsch, *Shakespeare and Experience of Love*, 110-11. See also Howard C. Cole, *The All's Well Story from Boccaccio to Shakespeare* (Urbana: Univ. of Illinois Press, 1981), 125.

18. *Shakespeare and Experience of Love*, 141-42.

19. Sir Francis remonstrates,

> My brother Frankford showed too mild a spirit
> In the revenge of such a loathed crime.
> Less than he did, no man of spirit could do.
> I am so far from blaming his revenge
> That I commend it. Had it been my case
> Their souls at once had from their breasts been freed.
> Death to such deeds of shame is the due meed. [xvii.16-22]

20. Coppélia Kahn, *Man's Estate*, 104, thinks Petruchio "a stereotype, animated like a puppet by the *idee fixe* of male dominance," and sees Kate as "realistically and sympathetically portrayed as a woman trapped in the self-destructive role of a shrew." I find Petruchio a somewhat more complex personality than she does, and see him as the character "trapped in the self-destructive role."

21. *Man's Estate*, 117. See John C. Bean, "Comic Structure and the Humanizing of Kate in *The Taming of the Shrew*," in Lenz, Greene, and Neely, *Woman's Part*, 65-78.

22. *OED*, s.v. "conformable."

23. *Wooing, Wedding, and Power*, 55.

24. Claudio's playfulness in the face of Hero's death is made more distasteful by our knowledge that "cat" was a slang term in the sixteenth century for "prostitute" (*OED*, s.v. "cat").

25. *Shakespeare's Comic Sequence* (New York: Barnes and Noble, 1979), 77.

26. *William Shakespeare* (Oxford: Basil Blackwell, 1986), 30.

27. J. Dennis Huston, *Shakespeare's Comedies of Play* (New York: Columbia Univ. Press, 1981), 138.

28. See, e.g., Huston's introductory chapter in *Shakespeare's Comedies of Play*; also Muir, *Shakespeare's Comic Sequence*, 78; and for related comments see David Daniell, "The Good Marriage of Katherine and Petruchio," *ShS* 37 (1984): 23-31.

29. *Antic Fables* (New York: St. Martin's, 1980), 95.

30. Riemer, *Antic Fables*, 95.

31. Everett, "Much Ado about Nothing," 319-35, thinks Beatrice and Benedick "fools" in the best sense of the word. For her, "The fools of the play have become the heroes" (328). Everett's excellent article is a relatively early feminist reading of the play and is not nearly well-enough known.

32. *Shakespeare's Division of Experience*, 127.

33. *Still Harping on Daughters*, 113.

34. *Antic Fables*, 95-96. See also Everett, "Much Ado about Nothing," 333. It is difficult to understand how Howard Felperin can conclude that although Orlando must save his brother from a lioness, "few, if any, of the protagonists of the comedies are called upon to exert a comparable moral effort" (*Shakespearean Romance*, 59).

35. "Rival Lovers in *Merchant of Venice*," 109.

36. Geary, "Nature of Portia's Victory," 64.

37. Ibid., 65. See also Horwich, "Riddle and Dilemma," 191-200.

38. Hyman, "Rival Lovers in *Merchant of Venice*," 112. See also Tennenhouse, "Counterfeit Order," 54-69.

39. *Shakespeare and the Problem of Meaning* (Chicago: Univ. of Chicago Press, 1981), 19, 17. C. L. Barber finds the ring plot "a slight business" in *Shakespeare's Festive Comedy*, 186, and John Russell Brown, anticipating Rabkin, calls it "the game of the rings" in *The Arden Shakespeare: The Merchant of Venice* (1955; rpt., London: Methuen, 1981), lviii. On the other hand, Harry Berger, Jr., in "Marriage and Mercifixion in *The Merchant of Venice*: The Casket Scene Revisited," *SQ* 32 (1981): 155-62, thinks Portia's seriousness in asking Bassanio for the ring so great that it shows us "how a culture dominated by the masculine imagination devalues women and asserts male solidarity against feminine efforts to breach the barrier" (161).

40. *Love's Argument*, 78.

41. *Shakespeare's Development*, 178.

42. Eric Partridge, *Shakespeare's Bawdy* (New York: Dutton, 1955), 203.

43. *OED*, s.v. "thing." Shakespeare puns on this meaning when Petruchio calls Kate, "My horse, my ox, my ass, my any thing" (III. ii. 232).

44. Brown, *Arden Shakespeare: Merchant of Venice*, lviii.

45. *Love's Argument*, 79.

46. Horwich, "Riddle and Dilemma," 199.

47. Neely, *Broken Nuptials*, 6.

48. *The Crown of Life* (Oxford: Oxford Univ. Press, 1947), 96. See also the splendid article by Jonathan Smith on "The Language of Leontes," *SQ* 19 (1968): 317-27: "The deaths [of Hermione and Mamillius] are 'purges', and there is a swift and subtle modulation in the language. The crude, coarse, and spasmodic movement gives way to

a calm, integrated resignation. A smoother, more regular, more relaxed verse takes the place of the jerky, elliptical tension in which the Latinate and the 'low' had kept uneasy company. Under a genuine grief the language has found its right level" (325).

49. *Alcestis,* in Way, *Euripides,* lines 354-55.

50. *Shakespeare: The Last Phase* (Stanford: Stanford Univ. Press, 1955), 190.

51. *Shakespeare's Development,* 219.

52. *Shakespeare: Last Phase,* 192.

53. Knight, *Crown of Life,* 127.

54. Neely, *Broken Nuptials,* 191ff, discusses Perdita as the "issue."

55. Webster, *Duchess of Malfi,* I.i.344-47.

56. *Arden Shakespeare: Cymbeline,* 145.

57. *Shakespeare's Comic Sequence,* 161, 210. Joyce Sexton sees Posthumus's repentance as "unprepared for, 'unrealistic', and illogical," in *Slandered Woman in Shakespeare,* 74. Robert Grams Hunter, in *Shakespeare and Comedy of Forgiveness,* 161, thinks Posthumus deserving of forgiveness because he forgives his wife, and criticizes Nosworthy's response, which he feels betrays "a lack of sympathy with Posthumus' moral and spiritual condition."

58. Teichman, *Illegitimacy,* 132.

59. Hunter, *Shakespeare and Comedy of Forgiveness,* 143.

60. Knight, *Crown of Life,* 202.

61. Ibid., 191.

62. Hunter, *Shakespeare and Comedy of Forgiveness,* 171.

63. Ibid., 171.

64. *Prefaces to Shakespeare* (Princeton: Princeton Univ. Press, 1963), 2:78.

65. *Arden Shakespeare: Cymbeline,* xxxvii.

66. Ibid., 17.

67. *Reinventing Womanhood,* 146.

68. Felperin, *Shakespearean Romance,* 183.

7. *"The Marriage of True Minds"*

1. *Shakespeare and Nature of Women,* 80, 93.

2. *Still Harping on Daughters,* 49.

3. Ibid., 145.

4. 43, 42.

5. *Broken Nuptials,* 57.

6. Ibid., 24.

7. See "Argument of Comedy," 79-89.

8. *Subject of Tragedy,* 31.

9. *Prefaces to Shakespeare,* 4:96.

10. *OED,* s.v. "interrogatory."

11. Granville-Barker, *Prefaces to Shakespeare,* 101.

12. Hardin Craig, for example, in *Complete Works of Shakespeare,* lists him in the dramatis personae as "a person representing Hymen," as does Anne Barton, in *Riverside Shakespeare,* though under what authority one can only guess, for the First Folio text, the definitive one, introduces Hymen with the simple stage direction, "Enter Hymen." Agnes Latham, in *The Arden Shakespeare: As You Like It* (1975; rpt., London: Methuen, 1977), begs the question by noting that "it is left to the producer to decide whether the masque shall be plainly a charade got up by Rosalind, or whether it is pure magic, like the masque in *The Tempest,* in which the actors were 'all spirits'" (note to IV.iv.106). George Lyman Kittredge, ed., *As You Like It* (Boston: Ginn, 1939), feels "We need not trouble ourselves to enquire who or what Shakespeare's Hymen actually is" (note to V.iv.113), and quotes Capell who thought Hymen a forrester

impersonating the deity. In any event, the possibility that Hymen is a god was one that Kittredge could dismiss by distancing himself from the Elizabethans, to whom, he suggests, a mixture of "the actually supernatural with real life" "gave no offense" (note to V.iv.113). Howard Felperin, in *Shakespearean Romance*, 65, feels that Hymen's appearance, "though unanticipated and unexplained, perfectly embodies and expresses the holiday humor which pervades the closing scene."

13. Kittredge sees "reason" as the subject of "diminish," and "wonder" as the object, "that a reasonable explanation may diminish your amazement," and Agnes Latham, *Arden Shakespeare: As You Like It*, seems to agree, suggesting that "the purpose of the song is to give the astonished company time to hear each other's stories without imposing them on the audience, to whom they are not news." "Wonder," however, is surely the subject of "diminish," and "reason" the object, for the audience is as clearly in the dark as are Orlando, Duke Senior, et al.

14. *Shakespeare's Problem Plays*, 134.

15. Ibid., 134-35.

16. Ibid., 136. For a cogent argument on the play's unity based on thematic concerns see Lawrence W. Hyman, "The Unity of *Measure for Measure*," *MLQ* 36 (1975): 3-20; also Trombetta, "Versions of Dying," 60-76.

17. *Shakespeare's Problem Plays*, 102-3.

18. For Neely (*Broken Nuptials*, 87), Helena has the "name" wife but is "not the thing" for "these remain separate. They are potentially mediated, however, by the child that kicks within her."

19. Trombetta, "Versions of Dying," 74.

20. "Characters of Shakespear's Plays," 4:357, 355.

21. *Evolution of Shakespeare's Comedy*, 97.

22. Ed., *Pericles*, in *The Complete Pelican Shakespeare* (Baltimore, Penguin, 1969).

23. *Shakespeare: Last Phase*, 19.

24. *The Arden Shakespeare: Pericles* (London: Methuen, 1963), xci.

25. Ed., *Pericles*, in *Riverside Shakespeare*, 1481.

26. Champion, *Evolution of Shakespeare's Comedy*, 97.

27. Smith, *Riverside Shakespeare*, 1481.

28. *The Singularity of Shakespeare* (New York: Barnes and Noble, 1977), 86.

29. Gourlay, "'O my most sacred lady'," 390.

30. Way, *Alcestis*, 4:1123. In his edition of *Alcestis*, A.M. Dale simply says, "The play is called *Alcestis* because the conspicuous story is hers" (Oxford: Clarendon, 1954), xxii. All references to *Alcestis* are to this edition.

31. See Erna P. Trammell, "The Mute Alcestis," *CJ* 37 (1941-42): 144-50; also Muir's brief remarks on *Alcestis* and *The Winter's Tale* in *Singularity of Shakespeare*, 78.

32. *Natural Perspective*, 75.

33. Ibid., 76.

34. Granville-Barker, *More Prefaces to Shakespeare*, 23.

35. Gourlay, "O my most sacred lady," 393. Peter B. Erickson, "Patriarchal Structures in *The Winter's Tale*," *PMLA* 97 (Oct., 1982): 819-29, holds an opposite view and cautions against sentimentality. Erickson sees the women in this play, for all their power, as firmly controlled by the governing patriarchy.

36. Hazlitt, *Characters of Shakespear's Plays*, 179.

37. Doran, *Endeavors of Art*, 327.

38. *Shakespeare*, 305.

39. See Traversi, *Shakespeare: Last Phase*, 79.

40. Carol Gesner, *Shakespeare and the Greek Romance* (Lexington: Univ. Press of Kentucky, 1970), 108.

41. Nosworthy, *Arden Shakespeare: Cymbeline*, note at V.v.262-63.

42. The engraving is reproduced in Schiffhorst, "Some Prolegomena," 17.

43. Wither, *Collection of Emblemes*, 28.

44. Nosworthy, *Arden Shakespeare: Cymbeline*, note at V.v.262-63.

45. The engraving, by Maarten van Heemskerck and Dirck Volckertszoon (c. 1555), is reproduced in Priscilla L. Tate, *"Patientiae Triumphus:* The Iconography of a Set of Eight Engravings," in Schiffhorst, *Triumph of Patience,* 116.

46. "Shakespeare through Contemporary Psychoanalysis," in Schwartz and Kahn, *Representing Shakespeare,* 31.

47. *Arden Shakespeare: Cymbeline,* lxxxiii.

Conclusion

1. Berners W. Jackson, "Shakespeare at Stratford, Ontario, 1975," *SQ* 27 (1976): 32.

Index